Human Smuggling

Significant Issues Series

SIGNIFICANT ISSUES SERIES papers are written for and published by the Center for Strategic and International Studies.

Director of Studies: Erik R. Peterson

Director of Publications: James R. Dunton

Managing Editor: Roberta L. Howard

The Center for Strategic and International Studies (CSIS), established in 1962, is a private, tax-exempt institution focusing on international public policy issues. Its research is nonpartisan and nonproprietary.

CSIS is dedicated to policy analysis and impact. It seeks to inform and shape selected policy decisions in government and the private sector to meet the increasingly complex and difficult global challenges that leaders will confront in the next century. It achieves this mission in three ways: by generating strategic analysis that is anticipatory and interdisciplinary; by convening policymakers and other influential parties to assess key issues; and by building structures for policy action.

CSIS does not take specific public policy positions. Accordingly, all views, positions, and conclusions expressed in this publication should be understood to be solely those of the individual authors.

❖   ❖   ❖

The Center for Strategic and International Studies
1800 K Street, N.W.
Washington, D.C.   20006
Telephone: (202) 887-0200
Fax: (202) 775-3199
E-mail: info@csis.org
Web site: http://www.csis.org/

Human Smuggling
Chinese Migrant Trafficking and the Challenge to America's Immigration Tradition

Edited by *Paul J. Smith*

THE CENTER FOR STRATEGIC & INTERNATIONAL STUDIES
Washington, D.C.

Significant Issues Series, Volume XIX, Number 2
© 1997 by The Center for Strategic and International Studies
Washington, D.C. 20006
Printed on recycled paper in the United States of America
August 1997

99 98 97   4 3 2 1

ISSN 0736-7136
ISBN 0-89206-291-6

Library of Congress Cataloging-in-Publication Data

Human smuggling: Chinese migrant trafficking and the challenge
  to America's immigration tradition / edited by Paul J. Smith.
      p. cm. — (Significant issues series, ISSN 0736-7136 ; v. 19, no. 2)
  ISBN 0-89206-291-6
    1. Chinese—United States.   2. Illegal aliens—United
  States.   3. Smuggling—United States.   4. United States—
  Emigration and immigration.   5. China—Emigration and
  immigration.   I. Smith, Paul J., 1965–   .   II. Series
  E184.C5H86   1997
  973'.04951--dc21   97-14610
                                                                       CIP

Contents

6

Immigrant Smuggling through Central America and the Caribbean   **134**

   Anthony M. DeStefano

7

Canada's Growing Role as a Human Smuggling Destination and Corridor to the United States   **156**

   Kenneth Yates

8

Safe House or Hell House? Experiences of Newly Arrived Undocumented Chinese   **169**

   Ko-lin Chin

Acknowledgments

I am deeply grateful to all of the authors for their time and commitment to this volume. I am especially grateful to the Carthage Foundation, whose generous financial support allowed this project and book to become a reality. Special appreciation is also extended to the following individuals who provided invaluable comments about the manuscript: Alene Gelbard of the Population Reference Bureau, Washington, D.C.; John Handelman of Washington and Lee University, Lexington, Va.; James Puleo of the Office of International Criminal Justice, U.S. State Department; Gerald Segal of the International Institute for Strategic Studies, London; and Shyla Vohra of the International Organization for Migration, Geneva.

I would like to thank my colleagues at Pacific Forum CSIS, including James A. Kelly, Ralph Cossa, Jane Skanderup, and Christina Hatfield, for their unwavering support and encouragement throughout this project. I would also like to thank my editor, Roberta Howard, for her expert guidance in transforming a rough manuscript into this present form. Finally, I must thank my two mentors on the subject of human smuggling, Admiral Lloyd Vasey (USN-Ret.), founder of Pacific Forum CSIS, and Captain Dennis Egan of the United States Coast Guard, both of whom encouraged me at the initial stages of this project.

Introduction

With the end of the Cold War, numerous strategic planners, futurists, and other professionals have speculated about potential security challenges that nations are likely to face in the coming century. Many experts argue that, in addition to traditional military threats, governments around the world will face a new class of security challenges that are transnational in nature. Examples of these new issues include global population growth and food security, environmental degradation, pandemics, transnational crime and terrorism, and international migration and refugee flows. Unlike traditional security issues, these transnational security concerns often emerge in subtle and protracted ways. Consequently, they may fail to elicit the same degree of urgency among policymakers compared with their more traditional counterparts. But, like a slowly metastasizing cancer, these new challenges can undermine societies at their core and, in the long run, may prove even more damaging than traditional warfare.

For the United States, at least two transnational issues have reached the highest levels of policy concern in recent years: organized crime and illegal immigration. Organized crime certainly is not new in America. But recent evidence of the "globalization" of organized crime, including a recent influx of new ethnic-based criminal gangs into the United States, suggests the onset of a more violent era of criminal activity. Senator John Kerry argues that a new "global criminal axis" exists throughout the world consisting of five principal powers: the Italian Mafia, the Russian mobs, the Japanese yakuza, the Chinese triads, and the Colombian cartels. For these and other gangs, the United States has become "the great prize . . . the prime market for imported narcotics, weapons, and vice."[1] Phil Williams of the University of Pittsburgh asserts that one reason for the proliferation of organized criminal activity throughout the world is the emergence of a borderless global economy: "criminal organizations carry on their activities in what for them is, in effect, a borderless world, while law enforcement is significantly constrained by having to operate in what is still a bordered world."[2]

Next to transnational organized crime, illegal immigration has also emerged as a thorny problem for the United States and other countries. The number of illegal immigrants residing in the United States may total 5 million, according to government estimates.[3] Moreover, illegal immigration may become an even greater problem for the United States as the scale of international migration grows around the world. In his book *Preparing for the Twenty-First Century*, Paul Kennedy argues that "in view of the imbalances in demographic trends between 'have' and 'have not' societies, it seems unlikely that there will not be great waves of migration in the twenty-first century."[4] Similarly, migration expert James Purcell, director-general of the Geneva-based International Organization for Migration (IOM), argues that increasing poverty and population growth in the developing world will spur increasing emigration and will place international migration on the top of policy agendas in the years to come.[5]

At first glance, global organized crime and illegal immigration would seem to be separate phenomena. But at least one criminal industry straddles both of these issues: human smuggling. Human smuggling is both an international migration phenomenon and a transnational crime problem. The United States has experienced human smuggling, especially from Latin America and the Caribbean region, for decades. In recent years, however, Americans have confronted an entirely new brand of human smuggling, this time originating from the People's Republic of China, that is earning billions of dollars annually and spanning more than 30 countries worldwide. The ethnic Chinese syndicates that facilitate this trade have displayed a degree of sophistication and technical savoir faire rarely seen in other criminal enterprises. They are agile, flexible, and mobile. Moreover, with a potential market base of more than 1.2 billion people, their earnings potential is huge.

This book is an attempt to study the growing problem of human smuggling from the People's Republic of China to the United States and other countries. Most of the chapters were first presented at a two-day meeting hosted by Pacific Forum CSIS in Hawaii July 26–27, 1996. Attending the meeting were representatives from the U.S. State Department, the U.S. Immigration and Naturalization Service, the U.S. Coast Guard, the IOM, the Metropolitan Toronto Police Service, and various

universities, nongovernmental organizations, and media. Participants were asked to address the problem of Chinese migrant
trafficking from three major perspectives: the "push" stage (reasons for and methods of departure), the "transit" stage (various
smuggling routes involved), and the "destination" stage (what
happens when Chinese nationals arrive in the United States).

First, it is important to acknowledge a problem that plagues
almost any study of crime or illegal immigration—the availabil-
ity of accurate and consistent data. Although the growth of illegal emigration from China has clearly been documented in
recent years, much uncertainty remains about the exact numbers
involved. Estimates of the number of Chinese smuggled into the
United States each year vary wildly—from a low of 10,000 to a
high of 100,000. A 1995 interagency report on human smuggling
asserted that perhaps up to 50,000 Chinese nationals were being
smuggled into the United States each year.[6] Similarly, it is
extremely difficult to determine the exact number of Chinese
migrants who are smuggled into Australia, Europe, Japan, Russia, and South America. In what appears to be the closest thing
to an official admission of large-scale Chinese emigration, Wu
Haode, deputy secretary general of the non-Communist political
party Zhi Gong Dang, reported in 1994 that more than 700,000
Chinese had left their homeland illegally in recent years. He estimated that about 200,000 were living in Asia illegally, 100,000 in
Europe, 150,000 in Russia, and 200,000 in the United States.[7]

A second issue that should be clarified at the outset concerns
the diversity of views the reader will encounter here. Many of
the authors disagree with one another on a number of issues.
Because human smuggling is an extremely complex issue—in
addition to the fact that the authors represent a variety of professional backgrounds—this disagreement and diversity of opinion is not only not surprising but justified. The authors' views
and opinions are theirs alone, of course, and not necessarily
those of their parent organizations or institutions.

The book begins with an examination of the "push" factors
that are currently driving Chinese to emigrate abroad. Chapter
one attempts to depict the global scope of Chinese migrant trafficking with specific examples from the past three years. The
chapter describes how Chinese migrant trafficking is but one
part of a larger growth trend in human smuggling, driven by
international migration pressures such as population growth,
economic disparities between countries and unemployment in

source countries. Factors that could fuel additional Chinese migration in the future, such as continued decentralization of political authority in China, are also discussed, as well as the complications that undocumented Chinese migration abroad is causing for China's relations with its neighbors, particularly Japan, and with the United States.

In chapter two, migration specialist Ling Li looks at the phenomenon of mass migration within China and how it relates, if at all, to human smuggling abroad. Li characterizes internal migration in China as "perhaps the greatest population movement in human history." He also argues that the human flow from rural areas to China's coastal regions will likely surge in the years ahead because of the growing economic disparities between the two regions. Given the enormity of this human tide, it might seem logical that a large flow of internal migrants could eventually leave China. Li does not believe that this will occur, however, partly because the financial costs of going abroad, plus distance from one's family and uncertainties about life in a foreign country, are substantial when compared with the possible economic gains to be achieved abroad.

Professor Jack Goldstone is less sanguine, however. Among other things, he argues that internal migration is just one of many "push" factors (including population pressures and growing rural unemployment) that will drive tens of thousands of Chinese abroad in the years ahead. Goldstone argues that China's economic development and opening to the outside world are, paradoxically, leading to greater emigration. This, he asserts, is because development operates unevenly on the economy, which in turn sparks internal migration and out-migration as individuals seek to make up for the income differentials that exist both within China and between China and other countries.

If one accepts the proposition that development can stimulate emigration, then the next question is what is the likely magnitude. For an answer, Goldstone looks at another developing country that is highly relevant for the United States—Mexico. About one million Mexicans (out of a population of 80 million) come from Mexico to the United States every year, even though Mexico's per capita gross domestic product is seven times higher than China's. Goldstone argues that if China similarly sent one-eightieth of its total population abroad, total emigration could theoretically reach 15 million per year, although this scenario is not likely to occur for various economic reasons. Nevertheless, the comparison perhaps explains why so many Chinese would want to leave at a time when their country is experiencing unprecedented economic growth.

The next section of the book focuses on the modus operandi of the smuggling syndicates that facilitate illegal migration out of China. The authors in this section discuss the origins of the human smuggling trade, its link to corrupt government officials around the world (including the United States), and the reasons why so much recent emigration has originated in two provinces, Fujian and Zhejiang. Journalist Marlowe Hood addresses these questions based on his interviews in China with potential migrants and with the family members of some Chinese who have already migrated to the United States and Europe. First, Hood argues that history explains much of the migration from Fujian and Zhejiang provinces. The historic migration from these two areas to America and Europe has created a web of ethnic networks that continue to sustain a steady flow of migration, both legal and illegal. Why do Chinese leave? Hood suggests that economic opportunity, not desire for political freedom or fear of political persecution, is the driving force. At one point, Hood interviews a Chinese villager who points to a picture of the Statue of Liberty. "For us, it doesn't mean freedom," he explains to the American, "it means opportunity." What kind of opportunity? The sort that allows Chinese in the United States to earn ten times what they would have earned in China. When will Chinese stop wanting to leave their country? As one Fuzhou-based entrepreneur explained to Hood: "When the income differential between China and the United States is 1:2 rather than 1:15 or 1:20, that is when Fuzhounese will stop going and even start to come back."

Dovetailing Hood's essay is a chapter by Willard Myers that proposes a theoretical framework of three basic phases to explain Chinese migration abroad. The first is the "economic phase" in which the most productive male members of a family migrate abroad and establish a base. This is followed by the "immigrant phase" during which the males who are living abroad use their accumulated capital to help members of their immediate family to migrate. Finally, there is a "relational phase" in which the seed population (in the destination country) assists in the migration of extended family members or village members.

Among other issues Myers explores is the so-called Taiwan connection to Chinese migrant trafficking, which he traces back to 1949 when Chiang Kai-shek's defeated Kuomintang armies were forced to flee mainland China for Taiwan. Myers' discussion of Taiwan's alleged role in human smuggling is particularly interesting given the 1995 U.S. government interagency task force report that strongly criticized Taiwan's lack of cooperation: "Over half the [smuggling] vessels interdicted since January 1993 were either Taiwan-flagged or have had Taiwanese captains and crew members. . . . More importantly, Taiwan has failed to enact laws to make migrant smuggling a crime."[8] Taiwan has long had a reputation as a haven for organized crime.[9] If future evidence confirms Taiwan's alleged "behind the scenes" role in Chinese migrant trafficking, it could have disturbing implications for future relations between the United States and Taiwan.

The final section of the book addresses the "destination phase" of Chinese human smuggling. Two chapters discuss the three major transit corridors into the United States—Canada, the Caribbean, and Central America. Kenneth Yates, a police detective and Asian crime specialist, describes Canada's growing role as both a migrant trafficking destination for Chinese and a transit zone for Chinese heading to the United States. He writes that Canada "has a reputation of welcoming almost everyone arriving at ports of entry, even though many government officials know that the majority of refugee claims are bogus." Many human trafficking organizations are exploiting Canada's lax immigration rules in order to deliver their human cargo into the country's major cities as well as to the United States. Yates describes the various methods used to transport illegal Chinese immigrants across the Canadian border into the United States, including land crossings via cars and trucks, high-speed boat rides across the St. Lawrence River, and even snowmobile rides.

If Canada has emerged as America's human smuggling gateway of the north, then the two southern gateways would have to be Mexico-Central America and the Caribbean. Journalist Anthony DeStefano details the various routes used by smugglers to bring human cargo into the United States via these gateways. He explains that smugglers view the entire region—especially the Caribbean—as America's immigration Achilles' heel. DeStefano argues that Central America and the Caribbean region are likely to continue playing a "transit zone" role for human trafficking into the United States because of the powerful economic factors that encourage the lucrative human trade.

Finally, Professor Ko-lin Chin addresses the issue that should concern most American readers: what happens to Chinese nationals once they have been smuggled into the United States? Chin describes in detail the "safe houses" used by smugglers to hold migrants until they pay their transportation debts. He describes the sorts of abuses that can occur in these houses, ranging from denial of food or water to shackling, extortion, torture, and sexual assault. Chin also details how migrants pay their smugglers and how paying on time can mitigate the abuse that is often suffered.

As for solutions to the problem of human smuggling, many participants at the original meeting suggested that there should be better coordination among U.S. government agencies in enforcing immigration and anti-alien smuggling laws. Some urged greater intelligence gathering and sharing among governments (e.g., Western Europe, Canada, and the United States) and more effective enforcement of labor laws in the United States (especially against "sweatshops" and similar businesses that thrive on the influx of smuggled illegal immigrants.) Other suggestions included the need for greater dissemination of information about the reality of human smuggling in the Chinese provinces where the smugglers operate, which would most likely involve a joint effort by the U.S. and Chinese governments.

Whether such proposals could effectively eliminate, or at least significantly curtail, human smuggling is uncertain. One fact, however, is clear: illegal immigration, like illegal narcotics, has both a "supply" and a "demand" dimension. Currently the United States has a huge appetite for cheap labor (as well as illegal narcotics). Perhaps it is a coincidence, but the rise of human smuggling from China (and elsewhere) into the United States has paralleled the growth of sweatshops and the emergence of an immigrant-driven "underground economy" in the country. As a 1997 Washington Post article noted, "Sweatshops have made a remarkable comeback in America, evolving from a relative anomaly into a commonplace, even indispensable, part of the U.S. garment industry."[10] In New York City alone, Chinese immigrants reportedly own about half of the city's sweatshops and tend to hire only other Chinese who are often toiling under a form of debt bondage to pay their smuggling fees.[11] Until the demand for cheap immigrant labor subsides in the United States, or until the U.S. government forces it to subside, human smuggling will likely remain a constant element in America's immigration tradition. From this perspective, it could be argued that human smuggling from China is largely a self-generated problem for the United States that will go away only when the U.S. government decides to seriously enforce its immigration and labor laws.

PAUL J. SMITH
Honolulu, Hawaii

Notes

1. John F. Kerry, "Organized Crime Goes Global While the U.S. Stays Home," *Washington Post*, May 11, 1997, p. C1.
2. Phil Williams, Testimony before the House International Relations Committee, reported in Federal Document Clearing House Congressional Testimony, January 31, 1996.
3. Eric Schmitt, "Illegal Immigrants Rose to 5 million in '96", *New York Times*, February 8, 1997, p. A9.
4. Paul Kennedy, *Preparing for the Twenty-First Century* (New York: Random House, 1993).
5. "Population-Migration: Rich Nations Get Ready, the Poor are Coming," Inter Press Service, October 20, 1995.
6. Presidential Initiative to Deter Alien Smuggling: Report of the Interagency Working Group (Washington, D.C., 1995).
7. "Global Chinese Migrants Top 700,000," Reuters World Service, March 16, 1994.
8. Presidential Initiative.
9. Sin-Ming Shaw, "Dealing with the Godfather," Asia Inc., May 1997, 50; "Taiwan Politics: Organized Crime Skyrockets," EIU ViewsWire (Economist Intelligence Unit), January 15, 1997.
10. William Branigin, "Reaping Abuse for What They Sew," *Washington Post*, February 16, 1997, p. A1.
11. Ibid.

1

Chinese Migrant Trafficking: A Global Challenge

Paul J. Smith

In the early morning hours of June 6, 1993, a Chinese human smuggling ship named the *Golden Venture* ran aground on a sandbar about 150 yards offshore Rockaway Beach in Queens, New York. As soon as the vessel hit the ocean bottom, crew members unlocked the cargo hold and, shouting at the passengers, ordered them to get out as quickly as possible. Of the roughly 300 passengers aboard the ship, about 200 complied with the commands and threw themselves into chilling 53 degree waters in hopes of reaching the shore. At least eight of them drowned. As for the migrants who survived and made it to shore, park authorities had spotted the ship, and within an hour officials from a variety of local, state, and federal law enforcement agencies were on the scene, apprehending and detaining the would-be immigrants. The 100 passengers who had remained on board the ship were eventually rescued by the U.S. Coast Guard.[1]

It would later be revealed that the Chinese passengers aboard the *Golden Venture* had endured incredible hardship in their efforts to reach the United States. Many had traveled from China across mountains in Burma to Thailand, where they had embarked on a three-month journey by boat. Once in the United States, their plight would not end. Many would request political asylum, yet only a few would receive it. In fact, almost four years later, 55 of the original *Golden Venture* passengers would be incarcerated in U.S. prisons, 80 would be freed on bond, and an additional 99 would be deported back to China. Only 30 would receive political asylum.[2] Finally, in mid-February 1997, President Bill Clinton reversed the government's policy and released the remaining *Golden Venture* migrants, although they would continue to be subject to federal supervision until their cases were adjudicated. The sudden change apparently was triggered by an article in the *New York Times* published earlier that month that depicted the plight of the Chinese migrants.[3]

Although Chinese human smuggling by ship had been going on for years (since 1991, for instance, the U.S. government had either intercepted or detected at least 17 freighters carrying several thousand Chinese to the United States), the *Golden Venture* somehow struck a nerve in the American psyche. Perhaps it was because the ship's arrival was so dramatic—and deadly—or perhaps it was because major television networks provided live, national coverage. Perhaps also it was because the *Golden Venture* landed only miles away from mid-town Manhattan, Wall Street, and the Statue of Liberty. Whatever the precise reason, the *Golden Venture* seemed to change how Americans viewed the issue of immigration.

For President Clinton, who at that time had been in office only five months, the arrival of the *Golden Venture* could not have been more ill-timed. Already, the president was sensing growing anti-immigrant sentiment throughout the nation. Unlike his immediate predecessors, Clinton was extremely sensitive to the political ramifications of immigration matters. Shortly after his election, he had announced that he would be continuing the Bush-era policy of forcibly repatriating Haitian refugees, despite a campaign promise to reverse it. Subsequently, the issue of illegal immigrants derailed the president's initial nominee for attorney general, Zoe Baird, when she revealed that she had hired illegal aliens to serve as a nanny and a driver. As governor of Arkansas, Clinton clearly understood the powerful backlash that unwelcome immigrants—in this case Cuban refugees—could evoke. Many attribute his gubernatorial defeat in 1980 to his perceived inability to prevent or control the Cuban refugee riots that erupted at Fort Chafee, Arkansas, in June of that year.[4]

Sensing the potential political consequences of the *Golden Venture's* arrival, President Clinton immediately ordered the National Security Council (NSC) to direct the U.S. response against the ethnic-Chinese smuggling syndicates. The NSC would later establish a task force involving 12 federal agencies to counter the human trade. During a press conference, one administration official stated that the fight against alien smuggling would require "increased use of intelligence assets" both within the United States and overseas.[5] One interagency plan presented to the NSC urged that the military be used to interdict migrant-smuggling vessels on the high seas and then detain the illegal immigrants on military bases. Another called for the use of worldwide intelligence agencies, space satellites (to track smuggling ships), and increased Coast Guard patrols.[6] The U.S. Navy was prepared to supply patrol planes such as Hawkeyes and P-3s equipped with modern detection technology should conditions warrant their use.[7]

On the legal front, both the White House and Congress began proposing changes to the nation's immigration laws. President Clinton proposed a series of political asylum reforms, such as "on-the-spot" administrative hearings at airports and all other ports of entry so that undeserving asylum applicants could be quickly deported.[8] He also appointed a widely respected immigration expert, Doris Meissner, as commissioner of the Immigration and Naturalization Service (INS), a post that had, until then, remained vacant. Several prominent congressional leaders also offered legislation designed to reform the nation's asylum laws. One senator proposed a law that would increase the powers of immigration inspectors, streamline asylum claims, and strengthen penalties against human smuggling.[9] Another proposed the death penalty for human smuggling-related kidnapping and sanctions against countries that failed to "cooperate adequately" in prosecuting organized crime syndicates.[10]

If the White House was viewing Chinese migrant trafficking as a national security threat, many Americans saw the phenomenon as an assault on the nation's venerated immigration tradition. Indeed, for many Americans, the *Golden Venture* symbolized what had gone wrong with the country's immigration laws. One newspaper captured this anti-immigrant sentiment when it editorialized that the *Golden Venture's* arrival "serves to underscore the country's unfortunate inability to control immigration from China and the host of other places in the world where natives want to leave—seemingly at any cost."[11] Another newspaper questioned the wisdom of granting asylum to Chinese nationals simply because they opposed their government's "one-child" reproduction policy: "Chinese are all political refugees, because they want large families. This is nonsense. They come because economic opportunity is greater in America."[12] Clearly, the arrival of the *Golden Venture* changed the way many Americans viewed their immigration tradition.

The following year, Paul Kennedy, the prominent Yale historian, and Matthew Connelly coauthored an essay for the *Atlantic Monthly* in which they compared the arrival of the *Golden Venture* with the fictional refugee ships described in Jean Raspail's controversial novel *The Camp of the Saints*:

If a short trip across the Adriatic seems a far cry from a passage from Calcutta to Provence, the voyage of the *Golden Venture* was even more fantastic than anything imagined by Raspail. . . . In the past most Chinese illegal immigrants came ashore on the West Coast or crossed into California after landing in Mexico. But the *Golden Venture* rounded the Cape of Good Hope and thus crossed some of the same waters as Raspail's imaginary armada.[13]

The *Golden Venture* as Prologue

Only a few months after the arrival of the *Golden Venture*, U.S. officials cautiously began to proclaim victory over the human trade. The number of ships carrying illegal Chinese immigrants to the United States had dropped off dramatically, a development that the INS attributed to tougher enforcement and the trickling of "horror" stories back to China.[14] There was also growing evidence that Beijing was cooperating with the United States by launching publicity campaigns throughout the country designed to discourage its nationals from leaving. The Chinese government also arrested and jailed many of the smugglers themselves.[15]

Soon, however, U.S. officials began to realize that the problem had not gone away. Instead of delivering immigrants aboard ships directly to the United States, the criminal gangs were increasingly relying on more circuitous routes via Canada, Central America, Mexico, and the Caribbean. Beginning in 1993, American officials began to recognize a fairly consistent pattern in the Caribbean region: as soon as one route was effectively cut off, the smugglers would simply exploit a less-used route. For example, in 1993 and 1994, a growing number of Chinese were arriving illegally in the United States via Puerto Rico. But as more and more Chinese were apprehended, smugglers began diverting their human cargo to less well-traveled "way stations" such as St. John in the U.S. Virgin Islands.[16] Officials in the Dominican Republic also realized that their country had become a major human smuggling corridor for Chinese nationals seeking to reach the United States via Puerto Rico.[17] An even more exhaustive smuggling route was uncovered by Florida authorities in late 1996 when they arrested a small group of Chinese nationals near Ft. Lauderdale; the migrants reportedly had endured a journey traversing Europe, South America, Cuba, Nassau, and the Bahamas before finally reaching the U.S. mainland.[18]

By the early 1990s, officials in Canada began to realize that their country had emerged as both a migrant trafficking destination and a smuggling corridor to the United States. In 1995, Canadian authorities were tricked by an imaginative scheme allegedly engineered by the son of a high-ranking officer in China's People's Liberation Army. The ruse began when an Ontario business group invited a delegation of Chinese businessmen from Yunnan Province to participate in a five-day seminar. Fewer and fewer of the Chinese guests showed up at the scheduled meetings, however, until the Canadians finally realized that nearly all of the Chinese had disappeared—many having departed for the United States.[19] Subsequent evidence revealed that the Canadians were unwitting partners in an elaborate multimillion dollar human smuggling operation that had planned to smuggle more than 900 Chinese into Canada, charging each of them Can$70,000.[20] Nearly a year later, Canadian officials discovered even more compelling evidence that their country had become a human smuggling gateway linking the People's Republic of China to the United States. In this case, police discovered a criminal syndicate that, since September 1994, had been smuggling more than 40 Chinese nationals every month from Fujian Province first to Hong Kong, then Bangkok, then to either Europe or South America, then Canada, and finally to the United States.[21]

By 1994, officials in the United States realized that the Chinese migrant trafficking organizations were far more sophisticated than anyone had originally anticipated. In June of that year—almost exactly a year after the *Golden Venture's* arrival—a U.S. intelligence report stated that Chinese smuggling organizations had "vastly expanded their elaborate networks of way stations around the world and [were] now capable of transporting tens of thousands of people to the United States." Smugglers were using an increasingly complicated series of air routes to ship their human cargo into the United States. One of the documented air routes, according to the report, originated in Thailand. From Bangkok, migrants would travel by air to New Delhi or Karachi, then to Nairobi or Johannesburg, and then to Buenos Aires or Rio de Janeiro. Finally, the migrants would fly from South America to either Madrid, Barcelona, or London, and ultimately the journey would terminate in New York City.[22]

The year 1994 would also be one in which officials in North America, Western Europe, and other regions began to recognize that Chinese migrant trafficking had ballooned into a multibillion dollar global enterprise affecting more than 30 countries. Like their American counterparts, authorities in Western Europe discovered in the early 1990s that they too were confronting rising human smuggling from China. In 1993, police in the Netherlands busted a lucrative Chinese immigrant smuggling ring based in Hong Kong that flew Chinese nationals to Western Europe and North America on regularly scheduled flights. Moreover, the gangs often coerced illegal Chinese immigrants entering the Netherlands to commit crimes, such as robbery, to pay their transportation fees.[23] Soon after, officials in Austria arrested 20 members of a migrant trafficking gang that was alleged to have smuggled illegal Chinese immigrants into Western Europe via Moscow and Prague. Italy, too, was becoming a Chinese migrant trafficking target. In 1995, Italian police "swooped" on 40 sweatshops found to be harboring more than 120 illegal Chinese workers who were toiling in dark, squalid conditions. A few weeks later, police in Belgium raided 20 Chinese restaurants suspected of being involved with human smuggling. In Spain, police broke up a smuggling operation that brought Chinese into Western Europe via Russia to work in sweatshops, restaurants, and brothels in Spain and other European countries.[24] Similarly, French police arrested 53 people in Paris and Lille for their role in a "wide-ranging network smuggling illegal Chinese immigrants into Western Europe" that used, among other things, stolen Icelandic and Belgian passports.[25]

Many officials in Western Europe blamed the rise of Chinese migrant trafficking into their region on loose border controls in Eastern Europe and the former Soviet Union. Chinese syndicates, like many organized crime gangs in the region, had exploited the loose borders to ship their human cargo to the West. The 1994 U.S. intelligence report cited above detailed how Russian organized crime gangs had forged powerful alliances with their Chinese counterparts to ship thousands of Chinese via the former Soviet Union and Eastern Europe to the West.[26] In 1995, for example, authorities discovered a Moscow-Prague-Western Europe route in which Chinese migrants would be flown to Moscow, taken by train to Prague, and then driven by car to either Germany or Spain.[27] A year later, officials from Russia's Federal Security Service—the domestic counterintelligence wing of the former KGB—uncovered a major Chinese human trafficking ring based in Moscow. As part of the crackdown Russian officials rounded up more than 150 Chinese who were staying in Moscow without registration.[28]

By 1996, it became clear that gangs were increasingly adopting the risky practice of packing Chinese immigrants into cargo
trucks to transport them across the former Soviet Union. In June
1996, for instance, authorities in Ukraine found 42 Chinese
locked inside a refrigerator truck, many of them suffering from
frostbite; officials discovered the truck only after villagers in
Uzhgorod, near the Slovak border, heard the Chinese pounding
against the truck's walls. Several months later, police officials in
the Belarussian village of Kozlovichi discovered about 80 illegal
Chinese immigrants in two sealed trucks driven by Czech drivers. Three months after that incident, Ukrainian guards in the
Lviv region intercepted 30 Chinese immigrants hidden in a
truckload of Christmas trees. In February 1997, police in eastern
Slovakia detained 28 illegal Chinese immigrants who had been
transported across the Ukrainian-Slovak border in a sealed
truck.[29]

Growing migration from China was affecting other regions
as well. South America, for example, had emerged as both a
destination region and a transit zone for smuggling into the
United States or Canada. In January 1996, the government of
Uruguay fired two high-ranking immigration officers because
of their alleged role in helping to facilitate the trafficking of Chinese immigrants via Uruguay into Argentina.[30] Eight months
later, authorities in Argentina arrested a Chinese national for
allegedly leading a ring that smuggled Asians illegally into that
country.[31] Most recently, police in La Paz, Bolivia, broke up a
Chinese gang of passport forgers—reportedly tied to high-level
Bolivian authorities—that used Bolivia as a "key bridge" for the
smuggling of Chinese nationals to third countries, particularly
the United States.[32]

Africa, too, was not immune from the Chinese human trade.
South African police in 1995 busted what they described as "the
country's largest immigrant smuggling ring," allegedly run by
eight Taiwanese nationals. The syndicate apparently was using
South Africa as both a smuggling destination and staging-post
to smuggle Taiwanese and mainland Chinese to the United
States or Canada. When police raided the syndicate's headquarters outside Pretoria, they found identity books, international
driver's licenses, fingerprint forms, and a large supply of food.[33]

For cultural and geographic reasons, many East Asian countries also found themselves facing waves of human smuggling
from China. Japan, South Korea, and Taiwan became major destinations. Due to their close proximity to China, Hong Kong and
nearby Macau emerged as both smuggling destinations and

staging posts to third countries. In late 1995, for instance, Hong Kong police busted a smuggling syndicate headed by a "middle-aged mother" that had locked 53 illegal immigrants into cargo containers for shipment to Japan;[34] in Macau, authorities discovered that illegal Chinese immigrants were using fake passports to pass through the Portuguese enclave's new airport in order to reach Southeast Asia.[35]

Japanese officials also often intercepted large groups of illegal Chinese immigrants arriving on boats and passenger airplanes.[36] In one case, Japanese coast guard officials intercepted a Japanese fishing vessel south of Nagoya that was found to be carrying 100 Chinese immigrants. The immigrants had apparently been transferred on the high seas from a Chinese vessel to the Japanese fishing boat. Such "high-seas transfer" tactics also occurred near South Korea. In December 1996, South Korean police intercepted a South Korean fishing boat carrying 62 mainland Chinese who had been transferred on the high seas from a Chinese vessel to the South Korean boat. Taiwan faced similar problems as hundreds of Chinese immigrants flocked to the island to find economic opportunities. In one dramatic case, Taiwanese police intercepted a Taiwanese fishing boat found to be hiding 41 illegal immigrants from China in its freezers.[37]

By the early 1990s, Thailand had also emerged as a major staging post for further smuggling to other East Asian countries, Western Europe, and the United States. Smugglers subsequently began exploiting neighboring Cambodia as a transit zone to many Western countries. In 1996, Cambodian police uncovered a major international crime syndicate that was smuggling Chinese nationals via Cambodia to Europe and the United States. In the Philippines, authorities nabbed nine Chinese nationals suspected of illegally entering the country as a means of ultimately reaching the United States. Singapore's government was forced to ban the practice of allowing Chinese citizens 48-hour visa-free visits once it discovered that syndicates were smuggling Chinese nationals into the country. In Malaysia, police reported that Chinese nationals were buying fake passports and using Malaysia as a gateway to the United States, Europe, and Australia.[38]

Migrant Trafficking: The Growing Crisis

Although Chinese migrant trafficking is large in scale, it is only one fraction of the overall global trade in humans. Around the world, smuggling organizations ranging in size and degree of sophistication are smuggling tens of thousands of people from poorer to richer countries. In the process, they are earning at least $7 billion per year, with the potential for even greater future profits.[39] Because smuggling humans is less risky than trafficking narcotics (due in part to dramatic disparities in criminal penalties), some gangs have reportedly abandoned the drug trade in favor of smuggling people.

Technically, human smuggling occurs when

- money (or other form of payment) exchanges hands; and
- a facilitator (or "trafficker") arranges passage across an international border; and
- such passage is illegal; and
- the movement is voluntary.[40]

Given that definition, human smuggling clearly is not a new phenomenon. For thousands of years, smugglers have traded in human cargo as part of the slave trade, the trade in indentured servants, and a variety of other contexts—nearly always involving financial gain for the smuggler.

Today's human smuggling differs from the past primarily because it is so inextricably linked to rising global migration pressures. Rapid population growth, widening economic disparities between countries, and a worsening global unemployment crisis are spurring scores of individuals to move across international borders to find employment, higher wages, or simply a better life. Thousands of others are fleeing their home countries involuntarily because of war, famine, environmental degradation, and other factors. As the scale of international migration grows, human smuggling is increasingly becoming its modus operandi.

Would-be immigrants are increasingly using the services of human smugglers for a variety of reasons: huge distances to be traveled; difficulty overcoming rising anti-immigrant restrictions (legal and physical) in many host countries; and difficulty adjusting to life in the host country (e.g., finding suitable housing and jobs). Sensing an increasingly lucrative opportunity, smugglers are coming forward to provide these services. Consequently, wealthy nations around the world are finding themselves serving as destinations for the human trafficking syndicates.

Immigration officials in both the United States and Canada, for example, are confronting an unprecedented influx of smuggled immigrants from a variety of countries. Along the U.S.-Mexican border, human smugglers known as "coyotes" charge $500 (and more) to transport Mexican migrants to Los Angeles, Houston, Seattle, Chicago, and other U.S. cities. Near the Dominican Republic, smugglers transport an estimated 20,000 migrants across the 90-mile-wide Mona Passage into Puerto Rico every year, leading the U.S. Coast Guard to order an increased presence in the region.[41]

In Western Europe, Moroccan smugglers are busy sneaking hundreds of their countrymen and others across the nine-mile Strait of Gibraltar into Spain. The Greek government estimates that annually smugglers traffick hundreds of illegal immigrants—primarily from Iran and Iraq—from Turkey into Greece using the Aegean Sea as their gateway. In Albania, human smugglers known as "ambassadors" have smuggled thousands of Albanian and non-Albanian nationals (Egyptians, Turkish Kurds, and residents of the former Yugoslavia, to name a few) from the port city of Vlorë across the Strait of Otranto to Italy.[42]

In Eastern Europe and the former Soviet Union, human smugglers are plying their lucrative trade with near impunity. Moscow has emerged as the major "clearinghouse" for illegal immigrants from Africa and Asia headed toward the West. The former Soviet republics of Ukraine, Belarus, and Lithuania have also become important transit zones to the West. In early 1994, a Ukrainian court sentenced four military helicopter pilots to jail terms for their role in running a human smuggling enterprise in which they charged Indian, Pakistani, and Afghan "passengers" several hundred dollars for a helicopter ride into neighboring Poland. Bulgarian police, meanwhile, uncovered human smuggling rings in their country trafficking Iraqi nationals into Greece.[43]

In many East Asian countries, too, human smuggling is a booming industry. Japan, with its high wages and attractive lifestyle, is attracting thousands of smuggled migrants from China and elsewhere in the region. To the south, smugglers use the Strait of Malacca to bring thousands of job-seeking Indonesians into Malaysia every year.[44] Thailand is considered East Asia's human smuggling "epicenter" as at least 2,000 immigrants—both Thai nationals and other nationalities—are smuggled out of the country monthly to third countries.[45]

Although many migrants are successfully transported by the smugglers to their destination country of choice, others must confront severe hardship during the journey and even after arrival in the target country. In many cases, smugglers injure or abuse their clients during the transportation phase. Immigrants transported aboard boats or ships are often forced to live in unsanitary conditions for long periods of time. When Italian police intercepted a Honduran-registered smuggling ship packed with Indian nationals in late 1995, they found what they characterized as extraordinary scenes: "dozens of panic-stricken illegal Indian immigrants in the dark, piled one on top of the other, cold, famished and in inhuman sanitary conditions."[46] Immigrants who are smuggled overland in trucks or vans often suffer a similar fate. When Hungarian police unlocked a container truck in the summer of 1995, they found 38 Sri Lankan immigrants, almost half of whom had died from heat and lack of oxygen. Investigators later revealed that the 20 survivors did not realize "where they were or that they had been sleeping on the dead bodies."[47]

Some of the worst abuse of smuggled immigrants has been documented among Chinese nationals. When U.S. Coast Guard officials intercepted the *Jung Sheng No. 8* fishing boat carrying 147 would-be migrants from China in July 1995, they discovered evidence of physical violence and sexual abuse. Many of the male passengers—some as young as 10 years old—reported being sexually assaulted by crew members. Thirty-five passengers were so mentally and physically abused that they seriously contemplated suicide.[48] As if their transportation alone was not harsh enough, many Chinese are kidnapped or abused by the same gangs hired to provide them safe passage. Shortly after their arrival in Vancouver, Canada, three Chinese women were abducted, threatened with rape, and forced to call their families in China and convey the threats and demands of their captors.[49] Another disturbing practice of Chinese smuggling gangs or their agents is to kidnap Chinese immigrants even after they have paid their transportation fees as a way of extorting additional money from either the immigrants or their families.[50]

Why Are Chinese Leaving?

Given the obvious risks inherent in human smuggling, why are so many Chinese so eager to go abroad when their country is experiencing an economic boom? It is perhaps understandable why Haitian immigrants would risk their lives to be smuggled to Florida, or Moroccans to Spain, or Iraqis to Greece. After all, many source countries are facing enormous economic challenges—widespread poverty, growing unemployment pressures, low wages, uncertain political environments.

China, on the other hand, is enjoying unprecedented economic growth—estimated at an average annual rate of 9 percent. The country is also witnessing a rising influx of foreign investment, the growth of private enterprises, and, in some regions, rising wages. In fact, the economic picture is so positive in certain parts of China—most notably Guangdong Province—that the government is facing its own illegal immigrant problem as workers from neighboring countries such as Sri Lanka and Vietnam flood into the country looking for jobs and higher wages.[51]

Yet, in many ways, the bright economic picture painted by many economists in China and the West tends to mask fundamental economic and social problems that China has yet to solve. First, China's prosperity, while impressive, is highly uneven. Although many coastal provinces are enjoying unprecedented prosperity, many inland provinces remain relatively poor. According to a recent World Bank estimate, more than 300 million Chinese—more than the total U.S. population—are considered to be living in poverty.[52] Compared with their counterparts in many of the neighboring "tiger" economies, Chinese earn relatively low per-capita incomes—estimated at $500 per year. One consequence of this growing economic disparity is a surge in internal migration as workers from China's poorer regions search for opportunities in the nation's cities and along its "Gold Coast".

Second, China faces an enormous challenge finding work for its burgeoning workforce, which numbers around 707 million and is growing by an estimated 14 million every year.[53] Consequently, unemployment pressures in China—both urban and rural—are expected to worsen dramatically in the next few years. A recent Chinese Labor Ministry report warned that up to 153 million people could be unemployed by the year 2000.[54] The issue is so sensitive in China that the government does not allow open discussions about "mass unemployment" in the country. When a domestic magazine, *Chinese Writers*, attempted to run a detailed exposé on the crisis, the government reportedly tried to shut it down.[55]

Third, China faces a population burden that is unmatched anywhere in the world, despite the country's strict one-child policy. Current predictions are that the nation's population should level off at roughly 1.6 billion by the middle of the next century, but even that scenario may be overly optimistic.[56] For example, the country's huge internal migrant population is undermining the government's ability to enforce the widely unpopular birth control policy.[57] Also, there is growing evidence of widespread noncompliance in many rural areas, where a strong cultural preference for male children as well as large families continues to persist.[58] Official corruption also has dampened Beijing's ability to limit the country's population. In 1995, for example, the Chinese government fired a village official in Sichuan Province accused of lying to the central government about his village's success at curbing its birth rate; during a three-year period, the official reported only 62 births—an apparent accomplishment for which he won several prizes—when in fact more than 110 children were born. Some Chinese experts estimate that up to 6 million "unregistered" births are occurring every year on top of the country's official growth rate of approximately 13 million per year.[59]

International migration is often explained by a basic "push" and "pull" model: "economic deprivation, high fertility, and unemployment (push factors) in lesser-developed countries work in concert with such elements as family reunification, higher wages, and increased demand for labor (pull factors) in industrialized countries to create an influx of immigrants."[60] If unemployment, low wages, and population pressures are "push" factors in China, then higher wages in the United States (or Western Europe or Japan), the presence of ethnic networks, and the existence of "sweatshops" (or similar businesses, including restaurants, that are willing to hire illegal Chinese immigrants) act as the "pull" factors behind Chinese migration.[61]

There is a common perception throughout China that no matter how good things are, things are better abroad. These ideas are imported via the media (satellite television and VCRs with shows like *Baywatch* and *Dallas*), visits from relatives who live abroad, and the growth of Chinese tourism abroad. The communications revolution in China often acts in tandem with the vast Chinese ethnic networks that exist throughout East Asia and the world. Centuries of migration have created large Chinese communities throughout the region, especially in Southeast Asia. Growing communication between those communities and relatives back in China helps to disseminate information about possible opportunities abroad.

Finally, there are the social and political factors that are contributing to growing human trafficking from the People's Republic of China. Since the implementation of Chinese reforms in the late 1970s, Beijing has steadily lost economic and political power to the nation's provinces.[62] Decentralization of power in China portends a possible increase in illegal emigration. Even if Beijing is sincere about its desire to limit illegal emigration, its directives and laws may be thwarted by local leaders—particularly in the coastal provinces—who have their own agendas. One manifestation of this trend is the rapid increase and proliferation of official corruption throughout China.[63] For smuggling syndicates, corruption provides a "channel" through which they can ply their trade. For the would-be emigrant, corruption is a way to bypass the long and arduous process that ordinary Chinese typically must endure simply to obtain a legitimate passport and permission to travel abroad.[64] One such instance of emigration-related corruption emerged in 1993 when three senior Xian city officials were arrested for providing fake travel documents that allowed 23 people to emigrate illegally overseas. In some areas of Fujian Province, some local officials have reportedly contracted with the "snakeheads"—alien smugglers—to have their own family members smuggled out of China for a discounted price. More recently, reports have surfaced that some Chinese officials are selling their official (green) passport to illegal immigrants; unlike regular passports, the official variety can be easily doctored with a razor and a substitute photograph.[65]

The Politics of Chinese Emigration

Throughout East Asia, there is widespread concern about the potential for mass migration from the People's Republic of China. Neighboring countries in particular are watching developments within China with an eye to whether they will increase pressures for illegal emigration. On China's northern border, it is the Russian government that is most concerned. Russian officials have argued that illegal Chinese migration into Russia's Far Eastern region could lead to the "peaceful loss" of that territory. En route to China in 1996, Russian president Boris Yeltsin stopped in Khabarovsk and promised local leaders and businessmen that he would raise the issue of illegal Chinese immigration with China's leaders.[66] Similarly, some central Asian states have reportedly voiced fears that illegal Chinese immigration into their regions might be part of a Beijing-conceived "plan aimed at long-term 'non-violent absorption' of the region."[67]

Immigration issues are also affecting China's relations with neighboring Japan. In October 1994, Japan's Maritime Safety Agency (Coast Guard) warned in its annual White Paper that Chinese snakeheads were teaming up with their Japanese counterparts to sneak illegal Chinese immigrants into Japan.[68] Nearly a year later, Japanese consulates in China asked the Chinese government to tighten emigration control "over Chinese citizens who try to smuggle themselves into Japan or stay illegally in Japan." The Chinese responded that Japan should speed up its issuance of business visas for Chinese and improve its treatment of Chinese nationals residing in Japan.[69] In February 1997, following a dramatic upsurge in human smuggling cases, the Japanese government once again formally asked China to curb the illegal migration of its nationals to Japan.[70]

Taiwan also considers the stream of illegal immigration from mainland China a major financial and political burden. According to a report published by Taiwan's official news agency, "the large number of illegal [mainland Chinese] migrants has inflicted a heavy financial burden on Taiwan"; among other things, Taiwan claims that it is spending an average of U.S.$5.46 million every year to pay for their temporary housing and repatriation transportation.[71] One reason for the high temporary housing costs is Beijing's reluctance (or delay)—its "snail's-pace progress," according to one high-ranking Taiwan official—in taking back its illegal immigrants.[72] Taiwan also considers illegal immigration from neighboring China a national security concern. In the past the Taiwanese government has accused Beijing of sending spies and saboteurs under the guise of illegal immigrants. These fears, legitimate or not, were bolstered in early 1996, prior to Taiwan's presidential elections, when Taiwanese police arrested 24 illegal Chinese immigrants carrying 100 rounds of ammunition, two Black Star handguns, and two kilograms of amphetamines.[73]

In many Southeast Asian countries, too, there is widespread concern about current and possible future trends in illegal Chinese emigration. In Singapore, elder statesman Lee Kuan Yew, in a 1994 interview with an international newspaper, warned that continued pressuring of China by the United States "on human rights could contribute to a breakdown of order in China that would drive millions of Chinese to seek refuge overseas."[74] In Vietnam, officials have reportedly "grown wary" of illegal Chinese immigrants working in Vietnamese villages near the Chinese-Vietnamese border.[75]

Illegal Chinese migration has also emerged as a sensitive issue in America's highly politicized and emotionally charged relations with China. Two issues in particular have recently complicated U.S. efforts to encourage Beijing to put a halt to the illegal exit of its nationals. First, U.S. trade policy toward China is fundamentally tied to Chinese emigration. According to the Jackson-Vanik amendment to the U.S. Trade Act of 1974, the president must certify that a nonmarket economy (e.g., China) allows freedom of emigration. Beijing argues that it does so. As one Chinese official stated,

> there is no problem with this in China, where there are no obstacles to emigration. The obstacle at present lies in the US' frequent refusal, on the grounds of current immigration trends, to grant visas to Chinese who want to go to the United States. So it is the United States that should relax controls in this regard.[76]

For Beijing, the premise of the Jackson-Vanik amendment—that China should allow its population to go abroad whenever and however it wants—contradicts recent pleas from Washington for Beijing to stop its nationals from fleeing. Washington's response is that U.S. laws establish annual quotas with regard to Chinese immigrants—which are easily filled—that act independently of the Jackson-Vanik amendment.

A sore point in Sino-U.S. relations has been the issue of political asylum. Since the Tiananmen Square incident in 1989, the United States has tried to show its disappointment with Beijing's behavior by granting political asylum, first to students and then to individuals who objected to the Chinese government's one-child population control policy. Most recently, for instance, Congress passed a law (Public Law 104-208) that defines opposition to China's birth control policy as a form of "political opinion" and thus grounds for receiving political asylum in the United States (although the law also limited the total number who could qualify under this new standard to just 1,000 individuals).[77] China has long claimed, however, that such policies on political asylum have actually had the effect of encouraging the human smuggling trade.[78] Beijing's position seems to be partly validated by evidence, reported anecdotally and in the press, that smuggling syndicates coach their immigrant clients on how to claim political asylum in the United States, including the appropriate English phrases to use.[79]

Conclusion

If immigration is not already one of the top issues in U.S.-China relations, it almost certainly will be in the years ahead. Although the number of illegal immigrants from China to the United States is relatively small compared with the number from Latin America and the Caribbean, the People's Republic of China, with its 1.2 billion inhabitants, looms as possibly one of the world's largest source countries for immigrants in future years. If the Chinese economy is unable to provide adequate job opportunities with wages comparable to U.S. levels, then emigration will likely remain an attractive option for thousands, if not millions, of individuals.

It could be argued that Chinese emigration is primarily a concern for China's neighbors, especially Japan, Russia, and Southeast Asia. Yet human smugglers have minimized the importance of geography. Current evidence suggests that whenever smuggling syndicates are facilitating illegal migration from China, the United States—in most cases—is the preferred destination, even if immigrants must first pass through Southeast Asia or Western Europe on their way to the "Beautiful Country" (*meiguo*, the Chinese word for America).

For Americans, human smuggling presents a moral quandary. On one hand, most Americans traditionally have wanted to offer compassion and refuge to strangers fleeing a hostile land. Simultaneously, however, many fear that excessive numbers of "guests" could spoil the party. Others fear that criminals are cynically exploiting the nation's goodwill only to increase their illegal profits. Not surprisingly, these mixed sentiments have resulted in an official U.S. government policy of "muddling through" the crisis. The question that Americans must ask is whether their immigration tradition, laws, and infrastructure are prepared for the massive demographic and economic changes that are occurring far beyond the country's borders.

Notes

1. The facts of this case are partly derived from, and described in detail in, *Yang v Maugans*, 68 F3d 1540, 1995 U.S. App. LEXIS 30649 (3d Cir Pa. 1995).

2. Sarah Jackson-Han, "Chinese Aliens Sparked Long-Term Immigration Crackdown," Agence France Presse, June 7, 1996; Celia W. Dugger,

"Dozens of Chinese From 1993 Voyage Still in Jail," *New York Times*, February 3, 1997, p. A1.

3. Celia W. Dugger, "Chinese Immigrants From Stranded Ship Are to be Released," *New York Times*, February 15, 1997, p. A1. The earlier article cited is also by Dugger, "Dozens of Chinese From 1993 Voyage Still in Jail" (see note 2 above).

4. Michael Kelly, "William Jefferson Blythe Clinton: A Man Who Wants to be Liked, and Is," *New York Times*, November 4, 1992, p. A1.

5. "White House Background Briefing on President Clinton's Initiative Against Trafficking," Federal News Service, June 18, 1993.

6. John Dillin, "Clinton Vows to Stem Tide of Illegal U.S. Immigration," *Christian Science Monitor*, June 21, 1993, 4.

7. Pamela Burdman, "Clinton Cracking Down on Human Smuggling: He Wants Stiffer Penalties, More Investigations," *San Francisco Chronicle*, June 19, 1993, p. A1.

8. Deborah Sontag, "On-the-Spot Hearings for Aliens are Considered," *New York Times*, July 22, 1993, p. A14.

9. Michael S. Arnold, "Calls to Change Asylum System Gain Urgency," *Washington Post*, June 13, 1993, p. A24.

10. Jerry Seper, "Roth Bill Targets Asian Gangs," *Washington Times*, June 11, 1993, p. A6.

11. "A Slow Boat From China; Better Control of Immigration is Essential," *Buffalo News*, June 9, 1993, 2.

12. Otis Pike, "Time to End Contradictions in U.S. Immigration Laws," *Minneapolis Star Tribune*, June 14, 1993, p. 13A.

13. Matthew Connelly and Paul Kennedy, "Must it be the Rest Against the West? Immigration and Relations Between Western and Developing Nations," *Atlantic Monthly* 274, no. 6 (December 1994): 61.

14. Dan Freedman, "Officials Say Big Boats no Longer Smuggle Aliens," *San Francisco Examiner*, December 29, 1993, p. A9.

15. Pamela Burdman, "China Cracks Down on Smuggling," *San Francisco Chronicle*, November 19, 1993, p. A1.

16. Ashley Dunn, "After Crackdown, Smugglers of Chinese Find New Routes," *New York Times*, November 1, 1994, p. A1; Lynda Lohr, "St. John Drop Point for Illegal Chinese Immigrants," Associated Press, August 12, 1995.

17. Santiago Estrella Veloz, "Chinese Emigrate via Dominican Republic," United Press International, February 21, 1996.

18. "Illegal Chinese Caught on Boat," *Fort Lauderdale Sun-Sentinel*, October 24, 1996, p. 12B.

19. Hugh Winsor, "Mounties to Search for 75 Chinese Businessmen," *Independent* (London), May 14, 1995, 2.

20. Alan Merridew, "Bid to Smuggle 900 into America," *South China Morning Post* (Hong Kong), October 1, 1995; Paul Kaihla, "Inside an Immigration Scam," *Maclean's*, October 2, 1995, 25.

21. "Canadian Police Dismantle Chinese Immigrant Smuggling Ring," Agence France Presse, November 6, 1996; John Ibbitson, "Canada a Pipeline for Smuggling Aliens," *Ottawa Citizen,* November 7, 1996.

22. Roberto Suro, "Chinese Smuggling Grows, Forcing U.S. Reassessment," *Washington Post,* June 2, 1994, p. A1.

23. Jeffrey Stalk, "Dutch Focus on Smuggling of Chinese," *International Herald Tribune,* May 7, 1993.

24. "Austrian Raid Nets Chinese Human Smuggling Ring," Agence France Presse, September 10, 1993; "Police Arrest 10 in Crackdown on Chinese Gangs in Rome," Agence France Presse, June 27, 1995; "Belgian Police Raid Chinese Restaurants," Reuters World Service, July 2, 1995; "Chinese Sweatshop Ring Busted in Spain," Deutsche Presse Agentur, October 16, 1995.

25. "French Dismantle Chinese Migrant Smuggling Network," Agence France Presse, March 5, 1997. Regarding earlier incidents in France, see "French Police Crack Down on Illegal Asian Migrants," Reuters World Service, December 3, 1996; "French Hold 20 in Chinese Immigration Ploy," Reuters World Service, February 14, 1997.

26. Suro, "Chinese Smuggling Grows" (see note 22).

27. "Police Break up Ring Smuggling Chinese into Spain, Europe," AP Worldstream, October 16, 1995.

28. "Police, Security Agents Crack Chinese Illegal Immigration Ring," AP Worldstream, November 21, 1996.

29. "Frozen Chinese Migrants Found on Ukraine Border," Reuters North American Wire, June 11, 1996; "Illegal Chinese Immigrants Detained in Belarus," Deutsche Presse Agentur, September 26, 1996; "Thirty Chinese Seized from Xmas Tree Truck," Reuters World Service, December 19, 1996; "Chinese Immigrants Returned from Slovakia to Ukraine," TASR News Agency [Bratislava] reported in *BBC Summary of World Broadcasts,* February 8, 1997, EE/D2838/C.

30. "Uruguayans Fired for Immigrant Traffic," United Press International, January 18, 1996.

31. "Chinese National Deported, Charged with Running Immigration Ring," Agence France Presse, August 29, 1996.

32. "Police Shatter Gang of Chinese Passport Forgers," Agence France Presse, February 20, 1997.

33. "S. African Police Smash Immigrant Smuggling Ring," Reuters World Service, March 16, 1995.

34. Patricia Young, "Human Snake Plot Uncovered, Court Told," *South China Morning Post* (Hong Kong), September 17, 1996, 3.

35. "Chinese Illegal Immigrants Target Macau Airport," Reuters World Service, June 5, 1996.

36. "Smuggling of Stowaways into Japan Rises Sharply," *Mainichi Daily News,* October 19, 1996, 12; "141 Illegal Immigrants Arrested in Japan," Agence France Presse, February 8, 1996.

37. "Japan Nets 100 Illegal Chinese Immigrants," Reuters World Service, December 12, 1996; "Chinese Caught Trying to Sneak into S. Korea,"

Reuters North American Wire, December 25, 1996; "Taiwan Nabs Chinese Illegals in Boat's Freezers," Reuters North American Wire, August 22, 1996.

38. On Bangkok, see Kim Gooi, "Bangkok is Asia's Hub for the Illegal Travel Business," Deutsche Presse Agentur, September 23, 1996; on Cambodia, see Niall Fraser, "Fugitives Head II Smuggling Ring," *South China Morning Post* (Hong Kong), January 8, 1997, 1; on the Philippines, see "Nine Chinese Arrested at Manila Airport," Deutsche Presse Agentur, October 18, 1996; on Singapore, see "Internal Affairs; Clamp Down on Visas for Tourists from China," Radio Australia External Service [Melbourne, May 1, 1996] reported in *BBC Summary of World Broadcasts,* May 2, 1996, EE/D2602/B; on Malaysia, see "Chinese Illegals Using Malaysia as Gateway to West," Agence France Presse, August 27, 1995.

39. "The New Trade in Humans," *Economist,* August 5, 1995, 45. One high-level U.S. military official estimates that the annual profits for human smuggling exceed $10 billion. See testimony of General Wesley K. Clark, Commander in Chief, United States Southern Command, before the U.S. House National Security Committee, reported in Federal News Service, March 20, 1997.

40. "Trafficking in Migrants: Characteristics and Trends in Different Regions of the World" (discussion paper submitted by the International Organization for Migration to the Eleventh IOM Seminar on Migration, Geneva, October 26–28, 1994).

41. Admiral Robert Kramek, Commandant, United States Coast Guard, speech to the National Press Club, reported in Federal News Service, August 5, 1996.

42. On Morocco, see Marlise Simons, "Jobless in Morocco, Looking North," *International Herald Tribune,* August 27, 1996; on Greece, see "Police Arrest 75 Illegal Kurdish Immigrants from Iran," AP Worldstream, October 8, 1996; on Albania, see Merita Dhimgjoka, "Albania's 'Ambassadors': Smuggling Poor into Italy," Associated Press, May 30, 1995; "Suspected Albanian Smuggler Killed in Boat Chase," Reuters World Service, April 24, 1996.

43. "Illegal Migration to West through Lithuania Increases," AP Worldstream, January 24, 1997; Galina Nekrasova, "Military Pilots End up in Jail for Smuggling People," TASS, February 14, 1994; "Bulgaria: Police Break up Ring Smuggling Illegal Immigrants," BBC Monitoring Service: Eastern Europe, November 15, 1994.

44. "Malaysia Rounds up Illegal Immigrants," United Press International, September 30, 1995.

45. Robert Horn, "Thailand a Key Crossroads in International People Smuggling," Associated Press, January 8, 1996.

46. "Italian Police Detain 55 Indians in Hold of Ship," Reuters World Service, October 30, 1995.

47. "Sri Lankan Truck Passengers 'Slept on the Dead'", Reuters, July 31, 1995.

48. Anthony M. DeStefano, "Chinese Turned into Sex Slaves," *Newsday,* August 23, 1995, p. A07.

49. "Alien-Smuggling Ring Uncovered in B.C.," *Gazette* (Montreal), July 16, 1995, p. E8.

50. Ashley Dunn, "New Type of Kidnapping Strikes Fear into Chinese Immigrants," *New York Times,* September 10, 1995, 45.

51. Tan Tarn How, "Guangdong Attracting Illegal Aliens," *Straits Times* (Singapore), June 24, 1995, 16.

52. "How Poor is China?" *Economist,* October 12, 1996, 35.

53. "China-Basic Data," *EIU China Hand* (Economist Intelligence Unit), May 1, 1996.

54. "China Labor: Unemployment Rises; Workers Leave State Enterprises," EIU ViewsWire (Economist Intelligence Unit), August 29, 1996.

55. "Mainland Factories Feel the Pinch," *South China Morning Post* (Hong Kong), November 30, 1996, 21.

56. "Jiang Zemin Warns of New Problems in Population Control," Agence France Presse, March 20, 1995.

57. Xiao Yu, "Young Women Threaten Plan to Control Numbers," *South China Morning Post* (Hong Kong), October 9, 1996, 10.

58. "Rural Behavior Undermines China's Family Planning Policy," Agence France Presse, February 13, 1995.

59. "China Fires Official over Birth Statistics," United Press International, September 30, 1995.

60. Kimberly A. Hamilton and Kate Holder, "International Migration and Foreign Policy: A Survey of the Literature," *Washington Quarterly* 14, no. 2 (Spring 1991): 192.

61. For a good discussion of "push-pull" international migration, see Philip Martin and Jonas Widgren, "International Migration: A Global Challenge," *Population Bulletin* 51, no. 1 (Washington, D.C.: Population Reference Bureau, Inc., April 1996); for a good recent discussion of "sweatshops" in the United States, see William Branigin, "Reaping Abuse for What they Sew," *Washington Post,* February 16, 1997, p. A1.

62. Gerald Segal, "The Muddle Kingdom? China's Changing Shape," *Foreign Affairs* 73, no. 3 (May-June 1994): 43.

63. Greg Austin, "The Strategic Implications of China's Public Order Crisis," *Survival* 37, no. 2 (Summer 1995): 8.

64. Ronald Skeldon, "Migration from China," *Journal of International Affairs* 49, no. 2 (Winter 1996): 434–455.

65. "Chinese Officials Arrested for Illegal Emigration Scheme," Japan Economic Newswire, November 6, 1993; Burdman, "China Cracks Down on Smuggling" (see note 15); Glenn Schloss, "Cadres in Passport Scam; Gangs Use 'Official' Documents to Smuggle Out Mainland Migrants," *South China Morning Post* (Hong Kong), August 21, 1996, 6.

66. "Yeltsin to Raise Issue of Illegal Chinese Immigration into Russia," RIA News Agency [Moscow, April 24, 1996] reported in *BBC Summary of World Broadcasts,* April 24, 1996, EE/D2595/B.

67. "Russia-China: Marriage of Convenience," *China Economic Review,* October 1996, 16.

68. "Japan Warns of Upsurge of Illegal Immigrants," Reuters World Service, October 28, 1994.

69. "Japan Calls for Tightened Emigration Control by China," Japan Economic Newswire, December 5, 1995.

70. "Japan Urges China to Curb Illegal Immigrants," Deutsche Presse Agentur, February 13, 1997.

71. Sofia Wu, "Illegal Mainland Immigrants Heavy Burden for Taiwan," Central News Agency, January 28, 1997.

72. Benjamin Yeh, "Beijing Urged to Speedily Take Back Illegal Immigrants," Central News Agency, January 28, 1997.

73. "Twenty-Four Illegal Mainland Chinese Immigrants Arrested," Central News Agency [February 7, 1996] reported in *BBC Summary of World Broadcasts*, February 8, 1996, EE/D2531/F.

74. Michael Richardson, "Singapore Fears a Chinese Upheaval," *International Herald Tribune*, May 27, 1994.

75. "Hanoi Orders New Permit for Foreign Workers," AP Worldstream, October 5, 1996.

76. Statement by Qian Qichen, China's vice premier and foreign minister, in "Qian Qichen on China-U.S. Relations" [Central People's Broadcasting Station: Beijing], *BBC Summary of World Broadcasts*, November 12, 1993, FE/1844/G.

77. Dugger, "Dozens of Chinese from 1993 Voyage Still in Jail" (see note 2).

78. "Chinese Spokesman Links Granting of Political Asylum to Migrant Smuggling," *BBC Summary of World Broadcasts*, June 4, 1993, FE/1706/I.

79. Merle Linda Wolin, "From China to America, via Moscow," *New York Times*, August 25, 1993, p. A15.

2

Mass Migration within China and the Implications for Chinese Emigration

Ling Li

In his recent bestseller *Megatrends Asia*, futurologist John Naisbitt predicted eight trends that will accompany the rise of a new, powerful Asia.[1] One of these is the migrant flows from the countryside to the cities, and China's *mingong* (peasant workers) wave, he observed, is perhaps the most spectacular movement.

Despite Naisbitt's impressionistic style, policy advisers from China's neighboring countries and the United States, and indeed anyone with an interest in the People's Republic of China, will no doubt share this vision. But in addition to internal migration flows, there is one added concern: alien smuggling. Perhaps not all "floating migrants" will take the next step and go abroad, but "if even a fraction of the 60 million chose to flee overseas, they could have a huge impact on neighboring economies."[2] A 1993 policy paper by the Atlantic Council and National Committee on U.S.-China Relations shared this concern:

> "The next decade could bring an internationally significant flow of migrants from the PRC. This is a prospect that China's neighbors view with apprehension and that could affect American economic interests and commitments to the well-being of some of the democratizing societies on China's periphery."[3]

The purpose of this paper is not to predict whether Chinese illegal migration to the United States will end or not. What is being attempted here is to provide a fuller picture of China's floating population and to examine whether there is a close correlation between alien smuggling activities and growing internal migratory flows.

China's "floating population" includes not only peasant workers but also urban professional transients, tourists, people on business trips, and others traveling for social and personal purposes. Because they come from different backgrounds, move for different reasons, and therefore have different impacts, grouping them together only confuses the discussion. As one researcher has noted, there is an "essential sameness" between China's floating population and migrant labor, who constitute from two-thirds to three-quarters of the totals in various studies.[4] In addition, rural-to-urban movements have dominated the migration streams.[5] Therefore, it seems appropriate to focus the discussion on the internal movement of peasant workers in China.

Some Historical Background

In China, as in most developing countries, the natural flow of migration in the absence of controls would be mostly to the city.[6] Since the mid-1970s, many countries have identified this urban-directed migration and spatial distribution as a severe problem.[7] Because of its centrally planned economy and explicitly stated urbanization policy, China had been able to control the flow of its population up until the early 1980s.[8] To understand China's past and present migration situation and its impact, one must also understand its urbanization policy, the household registration system, and rural economic reform.

China's policymakers believed that the growth of big cities should be controlled to avoid problems affecting urban housing, employment, and infrastructure. This passive attitude tended to minimize the government's failure in earlier periods to meet market demand and develop adequate urban infrastructure systems.[9] Whatever the causes, the government followed this line of reasoning and devised a policy strictly limiting the size of big cities.[10] With this goal in mind, the government enforced rigid residency rules, effectively tying peasants to the land. The introduction of the *hukou* (household registration) system in 1958 was as much for controlling migration as for the sake of political stability. Under the system, Chinese citizens are designated as either agricultural or nonagricultural. A person with nonagricultural registration is entitled to full urban employment, public housing, free medical services, and retirement benefits.[11] Ironically, this system actually increased the peasants' motivation to move because it further widened the already enormous traditional inequality in China between rural and urban dwellers.

Motivation alone is not enough, however. Although one technically could move anywhere in China, it was once practically impossible to do so without government approval and access to provisions for food and social services. This situation changed when the government initiated economic reforms in rural areas in 1978 and dismantled people's communes in 1983. Under the "family responsibility" system, established in the early 1980s, the government allocated quotas of crops to be produced by the collectives in various regions. A peasant household had to deliver the quota agreed to between the collective and itself; then it could claim the balance of the agricultural production for its own use.[12] The system, by rewarding individual initiative and efficient production, created a large surplus of rural laborers.[13] Subsequent reforms in urban areas led to the legalization of private enterprises, more relaxed employment policies, and the opening of urban free markets that traded virtually all daily consumer goods. Simultaneously, a flood of peasants began moving from rural areas to the cities.[14]

Scope and Characteristics of the *Mingong* Flow

Migration is usually defined as a change in residence over a significant distance. In China, however, because of the existence of strict residency rules, migration is characterized by an official change in household registration that is dependent on permission from authorities at both the origin and the destination.[15] Therefore the term *migrant* in China is generally reserved for permanent settlers. Those who move on a temporary basis and those who reside in a place for a prolonged period but without changing their registration are referred to as the "floating migrants," or the "floating population."

According to official figures, permanent migration stayed constant at an average annual rate of 18 per 1,000 in the 1980s.[16] Much of the increase in mobility can therefore be attributed to the growth of the floating population. At present, China has a rural labor force of more than 440 million. Of these, 330 million, or 75 percent, are engaged in farming. At the current rate of agricultural production, however, only around 200 million peasants are needed on the farm.[17] Encouraged in part by official policy, farmers in the early 1980s began to flock to nonagricultural sectors of the economy where they could earn higher incomes. Village and township enterprises, established in the early 1980s, had by the end of 1995 provided work for 126 million farmers from the time of their establishment.[18] At the same time, a great number of peasants had traveled many extra miles into China's booming cities to make a living. Current estimates of the year-round floating population throughout the country range from a conservative 40 or 50 million to a high of 100 million. The numbers 70 million and 80 million appear most frequently in official and scholarly sources.[19] A nationwide survey showed that peasant workers accounted for 60 percent of the floating population in large cities; small cities and towns have a much higher share of workers from the countryside.[20]

The hypothesis that migration declines with distance also holds true in China. According to a sample survey jointly conducted by the State Council and the Agricultural Ministry, the volume of intraprovincial migration is much higher than that of interprovincial flows, which account for only a little over one-third of the total. Of those intraprovincial floaters, nearly half move within their own county.[21]

Where transregional movements do take place, a significant portion of them are directed eastward. The eastern region's breathtaking growth in recent years certainly helps to keep its own drifting peasant workers occupied while attracting many more from the central and western regions. Guangdong Province's drifting labor force, for example, is numbered at around 12 million, roughly 6.6 million of whom are from other provinces. In many areas throughout the fast-growing Pearl River Delta, the number of floating peasant workers equals or even surpasses the local labor force. In the town of Changan, for example, there are 280,000 peasant workers, nearly ten times the local population of 31,000.[22]

While prosperous coastal cities are still the main destinations, poor northwestern provinces such as Xinjiang, Ningxia, and Gansu, where economic development programs provide many job opportunities, have also gained popularity.[23] Although the magnitude is still unclear, the movement is interesting because it apparently cannot be explained by income differentials.

In the early 1980s the term *mingong* referred to laborers from the countryside whom the government mobilized for major public works projects such as the building of bridges and dams.[24] Clearly, today's mingong are a different type of peasant worker. They are predominantly young and male. A sample survey of Chinese rural labor flows in 1993 found that 81.8 percent of those on the move are men, 58 percent are between the ages of 18 and 30, and 25 percent are between 31 and 40 years old.[25] Variations do exist, however. For example, of the 3.4 million registered peasant workers in Guangdong, migrant women account for 60.1 percent.[26] In export processing zones, women workers are considered more patient and careful and better adapted to working in production lines. Although their jobs still tend to be unskilled or semiskilled, peasant workers are now working in a variety of occupations either as self-employed or as individually contracted wage earners. Construction has provided more jobs for male rural migrants than any other occupation. Significant numbers of rural laborers also work in manufacturing, transportation, commerce, food service, and maintenance.[27]

Finally, an often-overlooked characteristic of rural-urban migration in China is that the rate of out-migration in the poorest regions is much lower than the rate in relatively well-off rural areas. For the former, such constraints as cost of transport and lack of social networks at the destination serve as powerful intervening obstacles in peasants' decisions to try their luck in the cities. According to a United Nations-assisted survey of 23 impoverished counties in China where per capita income is lower than 200 yuan, only 11.3 percent of working-age household members in the poorest households surveyed had worked elsewhere for more than one month during 1987–1989—the peak years of Chinese rural migration—while the figure for relatively well-off households in the same poor areas was 25.5 percent. In a separate survey of "ordinary"—not impoverished, not wealthy—rural areas in 10 provinces, conducted by sociologists at China's Wuhan University, the figure jumps to 51 percent.[28] Therefore, it is safe to say that most peasant workers are *not* poverty-stricken, desperate, or displaced persons who have been forced to flee their homes for survival.

Reasons for Leaving the Land

A Large Surplus Rural Labor Force

The rural economic reforms implemented since 1978 have provided rural households with strong incentives to economize their use of labor. This, combined with increasing agricultural mechanization, has led to a continuing decrease in average labor days per sown hectare (2.47 acres) for most crops. For wheat production, for example, the labor needed per sown hectare in 1985 was less than half that needed in 1978.[29]

While labor demand continues to contract, so does the amount of agricultural land available per rural household. Agricultural structural adjustment, soil erosion, and industrial and real estate development continue. Only 10 percent of China's land is now cultivated, providing an average of 1.24 *mu* (0.082 hectares) per head, one-fourth of the world average. At present, a farmer is entitled to 0.34 hectares of land in the countryside. Often, an entire year's worth of farm work can be completed easily within just a few months.[30]

To make matters worse, huge cohorts born in the high-fertility period from 1962 to the early 1970s began to enter the rural labor force by the end of the 1970s.[31] During the period 1979 to 1993, the rural labor force increased by nearly 140 million.[32]

Although the development of village and township enterprises beginning in the early 1980s greatly alleviated unemployment pressures in the countryside, these enterprises clearly had limited capacity to absorb workers. Many of them were inefficient and poorly managed. To survive increasing competition, the more successful ones opted for capital investment rather than for taking on new employees.[33] Whereas in the five years from 1984 to 1989 rural enterprises absorbed 12.6 million new workers a year, in the five subsequent years the number dropped to 2.6 million.[34]

Growing Rural-Urban and Regional Disparities

A typical industrial or construction worker in the late 1980s earned about 500 yuan more per year than a farmer earned. A transportation workers' salary was 700 yuan higher. Moreover, a worker's income included substantial bonuses and benefits.[35] Although peasant workers rarely receive the full benefit packages enjoyed by regular urban employees,[36] it is generally recognized that rural migrants are attracted to the cities by the expectation of higher wages rather than by the actual wages earned. In 1993, average annual rural income was 921 yuan ($106), a real increase of only 3.2 percent over 1992. In contrast, average urban income was 2,337 yuan ($240), up 10 percent. And there is no sign that this wage gap will be narrowed in the near future.[37]

Due to differences in resource bases and past development patterns, regional gaps existed even before the reforms. The gaps widened further in the 1980s, however, as the historically more developed eastern area of China became the chief beneficiary of the country's reforms.[38] Between 1978 and 1992, the average income gap between eastern and inland provinces widened by three times from 214 yuan to 724 yuan.[39] As table 1 shows,

Table 1
**Highest and Lowest Average Wages in China's Provinces,
1990 and 1994**
(100 = national average for the corresponding year)

	1990	1994
Highest		
Guangdong	136.9	158.2
Shanghai	136.3	167.9
Beijing	124	149.2
Lowest		
Anhui	85.4	81.3
Henan	85.3	77.4
Jiangxi	80.8	76.7

Source: Economic Information Daily, February 25, 1995, 4.

average wage earners in the three central provinces of Anhui, Henan, and Jiangxi were actually worse off in 1994 than in 1990, and it might not be a coincidence that those provinces are also major origins of transregional flows of peasant workers.

The situation has not improved much in the countryside in recent years. It appears that the exploitation of peasants continues unabated, especially in areas where "grassroots" democracy has not yet been established. Local officials often resort to illegal levies and extortion to fund new industrial projects.[40] Farmers who are caught in the "scissors gap" often complain about exorbitant prices for such basic commodities as fertilizer, pesticides, and machinery. In 1995, the state purchase price of farm goods rose by 19.9 percent, but the price of farming inputs went up by 27.4 percent.[41] Thus, despite greater productivity, rural incomes have actually fallen in many areas.

"Pull" of the Cities

Since China opened its doors to the outside world in the late 1970s, economic reforms have fueled rapid economic growth and created an unprecedented number of job opportunities in the urban areas. Keen on keeping down production costs to maintain competitiveness, many enterprises, state-owned and private alike, set out to recruit peasant workers, who were often accustomed to receiving few social benefits and comparatively lower wages. As it turned out, rural laborers were responsive and moved in great numbers to special economic zones and major coastal cities open to foreign investment, where opportunities were plentiful. For many young farmers, a factory job in the city is already a symbol of social promotion.

Even in cities with less spectacular growth and higher unemployment rates, often there was still a curiously strong demand for labor, especially for the demanding, relatively low-paying and low-status jobs disdained by urban natives. For example, in 1988 there was a recruitment quota for 3,102 workers in Zhengzhou's textile sector. One year later, more than 400 vacancies were still waiting to be filled, and in the past five years 1,222 textile workers have left their jobs for employment elsewhere. As a result, factories have had to resort to peasant workers to ensure normal production.[42]

Government Policies

Government policy has always had a significant influence on population movement in China. As mentioned above, the introduction of the family responsibility system is responsible, as much as anything, for the surging wave of peasant workers. Due to the change in market conditions resulting from economic liberalization, the peasants who began trickling illegally into the cities and towns were able to survive without official household registration because almost all daily necessities could be purchased in free markets.

Responding to these changes as well as to the needs of economic development, the government softened its former opposition to urbanization and carried out several policies in the 1980s to facilitate population mobility. In April 1983, the State Council passed regulations allowing peasants to work in market towns while retaining their rural household registration. This was expanded on in a 1984 circular that opened 60,000 market towns for peasants to reside in for business purposes, provided that they took care of their own grain rations and housing arrangements.[43] Starting in 1985, peasant workers were able to register for "temporary residence permits" in urban centers.[44]

Thus it appears that the flow of peasant workers is not entirely blind. A variety of "push" and "pull" factors have

worked together to bring about this mingong wave that is perhaps the greatest population movement in human history.

Impact of the *Mingong* Flow

Contributing to National Economic Growth

Many view the mingong wave as a necessary evil. For one thing,
it is extremely costly and inefficient to continue to tie a large
number of rural surplus laborers to the land—in fact, the flows
of peasant workers have effectively reduced unemployment
pressures in rural areas. At the same time, a stable yet flexible
and cheap labor supply has proved indispensable to the country's fast-growing economy.

In Guangdong, for instance, the system of market-oriented
production is largely built on migrants. Since the early 1980s, the
province has taken in more than 10 million workers from across
the country.[45] After a decade of currency depreciation, however,
peasant workers' nominal wages have actually not seen much
increase. Many *dagongmei* (working sisters) in southern Guangdong, for example, are still earning a monthly salary of around
500 yuan, a little over what was being paid 10 years ago.[46] This
might explain how Guangdong's producers of apparel, toys, and
electric gadgets can remain competitive in an export-oriented
economy.

In certain manufacturing sectors shunned by young urban
people, factories would actually have had to shut down had it
not been for the steady supply of peasant workers. It has been
estimated, for example, that if women migrant workers were let
go in Zhengzhou's six large textile factories, 30 percent of the
weaving and spinning machines would have had to be stopped,
creating an annual loss of 230 million yuan in output value.[47]

Having clothes tailor-made and goods repaired, buying a
quick meal, and hiring a baby-sitter used to be difficult to
achieve in the cities. With the relaxation of migration controls,
peasant workers have rapidly moved into the urban service sector to meet these and other demands. Without the need to
answer to the plans of state authorities, and with their ability to
respond promptly to the market, these workers have quickly
made their presence known in the cities. There have been anecdotal reports that city residents have complained about the
inconvenience they must experience during the Spring Festival,
when almost all "floaters" return home for their family reunions.

Fostering Rural-to-Urban Integration

Despite the Chinese Revolution's peasant origin, rural-urban inequalities persisted throughout the first three decades of the People's Republic. Although the more recent widening of the urban-rural gap pushed a great number of peasants farther afield, the movement might turn out to be part of the solution for this growing gap. In 1992, farmers from Anhui alone earned 7.5 billion yuan ($862 million), 45 percent more than the province's annual financial revenues.[48] In many impoverished rural areas, labor export has become the "pillar industry" for regional development.[49]

The potential of labor mobility to advance modernization and rural-urban integration is increasingly appreciated by many sending provinces, which is the reason for their positive efforts to strengthen the organization and protection of their peasant workers.[50] Even the mobility between village and town "introduces an element of modernization since it broadens the scope of peasant activities and establishes contacts between persons from different types of environments."[51]

Transregional flows of peasant workers have not only transformed the burden of rural surplus labor into wealth by increasing peasant incomes; they have also brought back to rural areas valuable human resources, although it is granted that some returnees are those who have failed. Successful peasants—with their newly acquired skills and ample financial savings—have certainly made an impact on local economies. Many have opened their own businesses. Of the 21,000 village and township enterprises in Anhui Province's Mengcheng, for example, 12,000 were established by returning peasant workers.[52]

Promoting Systemic Change

A more mobile population invigorates the economy with a freer flow of labor and knowledge. At the same time, it is also a sign of an open society. Sometimes, the government's efforts to manage the large flows of peasant workers made systemic changes unavoidable. For example, a study by the Policy Research Division of the CPC (Communist Party of China) Central Committee pointed out that transregional flows of the rural labor force have helped form a unified and open national labor market.[53] Such flows have also created pressure on the government to speed up the reform of residence and labor laws.

As rural laborers continue to hit the road, there has already been a de facto relaxation of migration policy. Increasingly, the role of the registration system in controlling migration is being called into question.[54] Although there is not yet a set agenda, the reform of the hukou system is under way, which many hope will end the artificial divide between city dwellers and country folks. Shandong Province, for instance, has decided to implement a localized hukou system for its cities and towns. Landless peasants and farmers turned factory- and service-workers can now apply for the localized city and township hukou with basically the same rights and obligations conferred on residents under the state administration.[55]

To tackle the root causes of the mingong wave and bring about a healthier evolution of the rural economy, the government has gradually institutionalized a series of reforms, including strengthening grassroots structures in rural enterprises and granting democratic power to village committees. Although the process of establishing new structures will take considerable time, there is little doubt that today's villages enjoy much greater autonomy than those of a decade ago.[56]

Burdening Infrastructure

In theory, urban services such as hospitals, schools, wholesale markets, and sewer and water facilities can be provided at lower cost per person for a concentrated population.[57] In this view, migrants may bring a city into a size range that allows for a more efficient provision of services. This is not necessarily true for large Chinese cities. One can probably talk about economies of scale in terms that the migrant addition to the labor force may result in greater specialization and increased labor productivity. As far as service provision is concerned, however, many cities in China have exceeded the optimal size range because of their weak infrastructures.[58] More migrants bring diseconomies of scale. And that could be the consideration behind the State Council's regulation that no work units should recruit new peasant workers during the month after the Chinese New Year.[59] Not only can the country's backward railway system not bear the burden, but the cities face severe difficulties in providing adequate housing, public transport, and other services to the predictable influxes of peasant workers around the time of the New Year Festival.

Challenging Social Order and Law Enforcement

The mingong wave also produces other side effects. Caught in an administrative vacuum, the floating population poses major challenges to law enforcement and social order. Living in a competitive and often unfriendly environment, peasant workers soon find out that the cities are not heaven, either. Although most do not channel their frustration toward antisocial activity, there is evidence that many more of them are committing crimes. In Shanghai, only 6.8 percent of committed criminals in 1983 were floaters. Six years later, the figure had soared to 31.4 percent. The seriousness of the crimes has also increased: in 1989, floaters were implicated in one of every three cases of murder or robbery in the cities.[60]

Peasant workers are also complicating family planning efforts. Because of the age selectivity of migration, the percentage of women of childbearing age has often been much higher in the floating population. A survey in Shanghai showed that peasant workers were 13 times more likely to break family planning rules than permanent residents.[61] In some areas, more than two-thirds of the unplanned births reported are in mingong families.[62] This is threatening to undermine the country's efforts to control population growth.

Implications for Illegal Chinese Immigration to the United States

The Continuing and Growing Mingong Flow

The development of rural enterprises has absorbed more than half of China's surplus farmers, but that still leaves 124 million idling at home and that number is expected to soar to 200 million by the year 2000. The Ministry of Agriculture plans to have 5 million farmers employed in newly established village and township enterprises every year during the Ninth Five-Year Plan.[63] Assuming that the plan can be successfully implemented—and taking into account as many as 100 million peasants already on the move—still leaves 75 million underemployed on the farm.

Given the natural economic advantages of the coastal regions, the income gap between these areas and the hinterland is almost certain to grow for many years. As long as this gap exists, rural laborers will continue to flow to the coastal cities. Despite periodic crackdowns by local authorities at the receiving end, the government has not been successful in putting a halt to the flow of peasant workers. Realizing that the growth of nonagricultural services alone cannot solve China's problems with rural underemployment, the central authorities are likely to continue the general policy of easing barriers to migration.

Illegal Migration as a Group Behavior

Group behavior refers to the phenomenon of different entities adopting the same pattern of behavior for various reasons. This can take place between as few as two persons or among a mass of two million. Therefore, without making a quantitative assessment the study of group behavior would have little social consequence. Some Chinese scholars have tried to apply the concept of population size as a means to study group behavior in such diverse situations as purchasing durable consumer goods and transforming economic systems in China.[64] A 1995 U.S. Interagency Working Group report identified southern Fujian Province as the main source of illegal Chinese migrants to the United States. Why is this trafficking so concentrated in one particular region? It appears that trafficking in Fujianese migrants also lends itself well to analysis using the concept of group behavior.

Population size influences group behavior in certain basic ways.[65] Generally, people's needs play an important role in triggering human behavior. The more people with similar needs, the more solid the basis for large-scale group behavior. Often, people gather information about the fulfillment of their needs through others' behavior. The intensity of such information often influences their decisions about whether to emulate the behavior. When there is a large population with similar needs, it is easier to achieve that level of information intensity necessary to incite group behavior. Moreover, when a particular group behavior develops to a certain level, it will create strong psychological pressures on others outside the group to follow suit. The larger the population size, the greater the scope of group behavior, and hence the heavier the pressure, which in turn magnifies the scope of the group behavior.

This is exactly what happened in southern Fujian, an area with a strong tradition of out-migration. *Zhoushui* (literally, walk the water) in the dialect of the region means going overseas to make a living. Just as peasants in northern China used to risk the journey to *guandong* (northeastern China) to escape famine or poverty, in southern Fujian it was once a common household survival strategy for one member of the household to brave the sea.[66] In some counties around Fuzhou, the coastal provincial capital, almost every household has one or more relatives abroad.

Fujian has been one of the fastest growing provinces in China and peasants' incomes have increased steadily. Still, their lives are not yet as comfortable as those of city dwellers, not to mention their relatives in the United States. When the U.S. government opened the door to political asylum to Chinese migrants in 1989, snakeheads (migrant traffickers, *shetou* in Chinese) strengthened their operations, and small streams of illegal migrants began to reach American shores. Initial success stories were plentiful. In other parts of China, peasants commonly hear stories, as presented by the Chinese press, about the "dark side" of American society. In Fujian, personal accounts from those who made it to the "golden mountain," along with the new apartment blocks built with migrant remittances, speak more eloquently. Even some local officials became convinced that illegal migration was beneficial to investment and income-generation.[67] Those who stayed behind began to feel real pressure to follow the early trailblazers. As one journalist noted, in the areas where most illegal migrants originated, "people look down on you if you haven't the heart to go abroad, and no girl will like you if you don't give it a try."[68] Thus more and more local residents were at the same time lured and pushed to take part in this group behavior.

In the theory of group behavior, there is also a hypothesis that people's needs and order of preference can be influenced by others. A susceptible "peripheral population" whose demand structure deviates from that of a certain group will also participate in the group behavior under certain conditions. In the face of China's growing floating population, it is not surprising that many are wondering: Do peasant workers in other parts of the country constitute such a "peripheral population" that will eventually follow the path of Fujianese illegal migrants? This paper would argue that although worrying signs exist that may give rise to legitimate concerns, such concerns are unlikely to materialize, and there is very little correlation between the flow of peasant workers and illegal emigration from China.

Some Cause for Concern

The very fact that peasant workers are on the move makes them more susceptible to the false promises of illegal migration. It is generally recognized that migrants tend to be positively selected with respect to youth and education and that they are usually highly motivated and willing to take risks.[69] As one of the top beneficiaries of China's reform and open-door policy, Fujian has the fifth highest intraprovincial mobility ratio in the country: for every 1,000 residents, 27 were on the move within their home province between 1985 and 1990.[70] As these peasant workers move to the areas where snakeheads operate, they will become aware of and may be tempted to take advantage of "opportunities" to go abroad. In other words, the very presence of these people who come from the same region and share the same dialect and tradition increases the size of the population base for group behavior.

As for peasant workers who underwent a two- or three-day trip from inland provinces to coastal cities, they might have even more reason to embark on the perilous journey abroad. The environment they find themselves in, according to the observations of sociologist Dorothy Solinger, "runs from chilly to frigid":

> Granted, many of them may not mind the harsh living conditions if their only motive is to scrape together capital that will be enjoyed back on the farm. But some untold proportion are camping down in the cities with some measure of permanence, and for them, the closed class order, the biased ownership structure, the irregular labor market, the party-dominated political system, the flimsy patronage networks, the elitist educational system, the barren housing market, and the snobbish citizens are bound to rankle.[71]

And the author concluded: "Integration for the floating population is blocked, stymied, or distorted." For those who do not wish to go back to the land, this prospect is certainly very grim and might push them from the "periphery" closer toward the center of action. Although some cities have started the practice of selling permanent residence cards, the price is universally high.[72] Compared to the fee of 50,000 yuan required of each individual migrant worker to live in Beijing, the normal 10 percent up-front payment of trafficking fees does not seem so high after all.

Recent studies, however, as the above-cited paper cautions, have focused on the lives of peasant workers in the big cities. But the majority of the movers are moving within the countryside and to medium and small cities and towns.[73] Besides, the situation is not immutable. The decline of the urban benefit provision system and impending reform of the hukou system indeed suggest otherwise. And, as the following discussion will argue, the step from migration within China to illegal migration abroad might prove too big for many peasant workers to take.

Does the Correlation Exist?

For many of China's peasant workers, making the decision to search for better-paying jobs in the cities is a rational process. According to a survey of peasant workers in Guangdong, a majority (85.3 percent) had their job assignments and work unit arrangements prepared before they arrived. Less than 10 percent could not find employment within a week of their arrival at their destination.[74] Besides, peasant workers tend to flow within the networks formed by relatives and friends who help one another with relocation and any other difficulties. As discussed above, most move for economic reasons and send remittances home regularly. During the Chinese New Year, everyone vies for a ticket back home for the yearly family reunion. This is vastly different from the "blind and dangerous flow" that was sometimes portrayed in the media.

When the "opportunities" of illegal migration find them, peasant workers will confront the same decision-making process: What are the prospects of finding a job abroad? How much more can I expect to earn? How much do I have to pay the snakeheads? How do I value the experience abroad? What is it like living in a strange country? Only when the expected future income differentials and perceived non-economic benefits are believed to be sufficient to offset the cost of the journey and other perceived costs will the potential migrant decide to make the move. These calculations may sound too complicated and unrealistic, but interviews with returned or aspiring migrants have revealed that such calculations not only are common, but often involve all family members.[75]

Expected future employment and income differentials. Extreme income disparities between China and Western countries such as the United States are major "pull" factors that influence migrants' decisions. In 1993, Fujian Province reported an increase of net rural per capita income beyond 1,000 yuan for the first time,[76] but a migrant working in a Chinatown restaurant in a Western country can probably save the same amount in a week to send back home. This income differential can be realized, however, only if the migrant can find a job. And just as only expected future incomes are relevant, it is the perceived possibility of finding work that affects the migration decision.

Researchers have documented that out-migration is heavily dependent on past migration traditions and existing social networks.[77] In China, peasant workers also rely heavily on social networks, especially those based on kinship and native place, for employment and survival at the destination. Formation of the *tongxianghui*—an association of people from the same native place—is a long tradition in Chinese society.[78] Although such formal organizations disappeared in many places some time ago, informal social networks do exist to strengthen the ties among *tongxiang* and promote their common interests. Every year after the Spring Festival, returning peasant workers often bring back with them their fellow villagers who also aspire to a life in the city. Introductions and arrangements by relatives and friends figure prominently in their search for jobs.[79] For migrants from regions with a strong tradition of emigration, similar types of assistance from the tongxiang are normally available. This is why almost all illegal Fujianese migrants have ended up in New York City, which already has a large Fujianese population.[80] Peasant workers from other regions, however, cannot hope to enjoy such benefits.

Cost of moving. According to commonly cited figures, illegal Chinese migrants are charged up to $35,000 per head for the journey to the United States.[81] Even if only a 10 percent up-front payment is sometimes required, that is still an exorbitant price beyond the means of most rural residents.

Many trafficked migrants from Fujian have had to resort to loan sharks after exhausting all resources from friends and relatives. Migrant trafficking is not a simple transaction between migrants and snakeheads; friends, relatives, and loan sharks are often the first link in a long chain of false promises, exploitation, and corruption. A common desire to emigrate, however, and the large amounts of disposable income available in origin areas

along the coast of Fujian have greatly facilitated its development.[82] Without the pool of overseas remittances and the access
to the trafficking chain, peasant workers in other areas may find
it difficult even to borrow enough money for the trafficking fees.

The high concentration of trafficked migrants in Fujian is
also related to the way in which trafficking networks operate.
Willard Myers of the Center for the Study of Asian Enterprise
Crime defines transnational ethnic Chinese criminal activity as
"a global trade in prohibited commodities and services conducted . . . among members of culturally recognized affinity
groups located from point of supply to point of destination."[83]
In other words, overseas Fujianese continue to maintain a strong
tie to their origin and kinsmen. They "do business" with their
own people, bound together by lineage and dialect. Snakeheads
are increasingly flexible about their methods of charging and
collecting fees. For example, migrants could become indentured
laborers, or fees could be collected at home after migrants successfully land abroad.[84] Such methods are difficult to enforce
when the client sources become diversified. Kidnapping for
extortion is an emerging crime afflicting Chinese migrants in the
United States, but almost all reported cases have involved only
Fujianese migrants.[85]

Perceived non-economic benefits and costs. In Fujian's countryside, where waves of emigration started as early as the seventeenth century,[86] having a family member abroad is not only a
source of income but also a source of great pride. Highly successful expatriates are "treated like kings" when they come back to
invest in their home country.[87] Getting out to see the world and
coming back to "glorify family and ancestors" becomes almost
an obsession in the area. Unlike Fujianese, however, most rural
laborers would be grateful just for the chance to live in a city.[88] It
is unclear how much more they would value the experience of
going abroad. The psychological costs of being away from home
and living in a foreign, uncertain environment are certainly
much greater than those associated with migrating within one's
own country.

One of the common risk-aversion strategies for rural migrants is to maintain a base and strong ties with their home communities while taking advantage of employment in other areas,
and Chinese peasants are no exception.[89] Surveys have indicated that up to 99 percent of peasant workers choose to keep
their "responsibility fields" in the family.[90] In the absence of a

rural social safety net, the fields serve as a form of insurance policy.[91] At present, when China is still able to maintain a high economic growth rate, it is still relatively easy for peasant workers
to find employment in the cities. When they cannot, at least they
have their land to come back to. Moreover, most peasant workers have to support their parents back home, and the married
ones have often left their spouses and children behind. These circumstances greatly reduce the "blindness" and insecurity of the
flows of peasant workers. Compared with illegal migration to a
foreign country, internal movement poses considerably less risk
for would-be migrants.

Peasant workers from the same place tend to specialize in
the same trade. In Beijing, for example, it is common to see
young housekeepers and baby-sitters from Anhui Province,
while Xinjiang migrants have earned their reputation as shrewd
traders and money-changers. At the southern edge of the city,
there was a "Zhejiang Village" occupied entirely by people from
Zhejiang Province who mostly specialized in garment processing. Besides providing substantial initial assistance in terms of
apprenticeship and easier entry into the trade, the practice of
remaining with one's own people and engaging in the same
kind of activity provides a sense of security and greatly reduces
the perceived psychological costs of moving into an unfamiliar
environment. Field studies of Mexican and Colombian migrants
show that the attraction of staying with kin or friends is so
strong that the migrant will remain with them in peripheral
shanty towns even though this may limit the migrant's employment opportunities.[92] As discussed above, however, most peasant workers in foreign countries do not have such social
networks.

In summary, illegal migrants from Fujian and peasant
workers elsewhere form different groups with very different
individual, social, and regional characteristics. For most peasant
workers, although income differentials are a powerful "pull"
factor, the perceived difficulty in finding work, the exorbitant
trafficking fees, and the risks of living in an unfamiliar foreign
country are all intervening obstacles that appear to restrain them
from resorting to the snakeheads.

The Role of Government

Many critics of China predicted the collapse of China after Deng
Xiaoping's death and cited the floating population as one of the

potentially destabilizing forces and a source of refugees flooding China's neighbors should their predictions materialize.[93] The problem with such judgment is that it underestimates the country's resilience and the government's ability to adapt to new situations. Concerted efforts by the government in exercising macro-control and accommodating the flows of peasant workers could influence the level of illegal migration.

The flow of peasant workers is a historical trend brought about by the government itself in its effort to build a market economy. Even as security officials decry the urban crime wave caused by peasant workers, few deny their contribution to the national economy. At present, government strategies focus on developing rural enterprises and speeding up the development of towns and small cities.[94] This policy of macro-control and accommodation is likely to continue, partly because the reactive measures have proved ineffective and partly because gradualism and pragmatism have always been the hallmark of China's reform and open-door policy.

This is not to say that it will be an easy task for the government to achieve the orderly flow of peasant workers. In large cities, peasant workers still suffer from the inconsistency of the government's carrot-and-stick policy. Except during campaigns such as the recent "Strike Hard" anti-crime effort, their plight generally receives scant official attention. As a World Bank official conceded, "China's cities and towns are intrinsically capable of supporting these rural migrants, but it won't happen without an activist government policy."[95]

Recent developments indicate a silver lining, however. At the Rural-Urban Transformation Conference organized by the Ford Foundation in Beijing in June 1996, researchers and social workers advocated a more lenient policy toward the peasant workers, and policymakers at the conference appeared to be receptive. In a bid to accommodate hundreds of thousands of rural migrants relocating in urban areas, the State Council is spending U.S.$100 million to find or create jobs for them with assistance from the World Bank.[96] Other examples also point to the government's efforts to adapt to changing situations, with characteristic pragmatism. Some mingong sending provinces have started to implement a new rural social security policy. So far, 2 million farmers in Anhui and 3 million in Zhejiang have joined the rural pension plans, which were nonexistent before.[97]

Experiments such as this, if successful, are expected to spread gradually to other areas. Realizing the danger of growing inequality, the government has promised to give more importance to the development of central and western regions during the Ninth Five-Year Plan. Starting in 1996, state grain procurement prices were to be increased by 20 percent to narrow the gap between rural and urban incomes.[98] Important institutional reforms and holistic measures like these, it is hoped, will reduce the risk level of the mingong flow and make staying put at home a more viable choice.

Notes

1. John Naisbitt, *Megatrends Asia* (Beijing: Waiwen Chubanshe, 1996).

2. Craig S. Smith, "Tide of Migrants Erodes Stability in China," *Asian Wall Street Journal*, February 3–4, 1995. The figure of 60 million migrants in the quote was one estimate as of 1995. Today some experts estimate the number of internal, or floating, migrants in China to be as high as 100 million.

3. The Atlantic Council and National Committee on U.S.-China Relations, *United States and China: Relations at a Crossroads*, Policy Paper, David M. Lampton and Alfred D. Wilhelm, co-rapporteurs, Washington D.C., February 1993.

4. Dorothy J. Solinger, "China's Transients and the States: A Form of Civil Society?" *Politics & Society* 21, no. 1 (1993): 91–122.

5. Lang Sheng, "Zhongguo Liudong Renkou Xunsu Zhengzhang de Yuanyin yi Bianhua Qushi" (The reason for the rapid growth of China's floating population and its changing trends), in Ji Dangsheng and Shao Qin, eds., *Zhongguo Renkou Liudong Taishi yu Guanli* (The trends and management of population flow in China) (Beijing: Zhongguo Renkou Chubanshe, 1995).

6. Judith Banister, *China's Changing Population* (Stanford: Stanford University Press, 1987).

7. United Nations, *World Population Trends and Policies*, Population Studies, no. 79 (New York: UN Department of International Economic and Social Affairs, 1982).

8. Gregory E. Guldin, *Urbanizing China* (New York: Greenwood, 1992); J. Wang and T. H. Hull, *Population and Development Planning in China* (Sydney: Allen & Unwin Publishing, 1991).

9. Sidney Goldstein and Alice Goldstein, *Population Mobility in the People's Republic of China* (Honolulu: East-West Center, 1985).

10. R. J. R. Kirkby, *Urbanization in China: Town and Country in a Developing Economy 1949–2000* (New York: Columbia University Press, 1985).

11. Xiushi Yang, "Household Registration, Economic Reform and Migration," *International Migration Review* 27, no. 4 (1993): 796–818.

12. John K. Fairbank, *China: A New History* (Cambridge: Harvard University Press, 1992).

13. Goldstein and Goldstein, *Population Mobility* (see note 9).

14. Yang, "Household Registration" (see note 11).

15. Alice Goldstein, Sidney Goldstein, and Shenyang Guo, "Temporary Migrants in Shanghai Households, 1984," *Demography* 28 (1984): 275–291.

16. Yat-ming Siu and Si-ming Li, "Population Mobility in the 1980s: China on the Road to an Open Society," *China Review 1993* (Hong Kong: Chinese University Press, 1993).

17. Junsheng Chen, "The Problem of Surplus Rural Labor and its Basic Countermeasures," *BBC Summary of World Broadcasts*, Fe/2227, S1/7, February 14, 1995.

18. Xinhua News Agency, March 9, 1996, 14:04 GMT.

19. Kam-wing Chan, "Urbanization and Rural-Urban Migration," *Modern China* 20, no. 3 (1994): 255–281; *Beijing Daily*, February 20, 1994, 3; Xinhua News Agency, July 9, 1995, 03:30 GMT.

20. Mengbai Li and Yin Hu, *Liudong Renkou deui Dachengshi Fazhan de Yingxiang ji Duice* (The impact of the floating population on the development of large cities and counter-measures) (Beijing: Zhongguo Jiancha Chubanshe, 1991).

21. Chen, "Problem of Surplus Rural Labor" (see note 17).

22. Joint Workshop on Drifting Labor Force in Guangdong Province, "Zai Liudong Zhong Shixian Jingying Yimin—Guangdongsheng Wailai Mingong Diaoyan Baogao" (Elite immigration in flowing status—Survey of the drifting labor force in Guangdong Province), *Zhanlue yu Guangli* (Strategy and management), no. 5 (1995): 112–120.

23. Daniel Kwan, "Drifters Head North for Work," *South China Morning Post* (Hong Kong), December 7, 1993.

24. Jing He, "The Peasant Wave: Good and Bad News," *Chengshi Wenti* (Urban problems), no. 5 (1994): 39–41.

25. Jingsheng Wei, "Gaige Kaifan Yilai Woguo Nongcun de Renkou Yidong," (China's rural population movement since the reforms and opening) in Ji and Shao, *Zhongguo Renkou Liudong Taishi yu Guanli* (see note 5).

26. Joint Workshop on Drifting Labor Force in Guangdong Province (see note 22).

27. Xinhua News Agency, May 2, 1995, 03:06 GMT.

28. Chunyuan Zhang, "Nongcun Renkou Liudong yu Jingji Shouru de Zengzhang" (Rural population flow and income growth), *Zhongguo Renkou Kexue* (Chinese demography), no. 5 (1991).

29. Jeffrey R. Taylor and Judith Banister, *China: The Problem of Employing Surplus Rural Labor*, CIR Staff Paper, no. 49 (Washington, D.C.: Center for International Research, Bureau of the Census, 1989).

30. *China Daily*, May 17, 1994, 4.

31. Taylor and Banister, *China: The Problem of Employing Surplus Rural Labor* (see note 29).

32. Chen, "Problem of Surplus Rural Labor" (see note 17).

33. *China Daily*, November, 15, 1993, 4.

34. Jun Han, "Mingong Chao: Yige Kua Shiji de Nanti" (The wave of peasant workers: A cross-century dilemma), *Zhongguo Gongshang Shibao* (China business times), February 19, 1994.

35. State Statistical Bureau of PRC, *China Statistical Yearbook 1989* (New York: Praeger, 1990).

36. Dorothy J. Solinger, "The Danwei Confronts the Floating Population (or: The Socialist Work Unit Confronts Migrant Labor)" (paper presented at the annual meeting of the Association for Asian Studies, Boston, March 23–27, 1994).

37. *EIU* (Economist Intelligence Unit), *Country Report: China/Mongolia* (London: EIU, 1994, 2d quarter/ 1995, 1st quarter).

38. Taylor and Banister, *China: The Problem of Employing Surplus Rural Labor* (see note 29).

39. Xinhua News Agency, March 8, 1996.

40. Xiangdong Liu, "Nongmin Fudan Jianxiaoqu le ma?" (Has the burden on peasants reduced?), *Liaowang* (Outlook), no. 12 (1996).

41. *China Business Times,* March 25, 1996, 1.

42. Yimin Shen and Chengzhu Tong, *Zhongguo Renkou Qianyi* (China's population movement) (Beijing: Zhongguo Tongji Chubanshe, 1992).

43. Solinger, "China's Transients" (see note 4).

44. *People's Daily,* September 8, 1985, 4.

45. Xinhua News Agency, April 8, 1996.

46. Joint Workshop on Drifting Labor Force in Guangdong Province (see note 22).

47. Solinger, "Danwei" (see note 36).

48. *China Daily,* May 21, 1994, 4.

49. Changping Wu, "Cong Gaige, Fazhan, Wending de Gaodu Shenshi Nongmin Liuqian" (Examining peasant migration from the angle of reform, development and stability), in Ji and Shao, *Zhongguo Renkou Liudong Taishi yu Guanli* (see note 5).

50. Xinhua News Agency, January 10, 1996.

51. Sidney Goldstein and Alice Goldstein, *Permanent and Temporary Migration Differentials in China,* East-West Population Institute Paper, no. 117 (Honolulu: East-West Center, 1991).

52. Han, "Mingong Chao" (see note 34).

53. Policy Research Division, Communist Party of China (CPC) Central Committee, "Guanyu nongcun laodongli kua quyu liudong wenti de chubu janjiu" (Preliminary study on transregional flows of rural labor force), in Ji and Shao, *Zhongguo Renkou Liudong Taishi yu Guanli* (see note 5).

54. Cathy Chen, "China Seeks End to Rural-Urban Divide," *Asian Wall Street Journal,* April 25, 1994.

55. Hui Song, "Huji Zhidu Neng Buneng Gai, Zhenma Gai" (Can household registration system be reformed, and how?), *Zhongguo Xinxi Bao* (China information daily), May 16, 1994.

56. CNA (China News Analysis) (Taiwan), *Floating Around the Towns,* no. 1527, January 15, 1995.

57. D. Turnham and I. Jaeger, *The Employment Problem in Less Developed Countries,* (Paris: Organization for Economic Cooperation and Development, 1971)

58. Xinhua News Agency, December 3, 1994.

59. Yaming Sun, "Zhongguo Tielu Guonianguan" (Chinese railway spends the new year), *China Youth Daily,* February 20, 1995.

60. Shen and Tong, *Zhongguo Renkou Qianyi* (see note 42).

61. Jasper Becker, "City-bound Peasants on the Increase," *South China Morning Post* (Hong Kong), March 24, 1995.

62. Wei, "Gaige Kaifan Yilai Woguo Nongcun de Renkou Yidong" (see note 25).

63. Xinhua News Agency, March 3, 1996.

64. Shiding Liu and Jiyan Hu, *Qutong Xingwei Yu Renkou Guimo* (Group behavior and population size) (Beijing: Zhongguo Renkou Chubanshe, 1993).

65. Ibid.

66. Xing Zhou, "Difang Chuantong yu Minnan Fazhan" (Local tradition and the development of southern Fujian) in Gao Mingqun, ed., *Shishi Shang-gong Wenhua Yanjiu* (The study of commercial culture in Shishi) (Xiamen: Xiamen University Press, 1995).

67. Chengrong Guo and Hongxiong Wu, "Minguanyuan xi Toudu Nei-wei Yuanyin" (Fujian officials analyze the reasons for migrant trafficking), *Wen Wei Po* (Hong Kong), June 11, 1993.

68. Peter Woolrich, "The Secret Underworld of the Triads," *South China Morning Post* (Hong Kong), March 14, 1993.

69. Samuel A. Stouffer, "Intervening Opportunities: A Theory Relating Mobility and Distance," *American Sociological Review* 5, no.6 (1940): 845–867.

70. *China Population Daily,* July 8, 1991, 2.

71. Dorothy J. Solinger, "The Floating Population in the Cities: Chances for Assimilation?" (paper presented at the Conference on "City Living, City Lives: The Potential for Community and Autonomy in Post-Mao China," convened by the Woodrow Wilson Center, Washington, D.C., May 1–4, 1992).

72. *China Daily,* November 28, 1994, 4.

73. Solinger, "Floating Population" (see note 71).

74. Joint Workshop on Drifting Labor Force in Guangdong Province (see note 22).

75. Woolrich, "Secret Underworld" (see note 68); Seth Faison, "With Eye on Dollar, Chinese are Blind to Danger," *New York Times,* October 21, 1995.

76. *Wen Wei Po* (Hong Kong), March 23, 1994.

77. Sally Findley, *Rural Development and Migration: A Study of Family Choices in the Philippines* (Boulder: Westview Press, 1987).

78. G. William Skinner, "Introduction: Urban Social Structure in Ch'ing China," in G. William Skinner, ed., *The City in Late Imperial China* (Stanford, Calif.: Stanford University Press, 1977).

79. Solinger, "China's Transients" (see note 4).

80. Paul Mooney and Melana Zyla, "Braving the Seas and More," *Far Eastern Economic Review*, April 8, 1993, 17–19.

81. IOM (International Organization for Migration), *Trafficking in Migrants: An Overview* (paper no. 1, presented at the IOM Seminar on International Response to Trafficking in Migrants and the Safeguarding of Migrant Rights, Geneva, October 26–28, 1994).

82. United States Information Agency, *Beijing's Boat People: China's Response to the Problem of Illegal Emigration*, research memorandum prepared by Robert J. Levy, Washington, D.C., September 15, 1993.

83. Willard H. Myers III, Transnational Ethnic Chinese Organized Crime: A Global Challenge to the Security of the United States, Testimony before the U.S. Senate Committee on Foreign Affairs, Subcommittee on Terrorism, Narcotics and International Operations, April 21, 1994.

84. Guo and Wu, "Minguanyuan xi Toudu Neiwei Yuanyin" (see note 66).

85. Rone Tempest, "Emigration: In the South, Wave that Began in '89 Seems to Have Ebbed," *Los Angeles Times*, October 23, 1995.

86. Shen and Tong, *Zhongguo Renkou Qianyi* (see note 42).

87. James McGregor, "Fujian Gets Boost from Overseas Chinese," *Asian Wall Street Journal*, June 4, 1992.

88. Solinger, "Danwei" (see note 36).

89. Oded Stark and David Levhari, "On Migration and Risk in LDCs", *Economic Development and Cultural Change*, no. 31 (1982): 191–196.

90. Maoxiu Wang, "Woguo Nongye Laodongli de Zhuanyi" (The transfer of China's rural labor force), *Renkou yu Jingji* (Population and economy), no. 3 (1987).

91. Judith Banister, "China's Population Changes and the Economy," in *China's Economic Dilemmas in the 1990s: The Problems of Reforms, Modernization, and Interdependence*, Vol. 1 (1991), Study papers submitted to the Joint Economic Committee, Congress of the United States, 234–251.

92. Sally Findley, *Planning for Internal Migration: A Review of Issues and Policies in Developing Countries* (Washington, D.C.: U.S. Bureau of the Census, 1977).

93. Carl Goldstein and Lincoln Kaye, "Get Off Our Backs," *Far Eastern Economic Review*, July 15, 1993, 68–75; Robert Weil, "China at the Brink: Class Contradictions of 'Market Socialism,'" *Monthly Review* 46, no. 8 (1995): 11–28.

94. Xinhua News Agency, July 8, 1995.

95. Toh Han Shih, "Silver Lining Seen in Migration into Cities," *Business Times*, May 17, 1996.

96. "Migrant Labour: A Nation on the Move in China," *EIU Business China* (Economist Intelligence Unit), June 24, 1996.

97. Xinhua News Agency, April 1, 1996 and April 19, 1996.

98. "China Industry: New Focus on Farming Seeks to Up Grain Output," EIU ViewsWire (Economist Intelligence Unit), March 22, 1996.

3

A Tsunami on the Horizon? The Potential for International Migration from the People's Republic of China

Jack A. Goldstone

"Resolved: That a Committee of three Senators be appointed to investigate the character, extent, and effect of Chinese immigration to this country, with power to visit the Pacific coast for that purpose, and to send for persons and papers, and to report at the next session of Congress."[1]

Concern about the potential for Chinese emigration to the United States has been felt for more than a century. And for good reason. The 1877 congressional report cited above noted that China "is within four weeks sail of this port, and the price of passage is only $40, and from present indications I should judge that this people, if encouraged, will become the most migratory on the globe; for notwithstanding the comparatively short time their ports have been open to free commerce, some of their people may be found in every part of the civilized world."[2] Today, China is once again entering a period in which its ports have been "open to free commerce" for a relatively short time, since Deng Xiaoping's post-1978 economic reforms. As of 1990, 1.65 million persons of Chinese ancestry resided in the United States, the result of prior waves of China-U.S. migration.[3] Consideration of China's rapidly changing circumstances suggests that further waves of migration to the United States are likely.

International migration generally does not flow from countries that are too poor or too well-off. If a country is too poor, the bulk of its citizens will be too engrossed in scraping together a living, too ignorant of other opportunities, and too far removed from the transportation and communication networks that initiate, facilitate, and sustain international migration. If a country is sufficiently well-off, the costs and risks of migration are usually outweighed by staying at home. It is in the middle range, when a country is emerging from extreme poverty, building its infrastructure, and accumulating savings, but before the majority of its population have achieved a stable and comfortable standard of living, that international migration has generally surged.

The world must now brace for the fact that about 2 billion people in Asia are fast approaching that "middle range" that has often been marked by substantial international migration. In China in particular, current growth rates—combined with some specific features inherited from four-and-a-half decades of rule by the Chinese Communist Party—will create opportunities and incentives for millions to seek to emigrate. India and other countries of South and East Asia—with either populations or incomes growing more slowly than those of China—will be perhaps a decade behind, but will still contribute to the flow of people seeking livelihoods abroad.

Thus, even under favorable scenarios for political stability and economic growth in China, illegal migration from China to the United States is liable to grow by a factor of 6 in the next five years, and by a factor of 10 in the next decade, rising to perhaps 200,000 to 300,000 per year by 2005. Over the next 10 years, attempts at illegal immigration from all of Asia to the United States are likely to rise to more than half a million per year, or more than half the current level of illegal migration to the United States from Mexico. If political instability or economic slowdowns should develop in China, the number of migrants from China seeking entry into the United States could become comparable to or exceed the number from Mexico. The difficulties and contradictions facing China's regime make some such instability likely to develop, if not in the next decade, then soon thereafter, making a wave of immigration from China a major issue for the United States at some point in the next 10 to 15 years.

The Recent History of International Migration to the United States

As of 1978, Asia overtook North and Central America as the largest source of legal immigration to the United States, and it maintained that lead throughout the 1980s.[4] In the five years from 1985 to 1989, while 360,000 legal immigrants were admitted from Mexico, more than 250,000 were admitted from the Philippines, 174,000 from South Korea, 135,000 from India, and 130,000 from China. Moreover, the most rapid growth in legal immigration has been from Asia; whereas legal admissions from Mexico increased by just over 50 percent from the 1960s to the 1980s, those from the Philippines and from China doubled in the same period.[5]

This trend has been part of a worldwide expansion of Chinese migration. It is estimated that there were 12 million Chinese living overseas in the 1950s, rising to 22 million in the 1970s, 27 million in the 1980s, and 35 million in the 1990s.[6] Although natural increase among overseas Chinese accounted for the bulk of the growth to the 1980s, the larger recent increase implies a total emigration from China of roughly 180,000 per year in the last decade.[7] Two-thirds of the migrants live in Southeast Asia, including Hong Kong and Singapore; but in recent years, their numbers have been increasing most rapidly in North America and Australia.

If Asians lead legal immigration to the United States, that is not true of total migration, for illegal immigration, particularly from Mexico, swamps the numbers admitted legally. According to one estimate, in recent years the number of Chinese illegally smuggled into the United States (25,000 per year in 1987–1991) is essentially equal to the number legally admitted.[8] The number of illegal migrants from Mexico, however, may be as high as 1 million per year.[9] The total worldwide migration from China is still probably less than one-fifth of that number, and of this total just over one-quarter come to the United States. It must be stressed that all of these figures are my interpretations of extremely rough estimates. Still, it appears that current illegal immigration from China to the United States is at least an order of magnitude smaller than that from Mexico. The question facing the United States is whether Chinese-U.S. migration is likely to undergo the kind of massive increase that would bring it closer to Mexican-U.S. migration as a policy concern.

Theories of International Migration

Theories of international migration do not offer a single, clear, cause of migration. Instead, they point to a complex combination of factors that work on various levels. These factors include household structure, national occupational structure, international income differentials, internal income inequality, economic growth, the development of internal and international migrant networks, and the degree of international integration of communications, transport, and the economies of source and receiving societies.[10] Despite this complexity, it is possible to identify conditions under which international migration is likely to grow.

First, international migration is *not* caused mainly by poverty. Instead, "international labor migration largely originates in countries at an intermediate level of development, rather than in countries whose wages are lowest."[11] Development in poor countries, therefore, generally has the effect of *increasing* international migration. As Douglas Massey remarks, "In the short run . . . development does not reduce the impetus for migration, but only increases it."[12] For example, from the 1940s through the 1970s, large increases in U.S.-bound Mexican emigration coincided with rapid economic growth in Mexico; similarly, rapid economic growth in Puerto Rico during the 1950s and 1960s due to Operation Bootstrap was associated with high rates of out-migration to the U.S. mainland.[13]

Development generally increases international migration because economic development operates unevenly on the economy. In particular, the rapid development of agrarian economies implies rationalization and mechanization of agriculture. This in turn implies the replacement of labor-intensive, small-landholding agricultural production by more capital-intensive farming on larger commercial farms. This change leaves large numbers of peasant farmers—or certainly their offspring—without land and without their former livelihood. The size of this pool of unemployed rural labor depends on the initial number of small farmers, the population growth rate of these farmer (and former farming) households, and the rate of consolidation and mechanization of farming, which in turn depends in part on government policies regarding land use, price setting to favor farmers or consumers, and land clearing and irrigation.[14]

The first goal of these displaced households is to find employment. Their strategies for doing so generally reflect the following mix of costs and rewards: the costs of transportation and communication with local towns, farther cities, and international sites of possible migration; the likely income in each of these sites; and the anticipated political costs (border controls, ease of obtaining citizenship) in those sites. Because economic development almost always reduces the costs of communication and transportation at the same time that it displaces rural populations, it is virtually a general rule that "every country that has undergone economic development under a market economy has experienced emigration."[15]

If development makes migration necessary by displacing the landed population, and easier by reducing communication and transportation costs, a decision must still be made about the best destination sites: local towns, farther cities, or international emi-gration. Here, the risk/reward ratios come into play. Generally, more distant travel is justified only by higher anticipated rewards. Thus nearby townships may be easiest to reach, and from there it may be easiest to maintain communication with one's home community. But the income gained may be small. Farther towns may involve higher costs and risks to reach, but also offer higher potential incomes. Finally, international migra-tion offers the highest costs and risks, but also the highest rewards. For example, in China, incomes in average cities are more than twice those in rural townships and villages; incomes in major coastal municipalities such as Shanghai and Guang-zhou are 3 to 4 times higher than those in smaller interior cities; and average incomes in the United States and Hong Kong are 20 times higher than the average income in Shanghai.[16] Thus a rural migrant's choice of destination will be governed by his or her taste for risk. A low-risk, low-reward strategy implies local migration; moderate reward-moderate risk implies migration to a major city; and a tolerance for high risks to obtain high rewards will favor international migration. Indeed, to diversify their risk portfolio, households are likely to diversify their migration strategies as well, sending one or more household members abroad and sending others to internal migration sites.[17]

In addition, there is some evidence that migration is spurred not only by displacement and unemployment, but also by *relative* deprivation, or growing income inequality. That is, households that suffer increasing inequality relative to others may take higher risks to overcome that inequality including emi-gration.[18] Thus economic growth that raises all incomes but increases inequality is likely to increase international emigration, because the poorer households will have both increased resources to enable long-distance migration and increased incen-tives to use a higher-risk, higher-reward migration strategy to overcome their relative income deficit.

Migration thus usually results in separate streams of inter-nal and international migration. There is no clear link between the two streams, for it is not the case that internal migrants simply become international migrants.[19] Rather, international migration is part of a diverse migration strategy that includes both international and internal migration as a response to dis-placement of rural populations; the degree of international and internal migration will reflect the balance between the two of anticipated risks and rewards.

Information on those risks and rewards is transmitted by networks of communication with migrants who have already moved. Such information is crucial to the migration choice, and internal and international migration streams tend to form around networks or circuits of active migrants.[20] Once established, such networks both facilitate and target further migration. As Alejandro Portes observes, "international migration is simultaneously a network-creating and network-dependent process."[21] For this reason, if the conditions in the source country that are "pushing" migration (displacement of workers and low incomes relative to the destination country) are maintained, networks of transnational migrants develop a momentum that helps pull larger and larger numbers of emigrants along the established route, sustaining an increasing volume of immigration.

To sum up, the following economic and social conditions contribute to an accelerating trend in international migration:

1. Large-scale displacement of labor from secure local economic roles (most commonly small farmers) as a consequence of economic development.

2. National policies of land use, pricing, and land reclamation that disfavor small farmers, increasing the necessity for farming households to seek other livelihoods.

3. Infrastructure development that lowers the costs of travel and communication with potential migration sites abroad.

4. Increasing international economic integration that facilitates labor migration as part of patterns of international economic activity.

5. Large income differentials between international migration sites and internal sites (local towns and farther cities) that make international migration an attractive strategy as an alternative or complement to internal migration.

6. Established networks of migrants that facilitate job-finding and settlement transitions (raising expected benefits and lowering risks) for migrants.

7. Political policies in sending and receiving countries that minimize the costs of migration and increase the possible rewards (e.g., allowing travel abroad in sending countries, and allowing settlement, work, and eventual citizenship in receiving countries.)

One further factor that can become important is political uncertainty and turmoil. Loss of political stability can spur international migration directly to escape prosecution, danger, and violence. It can also spur it indirectly, as internal uncertainty raises the risks associated with internal migration or loss of central government control increases the ease of slipping past international borders. Political change, ranging from weakening of the government to overt political violence, can thus exacerbate international migration as well.

The question to ask is how many of the above conditions characterize China and whether they are liable to grow in the years ahead.

Economic Change in China and Its Relation to the International Economy

There is no question that China is undergoing rapid economic development. What is interesting is that China has only just begun, in the last two to five years, to experience the patterns of economic development conducive to growing international migration.

First, China is undergoing a population increase, moderate in rate but still massive in absolute terms, at the same time that it is undergoing a restructuring of its internal labor market and agriculture that is releasing not just tens but hundreds of millions from their ties to the land. Second, while townships and cities in China are absorbing the bulk of these displaced households and their offspring, large income differentials within China, and even larger differentials between incomes in China and incomes abroad, make international migration an attractive option for many. Third, international migration is also being facilitated by increasing integration with the world economy, including much freer travel and transpacific trade, as well as the infrastructure links provided by development. And finally, China has its own special economic problems, involving the system of household registration, state-owned enterprises (SOEs), and the erosion of state welfare provisions. These increase the obstacles to internal migration, promise to release yet more displaced labor, and reduce the state-provided incentives to remain in China. Altogether, these special problems, and their sudden emergence, are likely to exacerbate the trend to international migration.

People, Land, and Labor

The biggest spur to international migration in China—and elsewhere in Asia and the world—is the creation of a surplus rural labor force through the combination of population growth and changes in agriculture that separate people from the land. What is particularly startling in China is the sudden emergence over the past decade of a surplus rural labor force of almost 100 million people, a number that is growing so rapidly that it could reach 250 million by the end of this decade.[22]

In 1985, China's population stood at approximately 1.1 billion. In the last 10 years it has grown another 100 million to 1.2 billion, with much of this growth occurring in the poorer, more rural regions. Over the next 10 years, another 160 million will be added: the population will grow by about 15 million per year for the next 5 years, accelerating to 17 million per year in the 5 years thereafter as the large cohorts of women born during the pronatalist Mao period of the 1960s and 1970s reach their peak childbearing years.[23] Thus, by 2005, China's population will likely reach 1.36 billion, which means that even if there were no displacement from existing agricultural work, at least 260 million new people will be dependent on jobs created since 1985.

This growth has occurred, and seems likely to continue, despite China's strict one-child policy. Although the policy has greatly slowed China's population growth, it seems unlikely that its targets will be met or even that official figures on growth will be accurate. The policy is plagued by evasion, inaccurate reporting of births, and the government's inability to supervise a vast, new "floating population" that, as we shall see below, is outside the household registration system used to enforce the state policy on births.

China's one-child policy rests on the fact that all households must be registered with the state according to their residence classification—either urban or rural. Until 1996, all registered urban households were eligible for state-guaranteed work, schooling, food, and health care (the "iron rice bowl"), all of which could be reduced or rescinded as penalties for excess childbearing. Rural households were eligible for land, schooling, and health care, which provided similar leverage. Under such pressure, sharp falls in birth rates were obtained.

Yet, even where official figures indicate a sharp decline in births, there is evidence of evasion. For example, in several villages in Shanxi Province where researchers found low birth rates, the official figures for the male/female birth ratio are extraordinarily high (1.33 m/f for first births instead of the biological norm of 1.06).[24] This suggests that 25 percent of female births are "missing." Researchers[25] have shown that most of these "missing births" are not due to female infanticide or selective abortion; instead, 45 to 75 percent of them are "hidden" births, which evade official reporting, whereby female babies are sent to live with relatives or neighbors. Indeed, throughout China, the reported male/female ratio is abnormally high and is highest where the one-child policy appears most "successful," casting doubt on the validity of the official figures.[26] These may therefore undercount new births by anywhere from 2 to 10 percent.

Moreover, recent economic development has led to the erosion of the household registration system. During the last decade more than 100 million persons have left their place of residential registration (and their state-guaranteed benefits) to seek work in the private sector in townships and cities. This floating population is able to provide for itself through the market, often enjoying higher incomes (if less security), and is thus no longer subject to the same leverage and penalties for higher births. Even though these "floaters" will not have large families, the urge to have a son means that, on average, they will aim to have at least two children per household, or twice the state target.[27] As the size of the floating population grows, and as the market takes over more functions in China, the government's ability to enforce the one-child policy is certain to erode, and the cultural desire for sons is likely to move the average fertility rate closer to 2.0. For these reasons, China's population growth, rather than suddenly slowing further in accord with official plans, is liable to remain moderate, and perhaps increase, for a decade or more.

In the late 1970s, the bulk of China's population, some 800 million, worked the land. Migration to cities was tightly controlled, and collective farms rooted population to the land. But under Deng Xiaoping's land reform, land was leased to individual families to work as they saw fit. Initially, this reform led to a large increase in the application of labor to the land and to rising rural incomes. Even though landholdings per family were tiny—

less than two-tenths of a hectare, or less than half an acre, per person—the ability to diversify and specialize in different crop mixes, and the profit incentive, led to far higher returns.[28] Rural incomes grew rapidly, and the gap between urban and rural incomes, as well as the differences between incomes in different regions, diminished up to the mid-1980s.[29]

Further economic reforms, including the creation of special economic zones along the coast for foreign investment and the enormous growth of rural manufacturing in villages and townships, have changed this picture. As families grew, the tiny family farms had no use for their additional labor; greater returns could be had by sending family members to the villages and cities to earn salaries. Foreign and domestic investment in manufacturing grew to take advantage of this cheap labor; and with dynamic economic growth, regional and urban/rural income disparities returned. Although rural incomes continued to grow, urban and particularly east coast incomes grew much faster. The gap between annual rural per capita output in central and east China, which was only $52 in 1985, had grown to $214 by 1993. The ratio of urban to rural per capita incomes, which fell from 2.4:1 to 1.7:1 between 1979 and 1984, rose to 2.7:1 by 1995, higher than it had been before the beginning of reforms.[30]

At the same time, farmland has decreased by 10 percent or more in the last decade, because of land lost to erosion and, more significantly, the development of village enterprises, expanding cities and towns, and road and rail facilities.[31] Massive public works projects, such as the planned Three Gorges Dam and other power facilities, will displace further millions from their land. Farming opportunities have thus become fewer and less attractive at the same time that the rural population continues to grow. Of the 260 million "new" population that China will have added between 1985 and 2005, more than 200 million will be born to rural households, and for most of them farm work will be unavailable or unattractive.

In addition, further development of Chinese agriculture is not compatible with land holdings of .2 hectare per person. Model state farms, using larger inputs of capital and mechanization to boost efficiency, average 44 hectares per worker. It is thus estimated that as many as 270 million people could be removed from China's agricultural labor force without affecting production.[32]

It is impossible to estimate how many existing farmers will be displaced, or how quickly, as China's agriculture is modernized. What is clear from the experience of other nations, however, is that a massive shift of population off the farms is an inevitable part of economic development. The existing income disparities (in early 1995, average annual earnings were $91 in rural areas, $237 in cities, and up to $800 in the major east coast cities) suggest that a substantial number of rural dwellers will move off the land in order to equalize family incomes.[33]

Since 1985, when farm incomes again started to decline relative to urban incomes, it is estimated that between 60 million and 100 million people have left their rural residences and become part of a floating population, living from wage labor in the townships or cities. As much as one-quarter of the population of Beijing—more than 3 million out of 12 million—are migrants without permanent urban registration.[34] Migrants also are a large part of the workforce in Guangdong and Shanghai, which are magnets for peasants seeking work.

Estimates of the size of the "surplus" rural farming population in the year 2000 range from the current figure of 100 million[35] to an official Chinese estimate of 200 million[36] to academic estimates as high as 250 million.[37] By 2005, population growth and economic development could add another 100-150 million to that total. In other words, it is not inconceivable that the number of people "freed" from attachment to farming could rise from nearly zero in 1985 to 400 million in the 20 years to 2005, roughly half coming from new population growth and half from movement of the existing farming population.

Townships, Cities, and the World Economy

Where will 300–400 million people facing unemployment and underemployment in the agricultural sector look for work? In the last decade, they moved in increasing numbers to China's rural townships and urban centers. Fortunately, the vast expansion of rural manufacturing has provided employment for tens of millions of workers, while other tens of millions have found work in China's burgeoning cities.

The limits of easy growth in township and urban employment, however, may already be in sight. Recently, driven by complaints about crime and squalor and worried about their ability to maintain control of sprawling cities where migrants are "out" of the system of household registration, authorities have attempted to clamp down on migration to major cities. As part of these efforts officials have razed squatter settlements and imposed "registration" fees of thousands of dollars ($11,600 in Beijing) on migrants seeking permission to reside and work in those cities.[38] In addition, the rate at which township enterprises are adding workers has slowed considerably—competition from both international producers and more capital-intensive, higher-quality production in China's cities has reduced the opportunity for village enterprises to grow simply by adding cheap, unskilled labor.[39] The 100–200 million potential migrants expected in the next 10 years may thus find it harder to improve their conditions by local migration than did the 100 million migrants of the last decade.

Yet China's government is following policies likely to increase migration off the farms. Worried about inflation, the government has reimposed price controls that limit the returns farmers can get for their grain. Although China is trying to control migratory chaos by providing state-subsidized rural jobs as well as by restricting work permits in cities and encouraging urban state-owned enterprises to shed workers, the government lacks the resources to provide rural jobs at wages at all comparable to urban levels.[40] Thus efforts to discourage migration to China's cities are not likely to keep people on the farm so much as they will fuel efforts at illegal migration, both domestic and abroad. Indeed, by imposing up-front fees and other roadblocks to settlement in its cities, China is forcing a larger-than-otherwise stream of potential migrants to seek opportunities overseas.

China's increasing participation in international trade provides the opportunities and information necessary to facilitate international migration. Increased traffic at international ports, more legal traffic from China abroad, and better transportation and communication from China's interior to its borders all lower the costs and risks of movement abroad. It is thus not surprising that illegal migration from China—to Hong Kong, Europe, Asia, and the United States—is growing rapidly.[41]

While low-cost labor in China is a magnet for international foreign investment, the legal (and illegal) export of that labor to manufacturing abroad is equally attractive. The U.S. Labor Department has estimated that in the United States alone there are 11,000 "sweatshops" for cutting and sewing garments using low-cost, often Asian, labor.[42] Large income differentials between work in China and abroad and a vast floating population forced to migrate for work will combine to fuel a steady market for emigration abroad, especially when China's government, through imposition of registration fees and restriction of work permits, raises the costs and risks of immigration to China's cities closer to the costs and risks of international emigration.

China's Special Problems: Urban Registration, State-Owned Enterprises, and the Erosion of the Welfare State

In addition to the normal changes accompanying economic development—a growing displaced farm population and increasing integration with the world economy—China faces special problems because it is making a transition from a centrally controlled socialist economy. This legacy involves three interlinked factors in particular that may encourage international migration: the urban/rural registration system; state-owned enterprises; and the erosion of the welfare state.

As mentioned earlier, population movement in China prior to the 1980s was controlled by the system of registering all households by their place of residence, either rural (farming) or urban. State-provided welfare benefits, and even grain coupons to allow urban residents to obtain their daily rice, provided strong incentives to stay in one's place of registration. In the late 1980s and 1990s, these registration patterns were increasingly evaded and eventually loosened, as tens of millions found they could obtain needed goods and services more readily (and in some cases even become rich) by relying on the free market instead of the state. Opening small businesses or working in international or township enterprises, rural households "moved out" of the registration system. With this powerful link to their place of residence broken, they became free to consider migration in China or abroad.

But in the last two years, as China's government has become concerned over the breakdown of the registration system and the concomitant loss of control over the population, there have been efforts to "tighten up" the system again.[43] Restricting and imposing high costs on urban residence, limiting work permits, and even reinstituting grain coupons for urban households have made it more difficult for migrants to settle in major cities. Using the registration system as a tool for social and political control of urban growth, however, at the same time that population growth and agricultural reform in the countryside have made the rural side of household registration obsolete, distorts the normal trends to migration that accompany economic development and may divert migration abroad.

For urban households, registration was generally a key to lifetime employment and pensions by working at state-owned enterprises. Yet with integration into the world economy, these enterprises have increasingly become inefficient, loss-making operations. With more than 100,000 SOEs employing almost 100 million workers, state-owned firms are still the largest employers of China's urban labor. But this cannot last long. With one-third of these firms losing money and another one-third barely breaking even, there is no room for rapid expansion of employment in these enterprises; instead, there are questions whether even the existing level of work and benefits can be maintained. Reluctant to fire workers because of fears of unrest, state-owned enterprises are nonetheless putting workers on reduced-wage "rest" leaves. They are also being encouraged to drop the "iron rice bowl" of lifetime employment and instead put workers on five-year contracts, with wages tapped to provide the pensions, health care, and housing previously provided by the state.[44]

All of these measures are designed to reduce the pressure on the government of supporting workers in state-owned enterprises. At the same time, they make the urban registration system, which entitles workers to state-provided jobs and benefits, less attractive. Pushing urban workers out of SOEs at the same time that rural workers are being discouraged from taking urban jobs should help provide a steady stream of labor to growing private and foreign-financed enterprises. But it also makes it more likely that at least some urban workers will seek their fortunes abroad.

In sum, prior to the 1980s, China's population was virtually cemented in place by registration and welfare systems put together under Communism. These systems are now being selectively changed. On the one hand, urban registration is being enforced to help block and discourage rural migrants from moving to cities. On the other hand, the benefits that the registration system provided to urban residents are being slowly withdrawn, as the burden of providing welfare benefits to the SOE workforce becomes too great to maintain. The result is that neither the rural nor urban population will soon have incentives to stay in their current locations. Increasingly, China's urban workers are "left to fend for themselves in a half-reformed economy caught between the industrial relics of a centrally planned establishment and the impossibility of funding a much-needed welfare system."[45] While these problems are in some sense a normal "cost" of the adjustment to a free-market system, they also prompt some workers to seek better incomes abroad.

As noted, China's population growth and economic development will create, by 2000, a population of former farm families seeking work of about 200 million, and probably 300–400 million by 2005. Yet the economic sectors that have absorbed much of that population to date—township enterprises, work in the cities, and state-owned enterprises—are unlikely to grow as rapidly as they did in the past or are actively discouraging and shedding workers. At the same time, the gradual dismantling of the registration/SOE/state welfare system in the cities will add further tens of millions to the labor force seeking greater opportunities than they have in their present jobs.

There are essentially only two outlets for these hundreds of millions: working for private and foreign-owned enterprises or emigration abroad. Because it is unlikely that 100 percent of all families will find the first strategy most attractive and fully successful, some proportion of the growing labor force is likely to seek migration. What percentage that will be will depend in large part on political factors in China's future.

Political Change in China and Its Consequences for Migration

Scenarios for China's future following the demise of its dominant figure, Deng Xiaoping, range from business as usual to collapse and civil war.[46] Attaching odds to any of these scenarios is something of a guessing game. Thus it seems wisest to consider several scenarios, along with their implications for emigration.

Can the Center Hold?

Current Party chairman Jiang Zemin has been working hard to consolidate his hold on power for the next decade. He has managed to curry favor with the People's Liberation Army by supporting PLA economic activities and larger defense budgets. He has also packed the politburo with supporters from his home base of Shanghai and has led a so-far successful campaign to discredit the rival Beijing faction in the Communist Party of China (CPC). Senior former general Yang Shangkun, once suspected as a possible leader of an anti-Jiang opposition, has appeared publicly to support Jiang. Many provincial governors, once a source of competition and conflict with the central leadership, have been replaced with compliant bureaucrats. In sum, Jiang seems to have been remarkably successful in overcoming deep fissures in the Party over the pace of democratization, economic reform, and military spending that were apparent at the time of the Tiananmen uprising in 1989.[47]

Theories of revolution point to the necessity of three sets of factors coming together to create the breakdown of a regime: state fiscal failures, divisions and competition among the elite, and popular grievances and mobilization against the state.[48] If Jiang has indeed been successful in overcoming divisions and competition among the central and regional elites and in consolidating support in favor of his leadership and policies, one of the essential conditions for state breakdown is gone, and the threat of a major collapse of government in China will recede in the near future.

Jiang's policies seem clear.[49] He seeks to maintain and restore the primacy of the central party decision-making apparatus in Beijing by diverting more revenue to the central government, appointing compliant regional governors, limiting political dissent and any movement toward democracy, leading an aggressively nationalist foreign policy (including strengthening the army and claims to Taiwan and other regions in the South China Sea), maintaining and supporting state-owned enterprises, and using central economic controls to shape the economy, restrict price movements, and limit and direct internal migration. Two questions arise regarding these policies: (1) Are they the correct policies to continue economic growth while maintaining Party control, and (2) are they a consistent package that can be reasonably implemented?

In the near term—perhaps for up to 10 years—the answer to both questions is yes. Judging from the experience of South Korea, Taiwan, and Mexico—three countries that sought economic growth under restrictive, authoritarian one-party states only to encounter strong pressures for democracy—the economic threshold at which pressures for greater democratization become irresistible is still distant for China. Korea and Taiwan, which have made the transition to democracy, have per capita incomes in excess of U.S.$10,000 per year. Mexico, which is just beginning to face strong pressures for democratic reform, has a per capita income of just over U.S.$3,500 per year.[50] China, on the other hand, has a per capita income of just under U.S.$500 per year. There is room for considerable income growth before

China reaches the level of economic development that spurred political liberalization in Korea, Taiwan, and Mexico.

As long as no major foreign policy or domestic violence incident scares away foreign investment, and as long as the CPC bureaucracy and military remain united behind Jiang, the goal of maintaining economic controls also seems possible. Containing inflation will be difficult, and controlling migration near impossible, without some safety valves. As in the case of Mexico, emigration may help provide that safety valve. The government is already encouraging Chinese workers to move to Tibet and Xinjiang, the most un-Chinese regions controlled by the Chinese state;[51] and there is some evidence of complicity by local officials in migration abroad.[52]

The biggest task for the government in this "united leadership, stable economic growth, strong central control" scenario will be managing regional inequality and autonomy. The continued flow of foreign investment to the coastal regions, where the most labor, capital, and infrastructure for international trade are already in place, will make overcoming the disparity in incomes between the east coast and the western and northern regions difficult or impossible. This disparity will be a powerful "pull" for migration from the overpopulated rural farming regions throughout the country, particularly in the north and the west. In addition, regional and local governments are setting higher targets for investment and growth than are compatible with the central government's goal of restraining growth and pressure on prices.[53] Nonetheless, as long as the central government can count on military and bureaucratic support to enforce central authority and can keep migration within "moderate" bounds, such tensions should not reach disruptive levels.

One clear implication of this scenario is that international migration will increase. It is unlikely that Chinese authorities can follow policies that will both reduce opportunities for farm employment (modernizing and mechanizing agriculture, increasing farm size, limiting the rise in grain prices thus forcing out inefficient producers) *and* restrict immigration to cities (restricting work permits, reintroducing grain coupons, and charging high fees for urban residence permits) without greatly increasing the flow of migrants seeking greater opportunities abroad. And, as noted, increasing incomes, rising inequality, improved transportation and communication infrastructures, and growing international trade should *increase* the number of individuals and households who find the high-risk, high-reward path of international emigration feasible and attractive.

Thus, even under the most favorable political scenario, out-migration from China should continue to increase, probably with assent (if not encouragement) from officials. How large would the flow be, and how much of it would come to the United States?

Currently, it is estimated that combined legal and illegal migration to the United States from China in the early 1990s was 50,000 per year, out of some 180,000 total emigrants per year. At that time, China had a floating population of roughly 100 million. Assuming that the floating population increases to 200–250 million by 2000, and to 300–400 million by 2005, and that the tiny percentage of total migrants seeking opportunities abroad (currently 1.8 per 1000) increases between 20 and 50 percent as a result of the Chinese policies described above, the total number of external migrants would increase, roughly, to somewhere between a conservative 430,000 per year and an upper estimate of as much as 675,000 per year by 2000, and to between a conservative 650,000 and an upper estimate of 1.1 million by 2005.

Because the current percentage of total migrants seeking international migration is currently so small, these numbers could conceivably double, or even triple, in the next 10 years. Mexico currently sends at least 1 million of its 80 million population to the United States each year, although its gross domestic product per capita is seven times as high as China's. As China gets richer, if it similarly would send one-eightieth of its total population in search of greater economic opportunities abroad, total emigration would reach an astonishing 15 million per year. Of course, this is unlikely to occur, given both China's higher rate of economic growth and lower levels of income. Yet if economic growth suddenly slowed in China or if incomes rose but great inequality and massive rural underemployment persisted, the above estimates of roughly one-half million to 1 million total Chinese emigrants per year could be low by an order of magnitude.

If the eventual destination of about 30 percent of China's emigrants remains the United States, the total number of Chinese immigrants seeking entry—both legal and illegal—would increase to roughly 130,000–200,000 per year by 2000 and 200,000–330,000 per year by 2005. If quotas for legal migration from China remain at the current level of under 30,000 per year, then attempted illegal entries would increase over today's levels by about a factor of 6 by 2000 and by a factor of 10 by 2005. This would still be less than one-third of the current illegal migration from Mexico. Nonetheless, because of the association of illegal immigration with other kinds of smuggling and because of its geographic concentration (illegal Chinese migrants from Fujian enter mainly in New York; those from Guangdong, mainly in California), this increase could have significant impacts on law enforcement and immigration efforts in those areas.

It should be noted that India's population is growing faster than China's and should surpass China's sometime early in the next century. Other smaller countries, such as South Korea, Malaysia, Thailand, and the Philippines, are also growing in income and have well-established immigration streams to the United States. Although British Commonwealth countries (Canada, Britain, South Africa) will likely remain the preferred destination of migrants from India and Malaysia, the United States will likely remain the preferred destination of migrants from Korea and the Philippines. None of those countries, however, are in quite the same situation as China. India is not growing as fast economically, and its rural population is not being discouraged from urban migration for political reasons as is China's. In Korea, Thailand, and Malaysia, the differential between local and U.S. income levels is diminishing, reducing the incentives for migration. Only the Philippines, with its established network ties to the United States, remains at a level of income and development associated with rapidly rising emigration. Nonetheless, it seems likely that the *total* number of people seeking migration to the United States from all non-Chinese Asian nations could approach the numbers from China, due to the same combination of economic development, displacement of the rural population, and still-large local/U.S. income differentials. If all other Asian migration to the United States reaches several hundred thousand per year in the next decade (in 1990–1991, *legal* migration to the United States from the Philippines, South Korea, and India totaled 110,000 per year),[54] total Asian migration to the United States, most of it illegal, could approach the magnitude of illegal immigration from Mexico within the next 5 to 10 years.

Potential for Conflict

The above scenario assumes a highly favorable internal economic and political situation in China. But such a situation cannot be taken for granted. Several threats loom on the horizon. Two of the elements of a state breakdown—state fiscal difficulties and popular grievances and mobilization—are already well entrenched in China. And a number of political pitfalls—labor difficulties at state-owned enterprises, management of internal migration and the farm economy, and treatment of Hong Kong and Taiwan—could disrupt Jiang Zemin's smooth consolidation of power, leading to factional struggles and possibly to widespread uprisings and conflicts.

Moreover, in the longer term, it seems unlikely that continued central control of the economy by the Communist Party will be compatible with growth of the private and foreign enterprise sectors. If, by 2015, China's population rises to 1.5 billion and more than two-thirds of that population is employed in the private sector rather than in SOEs and on state-leased farms, the ability of the CPC to tightly control the population will diminish sharply.[55] At that point, struggles for democratization and decentralization are sure to mount.

One of China's chief difficulties during the next 5 to 10 years will be solving its fiscal crisis. In the last decade, the share of national tax revenues taken by the central government has fallen from nearly 60 percent to just over 30 percent.[56] In the next five years, Jiang Zemin's government seeks to reverse this pattern and restore the central government's take to 60 percent by instituting major tax reforms.[57] If the central regime is unsuccessful in this attempt, it faces a fiscal meltdown, as government debts have already risen tenfold in the past decade and annual deficits now equal at least 10 percent of annual revenues.[58] The government needs massive amounts of funding to restructure its banks, continue support of loss-making state-owned enterprises, maintain a vast army, and meet enormous infrastructure needs. If tax reforms meet with either failure or increased hostility from provincial elites, the foundations of strong central rule will remain in peril or sharply weaken. It should be recalled that the English Revolution of 1640 and the French Revolution of 1789 both began with efforts by the central regime to increase its revenues through changing tax systems that were piling up debts and running chronic deficits.[59]

In addition to fiscal stress, it is often unappreciated how much popular protest and mobilization have continued in recent years, even after the repression following the Tiananmen uprising in 1989. Efforts to reduce security and benefits to workers at SOEs, and fraud and failures to meet obligations on the part of grain purchasing agents dealing with farmers, have provoked numerous local revolts against state authorities. According to an official Chinese government report, in 1993 the countryside experienced more than 6,000 protest events that resulted in severe damage to persons or property, including 900 that involved at least 500 participants and more than one township and 21 that enlisted at least 5,000 participants. A total of 8,200 county officials were injured or killed in these conflicts, 560 county-level offices were ransacked, and 385 security personnel lost their lives. According to the same report, in the first four months of 1994, the violence escalated, with another 5,000 township and county government personnel suffering injury or death in local protests. The report noted that "in some villages, peasants have spontaneously founded organizations of various types, including religious or armed organizations, to replace the party and government organizations. They have established taxation systems of their own."[60] In general, a powerful legacy of popular protest exists in China, stemming not only from traditional secret societies and local peasant traditions, but also from the workers and popular revolts promoted by Mao during the cultural revolution, and during other episodes of "power restructuring"[61] under the Communist regime in which workers and peasants engaged in confrontations with authorities over policy reforms.

As if coping with current financial problems and unrest is not difficult enough, Jiang Zemin's plans for maintaining Party control require restructuring taxes, curbing local autonomy, maintaining SOEs while reducing their staffing, security, and benefits, and reasserting control over procurement of grain and its pricing. All of these measures are painful to portions of the populace, and will be tolerable and effective only if carried out without blatant corruption and injustice. Unfortunately, China's government is, at present, famously corrupt.[62] Such corruption has produced elite evasion and popular protest whenever the kind of reforms envisaged by Jiang for the next five years have been attempted. If Jiang's policies trigger yet larger protests in the next five years, or fail because of elite evasion of state commands, opposition factions could be emboldened to challenge Jiang's leadership.

Finally, the future of Hong Kong and Taiwan pose serious pitfalls to the regime. In 1996, China blustered and engaged in dangerous military provocations with regard to Taiwan on the eve of Taiwan's presidential elections. If such provocations increase and Taiwan continues to move toward independence, Jiang (and his allies in the military) could be discredited. Or the provocations could trigger a retreat from foreign investment, causing the country's economic growth rate to slow by a few percentage points. Although not disastrous for the regime, such an economic slowdown could have a major effect on emigration by reducing domestic absorption of the surplus rural population.

Poor relations with Hong Kong could have the same effect. So far, the signs are that China will not respect the rule of law and will censor the press and suppress democracy and dissent in Hong Kong. In addition, private corporations in Hong Kong have been pressured to make deals that shift significant interests to ownership of Chinese state-owned enterprises. One can easily envisage several negative scenarios arising from this pattern. If Hong Kong's democrats and dissenters can be readily exiled or imprisoned without provoking further protests, all will be well for Beijing's rulers. But if Hong Kong's democrats are not repressed and protest spreads to the mainland, or if the repression in Hong Kong is brutal and bloody, foreign investment is again liable to retreat and Jiang's government to suffer.[63]

Finally, even if Jiang's policies succeed in the short run, the kind of economy and regime they seek to create may not be compatible. In the past, autocratic regimes that have sought to combine a closed, centralized, and non-democratic political system with an economy that shows rapid industrialization, massive gains in education, and sharply increased international communication and trade have sown the seeds of a revolutionary confrontation between state and society, despite experiencing rapid economic growth and histories of strong central government; Iran under the Pahlevi Shahs and Czarist Russia are cases in point.[64] Even the neo-authoritarian states of South Korea, Taiwan, Malaysia, and Singapore have allowed a disciplined limited political opposition to incubate, providing a basis for an eventually peaceful transition to greater democracy, and insisted on the rule of law, keeping political corruption at moderate levels. Even Thailand's corrupt military regimes have been restrained by its monarchy. But Jiang Zemin's faction, apparently rendered fearful by chronic disorders and the Tiananmen revolt, seems determined to tolerate no further democratization or any organized dissent or opposition, and to insist on Politburo edicts, rather than a stable rule of law, as the basis for governance. Such a system has never long survived the development of a modern industrial economy, and its leaders' efforts to hold onto power have generated revolutionary conflicts.

Any of the above scenarios for increased conflict—greater local disorders due to corruption in government, local elite resistance to central government efforts to increase its share of tax revenues, missteps over Hong Kong or Taiwan—could lead to defections from Jiang's leadership and a power struggle in the Chinese Communist Party, similar to those that occurred over Mikhail Gorbachev's efforts at reform in the Soviet Union. Moreover, the eventual incompatibility of a strict Communist regime with a predominantly private, developed, internationalized economy suggests that even if Jiang succeeds in his goals and the government can avoid pitfalls for the first decade of the next century, conflicts are more likely, not less likely, in the second.

Guessing the Future of Chinese Emigration: Big, Bigger, Biggest?

Even under the most favorable scenarios for China's political system and economy, illegal immigration from China to the United States is likely to rise during the coming decade.

If, however, any conflict scenarios develop, these numbers could increase even further. Political disorder and uncertainty generally increase international emigration. Almost one million emigrants have come to the United States from Central America since the 1970s, mainly in response to political conflicts in that region.[65] Legal migration from the Soviet Union to the United States increased by a factor of four between the early 1980s and the early 1990s in response to political restructuring and conflicts under Gorbachev.[66] In the next decade, conflicts between the central and local authorities, between the state and workers and peasants, and between the Beijing regime and Hong Kong or Taiwan, as well as any other difficulties that lead to a sharp slowdown in investment or economic growth, could raise attempted emigration from China to the United States to levels approaching one million per year or more. And further down the line, after 2005, is the possibility that a more serious confrontation between a conservative Communist regime and its advancing civil society is likely, which could send tens of millions of Chinese emigrants out into the world.

Douglas Massey has warned that

> China's movement toward markets and rapid economic
> growth may contain the seeds of an enormous migration.
> Even a small rate of emigration, when applied to a country
> with more than a billion people, would produce a flow of
> immigrants that would dwarf levels of migration now
> observed from Mexico. Social networks linking China and
> the United States are now being formed and in the future
> will serve as the basis for mass entry. Immigration from
> China, and other populous rapidly developing nations in
> Asia, has an unrecognized potential to transform America's
> ethnic composition.[67]

Unless things go badly wrong in China, Chinese emigration
to the United States is not likely to dwarf that from Mexico any-
time soon. Asian migration as a whole, however, will become
increasingly significant compared with that from Mexico, reaching perhaps one-half the current level of Mexican immigration
within the next 10 years. And if major conflicts should arise in
China—and many scenarios suggest that such conflict is likely
sooner or later—a surge in attempted migration to the United
States is likely that could indeed exceed current illegal migration
from Mexico.

Aristide Zolberg has warned that continued "North/South"
income differentials and population growth in the developing
world will sustain pressures for a wave of south-to-north migration into the next century.[68] Considering, however, the low but
rapidly rising average incomes, strong population growth, rising
inequality, existing migrant networks, increasing international
economic integration, and massive displacement of rural farming populations in China, India, and other nations of Asia, the
world may be facing an "East-to-West" wave of migration of
equal or even greater proportions.

Notes

1. United States Congress, *Report of the Joint Special Committee to Investigate Chinese Immigration* (Washington, D.C.: Government Printing Office,
1877), iii.

2. Ibid, 2.

3. Dudley L. Poston Jr., Michael Xinxiang Mao, and Mei-Yu Yu, "The Global Distribution of Overseas Chinese Around 1900," *Population and Development Review* 20, no. 3 (1994): 631-645.

4. Wilawan Kanjanapan, "The Immigration of Asian Professionals to the United States: 1988-1990," *International Migration Review* 29, no. 1 (1995): 7.

5. Sharon Stanton Russell, "Migration Patterns of U.S. Foreign Policy Interest," in Michael S. Teitelbaum and Myron Weiner, eds., *Threatened Peoples, Threatened Borders: World Migration and U.S. Policy* (New York: W. W. Norton, 1995), 63-67.

6. Alex P. Schmid, *Migration and Crime: Proceedings of ISPAC, United Nations Crime Prevention and Criminal Justice Program, Cairo May 1995* (New York: United Nations, 1995), 19; Poston et al., "Global Distribution" (see note 3).

7. Russell, "Migration Patterns," 84 (see note 5). Assuming a natural rate of increase for the overseas Chinese population of 2 percent per annum would account for the increase over 10 years from 22 million in the 1970s to 27 million in the 1980s, a period during which emigration was probably minimal. Continuing the same rate of natural increase from the mid-1980s to the mid-1990s would produce a total population of only 33 million, leaving a gap of 2 million to be filled by emigration. Annual emigration of 180,000 per year (again with a 2 percent per annum natural increase) over the decade would fill the gap. This number is consistent with Russell's estimate that more than 700,000 Chinese emigrated illegally in 1990–1993.

8. Paul J. Smith, "Illegal Chinese Immigrants Everywhere, and No End in Sight," *International Herald Tribune*, May 26, 1994.

9. Vernon M. Briggs, *Mass Immigration and the National Interest* (Armonk, N.Y.: M. E. Sharpe, 1992), 151. Estimating illegal immigration is fraught with difficulties. The data used here pertain to apprehensions at the border. Certainly, some of these include multiple apprehensions of the same individuals; just as certainly, other illegal migrants are not apprehended. Moreover, 90 to 95 percent of the apprehensions are Mexicans caught crossing the U.S.-Mexico border. Apprehension of other illegal entries, including visa overstays and illegal entry through air and seaports, is far less frequent. Thus, the apprehension data constitute a rough but not terribly misleading proxy for the minimum number of migrants seeking illegal entry from Mexico.

10. Douglas S. Massey et al., "Theories of International Migration: A Review and Appraisal," *Population and Development Review* 19, no. 3 (1993): 431–466.

11. Alejandro Portes, ed., *The Economic Sociology of Immigration* (New York: Russell Sage, 1995), 21.

12. Douglas S. Massey, "Economic Development and International Migration in Comparative Perspective," in S. B. Diaz-Briquets and Sidney Weintraub, eds., *Determinants of Emigration from Mexico, Central America, and the Caribbean* (Boulder, Colo.: Westview Press, 1991), 14.

13. S. B. Diaz-Briquets and Sidney Weintraub, eds., *Determinants of Emigration from Mexico, Central America and the Caribbean* (Boulder, Colo.: Westview Press, 1991), 4–5.

14. Alexander Monto, *The Roots of Mexican Labor Migration* (Westport, Conn.: Praeger, 1994), 12; Douglas S. Massey, R. Alarion, J. Durand, and H. Gonzalez, *Return to Aztlan: The Social Process of International Migration from Western Mexico* (Berkeley: University of California Press, 1987).

15. Massey, "Economic Development," 14 (see note 12).

16. Mark O'Neill, "China Faces 200 Million Unemployed Farmers by 2000," *Reuters World Service,* July 26, 1995; Martin Wolf, "A Country Divided by Growth", *Financial Times,* February 20, 1996; World Bank, *Workers in an Integrating World: World Development Report 1995* (Washington, D.C.: World Bank, 1995).

17. Diaz-Briquets and Weintraub, *Determinants of Emigration,* 6–7 (see note 13).

18. Oded Stark and Edward J. Taylor, "The Determinants of Undocumented Migration to the United States: A Research Note", in Diaz-Briquets and Weintraub, *Determinants of Emigration,* 189–214 (see note 13); Douglas S. Massey et al., "An Evaluation of International Migration Theory: The North American Case", *Population and Development Review* 20, no. 4 (1994): 699–751.

19. Wayne A. Cornelius and Philip L. Martin, *The Uncertain Connection: Free Trade and Mexico-U.S. Migration* (La Jolla, Calif.: Center for U.S.-Mexican Studies, University of California at San Diego, 1993).

20. Massey et al., *Return to Aztlan* (see note 14); Roger Rouse, "Mexican Migration to the United States: Family Relations in the Development of a Transnational Migrant Circuit" (Ph.D. dissertation, Stanford University, 1989).

21. Portes, *Sociology of Immigration,* 22 (see note 11).

22. Robert Weil, "China at the Brink: Class Contradictions of Market Socialism," *Monthly Review* 46, no. 8 (1995): 11–43.

23. Vaclav Smil, *China's Environmental Crisis* (Armonk, N.Y.: M. E. Sharpe, 1993); Su Xiaokang, "The Humanitarian and Technical Dilemmas of Population Control in China," *Journal of International Affairs,* 49, no. 2 (1996): 343–347.

24. Susan Greenhalgh, Zhu Chuzu, and Li Nan, "Restraining Population Growth in Three Chinese Villages," *Population and Development Review* 20, no. 2 (1994): 365–395.

25. Zeng Yi et al., "Causes and Implications of the Recent Increase in the Reported Sex Ratio at Birth in China," *Population and Development Review* 19, no. 2 (1993): 283–302.

26. Jiali Li, "China's One-Child Policy: How Well has it Worked?" *Population and Development Review* 21, no. 3 (1995): 563–585.

27. Ibid.; Zeng et al., "Causes and Implications" (see note 25).

28. Laurence J.C. Ma and Chusheng Lin, "Development of Towns in China: A Case Study of Guangdong Province," *Population and Development Review* 19, no. 3 (1993): 583–606.

29. Weil, "China at the Brink" (see note 22).

30. Ibid.

31. Smil, *China's Environmental Crisis* (see note 23).

32. Ma and Lin, "Development of Towns", 586 (see note 28); EIU (Economist Intelligence Unit), *Country Report: China*, May 21, 1996.

33. O'Neill, "Unemployed Farmers" (see note 16); Wolf, "A Country Divided" (see note 16).

34. Steven Mufson, "A Beijing 'Village' of Migrant Workers Fights to Stop Bulldozers," *International Herald Tribune*, November 28, 1995.

35. Su, "Population Control in China" (see note 23).

36. O'Neill, "Unemployed Farmers" (see note 16).

37. Weil, "China at the Brink" (see note 22).

38. Rajiv Chandra, "China: Rural Migrants No Longer Welcome in Overcrowded Cities," *Inter Press Service*, December 26, 1995.

39. Weil, "China at the Brink" (see note 22).

40. "China Enforces New Measures to Control Migratory Chaos," *Agence France Presse*, April 10, 1996.

41. Russell, "Migration Patterns" (see note 5); United States Information Agency, "Beijing's Boat People," USIA Research Memorandum, September 15, 1993.

42. "Sweatshops 'Growing Problem' in U.S., Reich Says," *San Francisco Chronicle*, May 25, 1996.

43. "China Enforces New Measures" (see note 40).

44. Teresa Poole, "Peking Fears a Backlash from 'Resting' Millions," *Independent* (London), June 20, 1996; Sheila Tefft, "Market Throws State Firms Over Handlebars in China," *Christian Science Monitor,* February 23, 1996.

45. Poole, "Peking Fears a Backlash" (see note 44).

46. Richard Baum, "China After Deng: Ten Scenarios in Search of Reality," *China Quarterly*, No. 145 (March 1996),: 153–175.

47. EIU, *Country Report: China* (see note 32); Willy Wo-Lap Lam and Frankie Fook-Lun Leung, "China After Deng," *East Asian Executive Reports,* September 15, 1995.

48. Jack A. Goldstone, *Revolution and Rebellion in the Early Modern World* (Berkeley: University of California Press, 1991).

49. EIU, *Country Report: China* (see note 32).

50. World Bank, *Workers* (see note 16).

51. Associated Press, "New Wave of Han Chinese Migrating to Far West China's Xinjiang," International News, January 13, 1996; Vivien Pik-Kwan Chan, "Tibet Fears Sparked by China Flood of Workers", *South China Morning Post* (Hong Kong), April 2, 1996.

52. United States Information Agency, "Beijing's Boat People" (see note 41).

53. EIU, *Country Report: China* (see note 32).

54. Russell, "Migration Patterns," 67 (see note 5).

55. Jack A. Goldstone, "China's Coming Collapse," *Foreign Policy*, no. 99 (Summer 1995): 35–54.

56. Weil, "China at the Brink" (see note 22); Lam and Leung, "China After Deng" (see note 48).

57. EIU, *Country Report: China* (see note 32).

58. Ibid.

59. Goldstone, *Revolution and Rebellion* (see note 48).

60. Cited in Elizabeth J. Perry, "'To Rebel is Justified': Maoist Influences on Popular Protest in Contemporary China" (paper presented to the Program in Agrarian Studies, Yale University, November 17, 1995).

61. Mark Lupher, *Power Restructuring in China and Russia,* (Boulder, Colo.: Westview Press, 1996).

62. Weil, "China at the Brink" (see note 22).

63. The risks that handling of Hong Kong will adversely affect China's growth are detailed in Bruce Bueno de Mesquita, David Newman, and Alvin Rabushka, *Red Flag over Hong Kong* (Chatham, N.J.: Chatham House Publishers, 1996).

64. Timothy McDaniel, *Autocracy, Modernization, and Revolution in Russia and Iran* (Princeton: Princeton University Press, 1991).

65. Susan Forbes Martin, "Development and Politically Generated Migration," in Diaz-Briquets and Weintraub, *Determinants of Emigration,* 215–239 (see note 13).

66. Russell, "Migration Patterns," 63–67 (see note 5).

67. Douglas S. Massey, "The New Immigration and Ethnicity in the United States," *Population and Development Review* 21, no. 3 (1995): 649.

68. Aristide Zolberg, "The Future of International Migration," in Diaz-Briquets and Weintraub, *Determinants of Emigration,* 319–352 (see note 13).

4

Sourcing the Problem: Why Fuzhou?

Marlowe Hood

Any policy response to a particular stream of illegal migration that does not take into account the source is bound to falter. This would seem axiomatic, and yet very little has been written about a region—Fuzhou—that has produced what is certainly among the most concentrated flows, both geographically and over time, of transcontinental clandestine migration in history. What amalgam of factors has motivated some 400,000 mainly rural dwellers from the northeast corner of Fujian Province in the People's Republic of China to "turn their backs on the family well" (*bei jing li xiang*) and embark on a perilous, hugely expensive journey to the other end of the world?[1] Are the same forces at work in nearby Wenzhou, China's other major fount of illegal emigration in the post-Mao era?

Even an intimate knowledge of these regions will not, of course, automatically yield answers, much less policy prescriptions for the North American and western European governments groping for a means both effective and humane to control their borders. But understanding the source may at least suggest whether the migrations unchained in these places are likely to continue or occur elsewhere.

The aim of this paper, then, is to highlight aspects of Fuzhou's past and present relevant to the extraordinary flow of clandestine migrants to the United States since the mid-1970s, and especially after 1986. It does not seek to draw direct causal links so much as to establish a context. The first of four sections reviews the region's physical and economic environment, and distinguishes between characteristics common to China's seaboard cities and those unique to Fuzhou. The second is, in effect, a digest of several dozen interviews—conducted in greater Fuzhou and Wenzhou in mid-1996—with Chinese who have been or are seeking to be smuggled abroad, and their families. Although not systematic, the testimony drawn from here avoids the distortions inherent in interviews with subjects already in the United States, especially those in detention.

The third section focuses on Wenzhou in Zhejiang Province to the north, a region that is to western Europe what Fuzhou is to the United States. The parallels are indeed striking, as is the apparently scant overlap in the migrant-trafficking networks that service these neighboring areas. But it is the differences, perhaps, that are most telling in so far as they may eventually help us tease out a model of long-range emigration from China during the reform era. Finally, the last section offers an admittedly impressionistic scheme of how the variables described might be assembled to answer the question in the title: why Fuzhou?

Fuzhou and Environs

Historians have described Fujian, a 125,000-kilometer band of seaside mountains dotted with a few patches of flat land, as "bandit country" and a hotbed of "rebellious ideas."[2] Compliment or insult, such epithets do evoke the province's distance from Beijing, physical and psychological, as well as its solid tradition of clandestine activity. This last redoubt of Ming loyalists in the mid-seventeenth century was also the birthplace of the *San Lian Hui*, the original Triad, and a center of sea-based smuggling of everything from salt to opium to silk. Now a new commodity—people—has been added to the ledger.

Admittedly, Fujian's outlaw past is only remotely linked to the illegal transport of migrants to the United States today, but not so the province's maritime tradition, which dates back at least to Zheng He's expeditions to South Asia and Africa during the early fifteenth century. For it was a handful of sailors and merchant marines from Fuzhou and neighboring Ma Wei, men like Alan Mansin Lau, a former president of the Fukien American Association, who planted the first seeds of Fuzhou's New York-based community by jumping ship in the United States during the two decades following World War II.[3] Exactly what these men—typically ages 35–40, married with children— planted was the desire to bring their families. But these hopes, frustrated during the first three decades of Communist rule by a virtual ban on emigration, lay dormant until a confluence of factors opened the doors—mainly back doors—to Fuzhounese seeking passage to America.

Like other cities in southern and coastal China today, Fuzhou, with 1.5 million registered inhabitants and a "floating population" of about 250,000, throbs with economic activity.[4] Despite its status as a provincial administrative capital (or perhaps, in this case, because of it), the city is part of the freewheeling and barely restrained capitalist growth especially characteristic of Guangdong and Fujian. The percentage of industrial output produced by private and nominally collective enterprises is far higher in Fujian than the national average, indeed higher than that of any other province except Guangdong. The scarcity of large state-run industry is not an accident but the result of a deliberate Maoist-era strategy designed to deprive a hostile Nationalist regime a scant 100 kilometers away of military targets.[5] This is no small irony, given that the post-Mao industrial and commercial boom in the Fuzhou region has been fueled in large measure by investment from and trade with Taiwan.

In fact, Taiwan's role in the Fuzhou-U.S. migration extends well beyond helping to shape the economic environment in which it became possible for individuals to undertake the journey of a lifetime halfway round the globe. Indeed, the connection to Taiwan—perhaps it is best called "the Taiwan connection"—has been at the core of the worldwide clandestine transportation network through which the traffic in smuggled human beings has flowed.[6] All of the at least 37 smuggling vessels with would-be migrants on board apprehended in or near North American waters by U.S. law enforcement from mid-1991 through mid-1994 were somehow linked to Taiwan: registration, crew, ownership, and/or home port.[7] More significantly— because transport by long-distance, oceangoing vessels never accounted for more than 10 percent of total smuggling traffic and came to a virtual halt by the end of 1994—the major hubs for smuggled immigrants, located in Latin America, are also run and controlled by Taiwan-born Chinese whose core networks extend from Fuzhou to Taiwan to lower Manhattan.

Relatively few U.S.-bound migrants originate from Fuzhou City itself. The vast majority come instead from greater Fuzhou and the surrounding counties of Lianjiang, Minhou, and Changle (the last reclassified in 1995 as a city). Farther south are two other areas whose able-bodied have gone overseas to toil as wage laborers, although less far afield: Fuqing natives head for Japan, while inhabitants of Pingtao Island go to Taiwan, both on smuggling boats owned and operated for the most part by Taiwanese. All of the above speak mutually intelligible but distinguishable variants of the Fuzhou dialect, which, as a whole, is sharply distinct from the Minnan dialect to the south and the Wu to the north. The registered populations of Changle,

Lianjiang, and Minhou are each about 600,000, while their surface areas are 656, 1,228, and 2,129 square kilometers respectively, the same size, combined with greater Fuzhou, as the state of Delaware. The Min River cuts through the region from east to west and hits the ocean where the Taiwan Strait meets the East China Sea.[8]

Fuzhou's burgeoning prosperity is plain to see, especially in the form of omnipresent construction of four- and five-story mansions rising from rice fields at the edge of nearly every village. But a closer look reveals that not all communities have prospered in the same way. The villages of Lu Xia and Cheng Xian, for example, provide a study in contrast. Both are well-off, but only one has sent a significant percentage of its native sons and daughters to America.[9]

Virtually all of Lu Xia's 400-odd households own and operate backyard factories, creating a helter-skelter patchwork of plastics recycling plants, jasmine tea factories, metal workshops, and rubber-thong manufacturers. The village is an environmental nightmare, but it is also a thriving beehive of private and collective entrepreneurship that employs more manual labor from Sichuan and Jiangxi than there are registered inhabitants. This would seem to be at least one reason why few from Lu Xia have opted to be smuggled to the United States: business is too good at home to justify such a risky—and costly—action. Another may be the village's proximity to Fuzhou, about 25 kilometers distance, which gives it easy access to materials and markets. Also lodged in Lu Xia's collective memory is the fact that two villagers who did go to the United States traveled on the *Golden Venture*, the cargo freighter that ran aground near New York City on June 6, 1993. That 10 of its passengers died, 47 were repatriated, and most of the rest were still in jail three years later seemed to have dampened enthusiasm to *tou du* or "steal passage," the Chinese term for being smuggled overseas.

A fourth bulkhead against a mass exodus may be the quality of Lu Xia's leadership. As of mid-1996, the village was run by a razor-sharp 31-year-old Communist Party secretary who was also by far the wealthiest private entrepreneur in town. This, he and others insisted, gave him the financial independence to act on behalf of the collective, unlike most of his colleagues in other villages who enriched themselves by plundering the communal coffers, extracting bribes, and exacting arbitrary fines.

That description, according to many residents, would better fit the anything-but-public-minded cadres of Cheng Xian, a slightly smaller village about 10 kilometers west of Changle City.

Indeed, Cheng Xian could be Lu Xia's mirror image: the same half-million-yuan houses sprout like summer bamboo, but there isn't a single factory, business, or enterprise in the village. "Our only industry is overseas Chinese," one villager noted wryly. Every household has at least one member in the United States. Money from relatives overseas has made Cheng Xian prosper, but it has also had the perverse effect of retarding economic development.

Indeed, many villages are devoid of most men and many women between the age of 18 and 45, while others are virtual ghost towns, populated only by old people caring for very young children whose parents are working in garment factories on the Lower East Side of Manhattan and Chinese takeouts scattered across the 50 states. But it is obvious that even less-depopulated villages, like Cheng Xian, are entirely dependent—economically, socially, even psychologically—on what have become their alter egos overseas.

As for corruption, it is Lu Xia, alas, that is the exception, not Cheng Xian. Official malfeasance has reached dimensions unprecedented during Communist rule and bolsters migrant smuggling in at least three ways, one direct and the other two more difficult to quantify. Its obvious role is in facilitating the organized, illegal exit of Chinese citizens from the PRC, an exodus that the local government has very little incentive to stop, and arguably a good reason to tolerate, given the vast amount of remittances and investment flowing back into the region, $100 million annually in Changle alone, according to local officials.[10] Only when people-smuggling became an international embarrassment were forces mobilized to halt the practice, and half-heartedly at that.

A subtler but even more important impact of corruption is the creation of an environment in which those who are either unable or unwilling to *la guanxi*—pull strings and open back doors—are locked out of the opportunities offered by China's booming, but profoundly corrupt, economy. How ironic, then, given the unsavory, crime-tainted reputation clandestine Chinese immigrants have acquired in the United States and Europe, that it is, to an important degree, precisely the honest toilers who cannot prosper amid China's hypercorruption who have opted to do their hard labor in a foreign land.

Finally, corruption that takes the form of arbitrary fines, illegal executions, and outright violence by local officials—harassment, in short—is another factor pushing people to seek their fortunes elsewhere. In one incident well known in the region, a 27-year-old woman, Ren Wanxia, was murdered inside the Xing Qi police station in December 1993 after protesting a minor fine and her body later dumped in the Min River. After multiple appeals and petitions to bring to justice the policeman who had killed her had failed, her older brother, deeply discouraged by his prospects in China, took a boat to New York and found a dish-washing job in a Brooklyn takeout.[11] Even if the overwhelming majority of applications for political asylum in the United States do not, in fact, meet the criteria for such status, the pervading atmosphere in China of unequal and corrupted access to opportunity makes the decision to leave that much easier.

Fuzhou—The People

At first glance, there would seem to be more reasons for rural dwellers to stay put than to pay a fortune ($35,000 in 1996), risking life and limb, to be ferried to a distant and increasingly inhospitable land for the privilege of working 12 hours a day in a sweatshop or a Chinese fast-food restaurant for years on end. In contrast to the mid-nineteenth century, when political and natural calamity within China coincided with post-slavery demand for cheap labor in the Americas, Fujian's economy—and with it the general standard of living—has improved dramatically over the last 15 years, while the governments of host countries have actively discouraged the arrival of immigrant workers. Average farmer income has increased severalfold during this period and is now dominated by earnings derived from private businesses and employment in township and village enterprises rather than from the production of grain sold to the state at fixed prices. The socioeconomic "push-pull" at work today is thus neither the same nor as clear as the dynamic that propelled able-bodied men from the Taishan district of Guangdong Province to America in the 1860s and 1870s.

But a closer look at the Fuzhou region reveals an interlocking chain of factors that has proven every bit as compelling as its historical antecedent. In assessing their quality of life, dozens of migrants and aspiring migrants interviewed take their measure not against the objective yardstick of a poorer past, but against their subjective expectations for the future. Such thinking is not, of course, unique to Fuzhou—it is a hallmark of China in the reform era. But the ambition to improve the family fortune that burns relentlessly at every level of Chinese society, restrained only by a sense of the possible, became one of the driving forces once migration to the United States entered that realm of feasibility. That it is a collective, family-based decision rather than an individual one makes it all the more tenacious.

When asked why Fuzhounese migrate, Chen Yuan, a 33-year old Fuzhou-based entrepreneur whose interests include real estate, computers, luxury hotels, construction, and media production, states the obvious: "When the income differential between China and the United States is 1:2 rather than 1:15 or 1:20, that is when Fuzhounese will stop going and even start to come back." A native of tiny Wenshi Village in Changle, Mr. Chen worked in New York from 1980 to 1988 before returning to set up his business empire, which has recently invested more than $100 million in a development project adjoining the Changle International Airport, scheduled to open in 1997. "Look at it this way—in terms of income potential for the average worker, one year in the United States equals 15 Chinese years."[12]

While only a partial answer, this is the one most often proffered by those explaining why they have gone or are seeking to go abroad: to make money. Chen Yuan, a U.S. citizen, is the exception because he became enormously rich and because he returned. But his example stands out on Fuzhou's horizon, as do, on a smaller scale, the modest but more tangible successes of *huaqiao* (overseas Chinese) who have sent back enough of their $1,000–$1,800 monthly pay checks from the United States to enable immediate family—once smuggling debts are cleared—to build the tile-and-concrete palaces that stand as irrefutable proof that going is worth the price of passage. Likewise, relatives returning from abroad to visit or do business, whose occasional and not always sincere admonishments not to follow in their footsteps are belied by the gold draped around their necks and the $1,000 mobile phones clipped to their belts. Almost by definition, the ones who haven't succeeded cannot afford to come back to bear witness to just how ugly life in the "Beautiful Country" (*meiguo*), as the Chinese call the United States, can be.

Liu Keguang, 28, one of Lu Xia's more successful entrepreneurs, had decided against going to America as of mid-1996, although he had bought a passport and an exit visa (50,000 yuan in bribes) just in case he changes his mind. He chose to remain because business—a backyard rubber-thong factory employing a dozen migrant workers—was thriving and likely to expand. Hu Leijing, 22, of Cheng Xian, by contrast, was simply waiting for his sister and brother-in-law in New York to save enough money to pay for his passage. Hu may have to wait a while longer than he expected. A May 1996 letter from his sister explained that she and her husband were looking for someone to transport their newborn daughter to China for a fee of $1,000 so that the mother could continue working. Moreover, because this first child was a daughter, Hu's departure would likely be further delayed. "If we had had a son, I would have been satisfied with one child, but now we will have to try again," the letter continued, distilling in a few words another core motive for venturing across the Pacific.

The fact that a woman (a daughter, from the parents' perspective) in China marries into her husband's family, combined with the rarity of retirement pensions in the countryside, has created an overwhelming incentive not just to have male offspring, but to direct them toward maximum income-earning situations. Thus it is often parents who effectively send their adult male children abroad and undertake to borrow the vast sums required to do so. (This is also why most rural families in China are willing to absorb exorbitant fines or pay bribes to circumvent the one-child policy). Working overseas is an especially lucrative option that happened, almost by historical accident, to be more open to Fuzhounese than to other regional and language groups in China who share the same imperatives. That New York is the address abroad, if not accidental, is certainly incidental.

Mr. Hu, one of three high-school graduates in his village, flips through the pages of an album with photos of his sister. He pauses before a postcard of the Statue of Liberty, as if struck by some previously unnoticed detail. "I don't suppose it means the same thing to me as it does to you," he says, addressing an American. "For us, it doesn't mean freedom. It means opportunity." Mr. Hu—bright, educated—failed twice to get into university and is earning $60 a month in a rubber-products factory. He has no *guanxi*, no back doors to open, no brothers abroad, and an impatient father who still plants and harvests the family's rice with his own hands while most of his neighbors have hired peasants from Sichuan to tend their fields and build their new, four-story houses.

In a context where "push" factors such as natural calamity, war, or persecution by the state are not dominant, as is the case in Fuzhou, a host of variables at the margin can sway an individual's decision about whether to be smuggled abroad. Besides access to business opportunities at home, a would-be migrant can be dissuaded by word of mouth about changing employment conditions in target countries, or by an especially cautious frame of mind, or by a previous attempt gone awry. When their efforts in 1986 and 1987 to go to Europe failed—one after a serious bout with dysentery in a Burmese jungle, the other after being caught moving across the Tibet-Nepal border—two men interviewed in 1996 had never tried again. But their cases were, perhaps, the exception rather than the rule: both had tried to exit China on their own, hoping but failing to link up with snakeheads—alien smugglers—in Bangkok or Katmandu, which meant neither had outstanding contracts to complete. Besides, by 1996 one of the two had saved enough money for a deposit on a smuggling fee. More typical, especially for the Fuzhou region, is the case of a young man from Hou Yu who had tried to reach U.S. soil five times (one of them on the ill-fated *Eastwood*, a cargo freighter carrying 527 PRC nationals that made it only as far as the Marshall Islands) and was preparing for his sixth attempt when we met. His bad luck was exceptional (and legendary), but his resolve was not.

One thing that does not seem to affect demand is cost: the price of passage had increased eightfold in 10 years, but as long as smuggled migrants know they can pay off the additional premium with an extra six months of work, cost is no object.

Wenzhou—Counterpoint

Greater Wenzhou and Qingtian County in southeastern Zhejiang Province together make up the second highly concentrated source of recent migration from China. Indeed, the Ou River basin and surrounding mountains dominate the flow of PRC migrants to western Europe almost as thoroughly as Fuzhou to the south has accounted for the growing mainland Chinese population in the United States.

From the most remote mountain villages to downtown Wenzhou's booming waterfront, the region, like Fuzhou, is permeated by its overseas connections. Rural and urban landscapes have been transformed by remittances, export earnings, and donations from wealthy compatriots "beyond the seas." Almost every township has native sons and daughters abroad, even if only a handful of locales have become famous *qiao xiang*, or emigration sources. The Chinese transliterations for European cities roll off tongues as easily as the names of neighboring counties, even if *Haiya* (The Hague) or *Duling* (Turin) remain abstractions despite a steady stream of letters from the relatives who have made homes (*jia*) in these places that, paradoxically, can never truly be home (*guxiang*).

Urban Wenzhou is a coastal city of more than a million people on the south bank of the Ou estuary, midway along the radius of a 15,000-square-kilometer semicircle of mountains (including Qingtian) half the size of Belgium, with a total population of about 7.5 million.[13] Within China it is famous as a beehive of small-scale entrepreneurship where tens of thousands of private enterprises dominate the local economy—and attempt to corner national markets in products ranging from buttons to lighters to electric-light switches—leaving only 5 percent of industrial output to state-owned, state-run factories. The city of Qingtian lies along the northern bank of the Ou River 50 kilometers upstream from Wenzhou and administers a population of about 500,000. With little industry and even less agriculture, the local economy depends, rather, on two resources: soft stones and tough overseas Chinese. Indeed, one is hard put to find someone of any age who doesn't have an immediate relative in France, Italy, Spain, Austria, or Holland.

The region as a whole is, like Fuzhou, physically cut off from the rest of China—the first-ever rail link is not scheduled for completion until 1998, and its first airport opened only in 1990.[14] Whether it is in spite of or because of this shared isolation, exceptionally large numbers of the area's inhabitants have sought their fortunes abroad. According to internally published official statistics, there were approximately 240,000 Wenzhounese and 60,000 natives of Qingtian living abroad by the end of 1995.[15] Because these estimates are based on the issuance of passports and exit permits, the actual number is certainly higher—perhaps by as much as half—since many of those entering Europe overland by clandestine means do not bother with costly exit procedures. If total numbers are underestimated, the official country-by-country breakdown is probably accurate in terms of percentage distribution, and corroborates research by Chinese and foreign researchers indicating that 75 to 80 percent of the overseas population live in western Europe. Unlike the Fuzhounese, however, another million Wenzhou natives have also set up manufacturing and commercial outposts throughout China, most notably in a southern suburb of Beijing known as "Zhejiang Village."

The saga of migration from southeastern Zhejiang to Europe begins more than a half a century earlier than that from Fuzhou to North America, and is itself marked by sharp internal differences between Wenzhou and Qingtian. Although Qingtian is far smaller than Wenzhou in area (2,500 square kilometers) and population, its European presence in the 1930s was 20,000 strong, several times the number from Wenzhou. It was also, between the wars, more widely dispersed, with sizable enclaves not just in France, but in Italy, the Netherlands, and Germany.[16]

At first glance, almost every point of comparison would suggest that the flow of migrants should have started and surged in Wenzhou rather than in its poor cousin to the west. Wenzhou's history as an active port dates back a millennium to the Sung dynasties and includes, in 1876, its forced opening to foreign ships and commerce, an event that engendered regular contact with the West even if concomitant trade was not on a par with other major entrepôts. The late-nineteenth century incursion of western imports dislocated the local economy and left thousands idle as demand abroad—especially in Europe—for labor increased, creating a potential match. Indeed, beginning at the turn of the century, a constant trickle of traders and laborers did find their way to Europe from Wenzhou. The numbers increased from a handful to several thousand during the 1920s and 1930s, some going by ship from Shanghai directly to Mediterranean ports, others by boat to Port Arthur and from there across Russia on the Trans-Siberian Railroad, which opened in 1904. But it was Qingtian natives who led the way overseas as early as the 1870s and whose numbers escalated steadily until the onset of World War II.[17]

There are three main reasons. One is engraved in stone—engraved, that is, in the semiprecious soapstone extracted from Qingtian's otherwise unyielding mountains, and which dozens of generations of carvers have fashioned into landscapes and figures from Chinese mythology, and which itinerant peddlers were selling in Europe by the late nineteenth century. It is surely no coincidence that the townships and villages closest to the soapstone deposits—Fangshan, Youju, Shankou—have consistently had the highest rates of emigration. Two other factors fueled migration from Qingtian to Europe during the early twentieth century, one a natural disaster and the other a man-made one. The latter was World War I. In 1917, France and England recruited more than 100,000 laborers—2,000 from Qingtian—to support their war efforts.[18] When the fighting was over, part of the Qingtian contingent stayed behind. They were later joined by relatives, and by compatriots fleeing the second disaster, a drought in 1929 that wiped out a grain harvest that, even in a good year, met only a fraction of Qingtian's consumption needs.

The onset of World War II effectively froze further emigration to Europe from both regions, with many Wenzhounese and Qingtian natives actually returning home in the late 1930s, although enough remained to form the core of post-war communities. During the first three decades of Communist rule, what had been an increasing flow of out-migration was reduced to a tiny trickle. As the Cultural Revolution's mixture of autarky and anarchy yielded in the mid-1970s to the juggernaut of externally oriented development that has persisted to this day, a wave of pent-up demand to reunite long-disrupted families and to seek economic opportunity abroad was released. Such was also the case in Fuzhou, but several factors gave rise to variations in what was arguably, at root, a very similar migration dynamic.

To begin with, relatives in Europe of would-be migrants from Wenzhou and Qingtian had already been abroad in significant numbers for decades, during which time many had started successful businesses and accumulated capital that could be used for transportation costs. The fact that most western European nations established diplomatic relations with China at the time of or before its admission to the United Nations in 1971 also opened the way for legal, if highly restricted, family reunification. The United States didn't recognize the PRC until 1979, a delay that helped push emigration from Fuzhou into illegal channels. Finally, the contiguous land mass between China and western Europe had a profound impact on the extent and nature of clandestine immigration, which grew exponentially in the mid-to-late 1980s as chain migration reached a peak even as countries of the European Union beset with unemployment moved to close their doors to foreign labor.

The logistical difficulty of traveling surreptitiously from Fuzhou to the United States not only dictated huge fees, but also led to the concentration of criminal smuggling in a handful of networks that, while ever-shifting and loosely articulated, had stable—and unmistakable—command structures. In the case of Europe, the added option of traveling by land, generally through the former Soviet Union, opened up the market for smuggling services to a much wider field of small-scale criminal entrepreneurs. It also made it possible for smuggled migrants to proceed in stages to their destination—which was, in any case, often defined more by shifting national immigration policies in Europe and the competence of one's "ox's back" (the local equivalent of Fuzhou's snakeheads) than by a specific geographic location—stopping along the way to earn money or, in some cases, changing plans and settling down. These differences with the Fuzhou experiences hold for all of southeastern Zhejiang, but there remain important distinctions within the Wenzhou exodus.

Urban Wenzhou has enjoyed an uninterrupted economic boom, with gross domestic product increasing by an average of 16 percent a year and per capita income by a factor of 10 since 1978—staggering even by China's breakneck standards. While a significant part of this growth has been fueled by overseas investment and exports, the majority of what by 1995 was an annual industrial output of 80 billion yuan was generated domestically. The implications for emigration are at least two-fold. First, by the early 1990s very few residents of Wenzhou City, which has perhaps the highest concentration of individual entrepreneurs of any Chinese city with more than a million people, sought to make their way abroad illegally. Those who did go went to do business more often than to earn hourly wages in a garment factory or restaurant. The income gap that once made European sweatshops beckon has diminished for urban Wenzhounese much as it has for their counterparts in Fuzhou.

But in the surrounding suburbs and countryside, although they have prospered too, the sirens of a 10,000 yuan-per-month paycheck were still a very powerful lure in 1996. Less than a dozen kilometers from downtown Wenzhou is the island of Qidu, a flat, dreary township composed of six villages all dotted with outsized and ostentatious *huaqiao* houses. The fact that Qidu's out-migration started in the 1930s, that it has generated considerable wealth, and that more than 50 percent of the island's 7,000 inhabitants are in France and the United States—unusually, in roughly equal numbers—has not dimmed the enthusiasm of those remaining for finding passage abroad, even to the point of entreating an unknown foreigner.[19]

Likewise for Li Ao, another of Wenzhou's famous *qiao xiang*, in nearby Rui An Municipality. Although the township has clearly prospered and enjoys the munificence of returned compatriots in the form of 12 kilometers of new roads, 7 bridges, 10 schools, a fresh-water reservoir, a clinic, and—appreciated above all by Li Ao's youth—a large movie theater, it is taken for granted by the few young men ages 20–30 still at home that they are Europe-bound.[20]

Increasingly restrictive immigration policies in EU nations, rather than discouraging new arrivals, have succeeded for the most part only in pushing undocumented Chinese from one European country to another or, at best, into central Europe. High unemployment rates in Europe also seem to have had little impact on Chinese-backed black market economies, which thrive at the margins of European industries burdened with extremely high labor costs. Chinese smuggling networks—described by law enforcement officials as the most sophisticated and thus the hardest to detect, much less shut down—were clearly expanding their operations into Europe as of 1996.

Why Migrate?

There are many competing and overlapping theories as to why people migrate long distances in the absence of catastrophic conditions. These explanatory models can be roughly grouped into four categories. The first emphasizes the drawing power of high wages and labor demand, with or without active recruitment by employers or their agents. It usually imputes a "rational choice" on the part of individuals weighing the pros (more money, potential for otherwise unimaginable wealth, access to better education for children) and cons (danger and expense of illicit travel, years of dirty, hard work, chance of apprehension) of going abroad. The shortcomings of this approach are what it fails to account for: forces that, sometimes invisibly, overwhelm individual choice; potential labor pools that do *not* respond to opportunity; the fact that migration flows sometimes continue even after the jobs have dried up.

A second set of theories focuses not on the individual or even the country in which he or she lives but on the increasingly global economic system in which both function. China's integration into the world capitalist matrix, for example, has caused major social dislocation domestically, giving rise to both the need (underemployment) and the means (rising income, access to transportation networks) to move abroad. The problem here is the inability to explain why half of village "X" is in New York while village "Y" five kilometers down the road is still intact or, indeed, why Mr. Chen decided to go while his similarly situated neighbor did not.

A third approach, rooted in sociology and economic anthropology, gives pride of place to the structure of kinship and family groups, examining the linkages, for example, within single-surname or two-surname villages, and the concentric circles of mutual obligation within family and regional groupings. This adds an important dimension to the picture, but often winds up explaining the process by which migration unfolds rather than the reasons it gets started in the first place. Finally, there are those who give culture an essential role, postulating the existence of a "culture of migration" in which communities in sending countries become dependent on and are shaped by their extensions overseas, mutating into new forms. While certainly true, it is nonetheless difficult to separate which changes in a given region are due to migration and which are due to other factors that may have nothing to do with communities abroad.

Many of the forces at work in these theories are described in terms of "push" and "pull" factors. In the case of Fuzhou, however, it may make more sense to work outward in concentric circles from the core motivation for migration: improving the economic position of the family. This goal, in turn, is reinforced by the hardwired sense of obligation especially strong among rural Chinese, first toward parents and children, and secondarily toward distant kin and relations. It is the core element of what itself became a driving force once the initial population was established in the United States: the desire to reunify the family.

A consistent order of migration within an extended kinship structure appears to be driven by a collective strategy to expand the economic base of the family. The original migrant, typically a married male in his late thirties, is followed by one or more brothers, his working-age sons, and then his sister's and wife's husbands, who themselves become the next link in an agnatic chain migration. The implication is that, for Chinese migration in general, "an economic strategy governs its order and progression, while bonds derived from *qinshu* (kinship) and *guanxi* (non-kin relationships) determine its extent."[21]

From here we can draw up our list of "push" and "pull" factors, some specific to Fuzhou, most not. On the "push" side of the ledger we find underemployment, low wages, corruption, lack of opportunity, special circumstances (crushing debt, business failure, a criminal record), and, in some cases, persecution by the state. On the "pull" side must be included high wages abroad (relative to China), the visible success of previous migrants, and Chinese and U.S. government policies that facilitate exit from China, entry to the United States, employment, and legal foreign residence.

There are at least three things to which would-be migrants must have access in order to leave and arrive by clandestine means, once the decision to do so is taken: money, transportation, and guanxi. In the case of most Fujianese bound for the United States, money came from relatives already in America or in China, transportation was provided by criminal enterprises, and guanxi was cultivated through assiduous networking and some good luck.

Finally, there is a set of circumstances—many of them particular, if not unique, to Fuzhou—that has created a context in which the United States-bound exodus could occur: the simple fact that Fujian is a coastal province, the proximity to Taiwan, a tradition of smuggling and clandestine activity, the prevalence of tightly knit kinship structures, including single-surname villages—all of these things have contributed to one of the most remarkable migrations of modern history.

Notes

1. How many have migrated from the greater Fuzhou area to the United States, and of these, how many did so illegally? Not surprisingly, there are no precise statistics available. Willard H. Myers III (author of chapter 5), based on 4,000 interviews, has calculated that 100,000 smuggled migrants arrived in the United States each year from 1990 through 1994, making up the vast majority of Fuzhounese in the United States. U.S. government estimates are less precise but are on the same order of magnitude. The Fukien American Association in New York estimates that there are 150,000 natives of the Changle administrative region alone living in the Tristate area (New York, New Jersey, and Connecticut).

2. Jonathan Spence, *The Search for Modern China* (New York: W. W. Norton, 1990).

3. Author's interview, conducted on April 2, 1993.

4. Li Jiefeng, ed., *Fujian Sheng Gonglu Jiaotong Tu Ce* (Fujian Province road and traffic atlas) (Fujian: Fujian Provincial Map Publishing House, 1993).

5. Simon Long, "Regionalism in Fujian," in David S. G. Goodman and Gerald Segal, eds., *China Deconstructs: Politics, Trade and Regionalism* (New York: Routledge, 1994).

6. Marlowe Hood, "The Taiwan Connection," *Los Angeles Times Magazine*, October 9, 1993.

7. U.S. Immigration and Naturalization Service (INS), "Chronology of Alien Smuggling by Sea" (unpublished), May 2, 1994.

8. Li, *Fujian Sheng Gonglu Jiaotong Tu Ce.*

9. Author's interviews, conducted in 1996.

10. Ron Tempest, "Chinese Exodus Apparently Slowing," *Los Angeles Times*, October 23, 1995.

11. Author's interview, conducted on July 8, 1994.

12. Author's interview, conducted in 1996.

13. Yin Peizhang, *Wenzhou Cidian* (Wenzhou encyclopedia), (Shanghai: Fudan University Press, 1995).

14. Jenny Ho, "Wenzhou Stands at Economic Crossroads after Miracle Years," *South China Morning Post* (Hong Kong), July 15, 1996.

15. "Qingtian Haiwai Huaren Jianshi" (A brief history of Qingtian's overseas Chinese) published for restricted circulation, Overseas Chinese History Exhibition Hall, Qingtian, Zhejiang Province, 1996.

16. Mette Thuno, "Origin and Causes of Emigration from Qingtian and Wenzhou to Europe" (paper presented at the Workshop on European Chinese and Chinese Domestic Migration, Oxford, July 3–5, 1996).

17. Ibid.

18. Live Yu-sion, "Les Chinois de Paris depuis le debut du siecle: Presence urbaine et actives economiques," *La Diaspora Chinoise en Occident*, ed. Michelle Guillon and Emmanuel Ma Mung, *Revue Europeenne des Migrations Internationales* 8, no. 3 (1992).

19. Author's interviews; also see Yin, *Wenzhou Cidian*.

20. Ibid.; also see Li Minghuan, "To Get Rich Quickly in Europe!—Reflections" (paper presented at the Workshop on European Chinese and Chinese Domestic Migration, Oxford, July 3–5, 1996).

21. See, in this volume, chapter 5 by Willard H. Myers III, p. 100.

5

Of *Qinqing, Qinshu, Guanxi,* and *Shetou*: The Dynamic Elements of Chinese Irregular Population Movement

Willard H. Myers III

It was warm that June evening in 1992 in Manhattan's China-town. I was an honored guest at a 15-course banquet hosted by a 29-year-old Fujianese, undisputed leader of one of the major "meeting and greeting" organizations that serve as the final link in the chain of every Chinese human smuggling enterprise. As he rose to speak, all eyes riveted on him. He began by reviewing his organization's accomplishments for the year, speaking in the Fuzhou subdialect of Northern Min, his distinctive cadence marking him as a villager. When he turned to the efforts of U.S. law enforcement to shut him down, staring directly at me, he said, "Immigration can do nothing."

One year later, on Sunday morning, June 6, 1993, the Cable News Network carried live coverage of the *Golden Venture*, grounded off Rockaway Beach while trying to land 286 Fujianese migrants in Manhattan. The specter of a smuggling vessel within sight of the Manhattan skyline, and the frantic efforts of rescuers to save 10 victims who drowned swimming ashore, administered a galvanic shock to a complacent, ineffective, disorganized, and frequently obstructionist law enforcement community and to the Clinton administration, both of them heirs to a conflicting set of policies designed to address China's treatment of human rights in the wake of Tiananmen Square.

Twelve days later, on June 18, 1993, President Bill Clinton publicly announced his response:

> I have today approved a plan of action to combat the problem of organized crime syndicates trafficking in alien-smuggling. The plan involves the coordinated efforts of 12 departments and agencies of the U.S. government, working in coordination with the White House Domestic Policy Council and the National Security Council. It responds to a major crime problem which has existed for almost two years but to date has been dealt with only on an ad hoc basis.

And in a manner reminiscent of Churchill's post-Dunkirk speech, he added,

> We will go after smugglers and their operations at the source. We will take measures to interdict and redirect smuggling ships when they are in transit. We will expedite procedures for processing entry claims and for returning economic migrants smuggled into the United States, and we will ask Congress to pass legislation to expedite this process further.[1]

The Immigration and Naturalization Service (INS) was out; the National Security Council (NSC) was in. The Central Intelligence Agency (CIA) was tasked with developing a plan to "identify the smugglers and disrupt their operations". The Federal Bureau of Investigation (FBI) was the lead enforcement agency on land and the U.S. Coast Guard (USCG) the lead at sea.

The FBI, which had referred to Asian crime as "emerging ethnic organized crime" and placed it last on its list of criminal priorities, assigned 100 agents to a single task—smashing Fuk Ching, the New York Chinatown gang deemed responsible for the *Golden Venture*, and arresting its 27-year-old Fujianese leader, Guo Liang Chi, known by his gang name Ah Kay. Ah Kay was, the FBI said, the boss of bosses and Fuk Ching was the gang of gangs behind "Chinese trafficking in alien smuggling." Given a defined mission and a visible target the FBI did what it does best—got its man, along with known members of Fuk Ching. On August 28, 1993, Ah Kay was arrested in Hong Kong and on August 29, 13 members of Fuk Ching were swept off the streets of Manhattan, all charged with extortion, kidnapping, and murder. Alien smuggling was effectively smashed, according to the FBI, by this single bold stroke.

Within days, Ah Kay was returned to New York and placed in a high-security cell at the Metropolitan Correction and Detention Center, within sight of Chinatown. In accordance with a negotiated agreement, he has remained there, serving as the FBI's Chinese "Deep Throat." For almost three years, vast enforcement and prosecutorial resources have been devoted to smashing what Ah Kay knew of the apparatus of Chinese global alien smuggling enterprises and Chinese crime. Indictments and prosecutions have swept elements of past alien smuggling ventures from the streets of New York, Los Angeles, San Francisco, and Seattle and removed the Cantonese criminal infrastructure from New York's Chinatowns.[2]

Since 1993, the tactical, legal, and regulatory landscape has been transformed, making it less hospitable to Chinese smugglers and to irregular Chinese migrants. Smuggling vessels carrying Chinese migrants are intercepted on the high seas, a jurisdictional no man's zone where the right to halt vessels is, at best, awkward under international law, but the United States has no asylum obligations as a signatory to the United Nations Convention and Protocol on the Status of Refugees.[3] Chinese migrants arrested on U.S. soil are detained in expanded prison facilities until completion of exclusion and deportation hearings before immigration judges, who have essentially eliminated China's policy of coerced population control as a ground for asylum.[4] Opportunities for Chinese migrants to gain temporary status have been foreclosed, leaving permanent residence as the only option.[5]

Penalties for alien smuggling have been increased from 5 years in prison to 10 years, 20 years in the case of serious bodily injury or jeopardy to life, and the death penalty or a life sentence in the case of a smuggling-connected death. The enactment of the Anti-Terrorism and Effective Death Penalty Act of 1996, on April 24, 1996, finally put teeth in President Clinton's 1993 promises. RICO (the Racketeer Influence Corrupt Organizations Act) was amended to add alien smuggling and crimes essential to or facilitating it to the list of felonies falling under the act. Authority for wiretaps and interceptions of oral communications have been extended to such crimes, and the criminal jurisdiction has been expanded to embrace the full limit of the territorial sea claimed by the United States. Aliens seeking admission can now be summarily excluded and deported and their asylum cases administratively determined before a nonjudicial officer while the alien is detained. Aliens found within the United States who have not been inspected or admitted receive exclusion, not deportation, proceedings, where they, not the government, have the burden of proof.

President Clinton's October 1995 security directive, PDD-42, declaring transnational organized crime a threat to the U.S. national security, unleashed the full panoply of foreign intelligence and enforcement resources against Chinese alien smugglers. Beijing's cooperation in stemming the migrant flow at the source has been secured despite the duplicity of the U.S. posture toward China—publicly threatening it with sanctions to curb its violation of human rights, while privately demanding that it prevent migrants from departing. And U.S. diplomatic coercion has had some effect in forcing transit nations to overcome their natural reluctance to expend their resources to interdict migrants bound for the United States.

By the end of 1994, U.S. arrivals of Fujianese migrants declined dramatically, and in 1995 they declined again. In the same period, the European Union (EU) experienced an unexpected influx of migrants from the coastal city of Wenzhou, producing a crisis atmosphere in Belgium, the Netherlands, and England.[6] Australia, which has long feared illegal immigration from Asia, but believed that geography and vigilance conferred immunity from it, has experienced an increasing trend of episodic marine landings by Sino-Vietnamese (ethnic Chinese-Vietnamese). And even nearby Japan has reacted with alarm to partnerships between Fujianese smugglers and Yakuza, which have produced 27 seaborne apprehensions involving more than 750 Fujianese migrants in the first five months of 1997—more than 30 times the number apprehended in 1990.

These outflows are a mere fraction of China's 1.2 billion population. But they have been enough to produce concern and fear in many nations, West and East, about China's ability to manage the difficult political and economic transitions it faces without triggering more and larger ones. There are many of them—political instability on Deng Xiaoping's death; closing, consolidating, or privatizing inefficient state-owned industries; resolving economic disparities between the industrial south and the agrarian north; and expanding its military capability without stirring hegemonic fears among its neighbors. China already has 180 million "redundant workers," and their ranks will swell to 200 million by the year 2000. On June 30, 1997, Hong Kong became a Special Administrative Region (SAR), Macao is to return to China in 1999, and the intractable issue of Taiwan is no closer to resolution.

To some, the most optimistic scenario is an increasing flow of irregular Chinese migrants and human smuggling as an institutionalized facet of global migration. Others, given to doomsday scenarios, envision a mass migration should China stumble badly in managing one or more of these critical transitions.

Are these scenarios more fanciful than real? Is irregular Chinese migration stimulated by economic and political conditions in China? Has irregular migration produced the smugglers or do the smugglers produce the irregular migration? Have toughened laws and increased enforcement in the United States made a difference? Has lax law enforcement shifted irregular migration to the EU? Was my Fujianese friend right, "Immigration can do nothing"?

Drawing on more than 4,000 interviews with smuggled Fujianese migrants, closed intelligence sources within Chinese human smuggling enterprises and law enforcement in the United States, Canada, the EU, Hong Kong, and Australia, and 14 years of intensive, first-hand observation and exposition of this phenomenon, this essay will endeavor to provide answers to each of these critical questions.

Kaishi—The Beginning

Chinese migration from just two coastal provinces, Fujian and Guangdong, has provided the source for the majority of the 55 million overseas Chinese living in virtually every country today.[7] Throughout more than 500 years of Chinese migration, the motivating force has been the pursuit of foreign economic opportunity. From the fifteenth to the seventeenth centuries many were entrepreneurs, and in the eighteenth and for much of the nineteenth centuries, most were coolies who served the labor needs of European colonial powers. Coolies were recruited and transported from specific entrepôts in Guangdong and Fujian, and this geographic selectivity created foreign Chinese colonies that had cultural, dialectal, and natal place homogeneity. Fujianese predominated almost everywhere, except in North America, England, and Hong Kong.

In each of these colonies, Chinese followed an immutable socioeconomic progression from laborer to manager to owner, or entrepreneur, gaining, in many countries, functional control of the economy. Universally, host societies reacted to Chinese economic competition by institutionalizing discrimination. Across the globe, from Jamaica to the United States and Canada in the Western Hemisphere to the Philippines, Indonesia, Malaysia, and Thailand in the Eastern Hemisphere, discriminatory laws contained common anti-Chinese provisions: forbidding transportation and migration, preventing naturalization, restricting entry to most occupations, and foreclosing investment in most economic sectors. Collectively, these laws prevented the expansion of Chinese colonies, isolating them from one another and, perhaps most critically, denying them access to natal villages in China. Chinese migration was essentially frozen, but the migrant spirit and the desire to reestablish natal place connections remained very much alive.

Cantonese speakers from Taishan in the Pearl River Delta region of Guangdong Province, imported to replace slave labor, formed a dialectally and culturally homogenous Chinese society in the United States and Canada. In 1873, the United States enacted the Exclusion Act, the first of a series of Draconian laws designed to restrict Chinese economic competition and halt further migration. Similar restrictive legislation was enacted in Canada, effectively closing North America to the Chinese. The U.S. bulwark of criminal and immigration laws that kept the "yellow hordes" at bay endured the repeal of the Exclusion Acts in 1942, yielding only with the equalization of hemispheric immigration quotas in 1965. Functionally, lawful migration from China to the United States resumed with the opening of diplomatic relations in 1979.

Houmen—The Back Door

With the U.S. front door closed de jure and de facto to lawful Chinese migration for almost eight decades of the twentieth century and effectively closed to most lawful Fujianese migration until 1994, finding a back door was the only rational response.[8] And for most of those decades, the back door was a merchant ship that made port in the United States, allowing Chinese crew to jump ship and stowaways to come ashore. Both Cantonese and Fujianese used the back door, the Cantonese to reunite families and the Fujianese to establish a migrant seed population.[9]

Through a process of accretion, the Fujianese established a male-dominated seed population that mirrored Cantonese society for much of the Exclusion era.[10] At the close of the 1960s, about 90 percent were married males 40 to 55 years of age whose wives, children, and other members of large extended families remained in Fujian. Many had been joined by their male siblings, who possessed identical demographic characteristics.

Like Cantonese migrants from Taishan, the Fujianese seed population was essentially source-homogenous; nearly all of them came from villages in Lianjiang, Changle, and Minhou, three counties that lie along the mouth of the Min Jiang River and border Fuzhou City, the provincial capital of Fujian. They were located in a narrow band on the northeast coast of the United States. New York, with its Cantonese Chinatown, was the cultural center and northernmost point; Washington, D.C., formed the southern boundary. In a pattern that would become the template for Fujianese migration, they labored in Cantonese businesses, pooled their capital with their siblings, and formed an embryonic group of Fujianese entrepreneurs.

Feixing Houmen—The Flying Back Door

By the start of the 1970s, the relatively small seed population of Fujianese was established and had accumulated enough disposable capital to permit the migration of other family members. But obstacles stood in their path—China's closed borders and lack of lawful U.S. immigration status barred legal immigration, and illegal migration as stowaways aboard a merchant vessel was too dangerous for women and children. The *feixing houmen* was the solution.

Then, as now, Hong Kong was the center of airlinks between the East and the West. The Cold War was still being waged, the Containment Policy still had relevance, and "refugees" escaping Maoist China were welcomed in Hong Kong. Here, they could obtain Hong Kong residence, travel documents (certificates of identity, or CIDs), and board an airplane to the West.

Crude Chinese human smuggling routes existed. They began across the globe in La Paz, Panama City, and Guatemala City, converged on Mexico City, and ended at the U.S.-Mexico land border. They were "mom and pop" operations capable of smuggling only small groups, not more than three to five persons at a time, and generally handled one person at a time. They were freestanding operations, with no established links to Hong Kong or China. They were an adjunct to the maritime back door, providing a means for Chinese ship-jumpers and stowaways in Central and South American ports to reach the United States. Knowledge of their existence was gained by word-of-mouth. Almost all were run by Cantonese—Chinese merchants, operating import-export businesses, who had developed connections and networks in the "shadow economy" that embraces licit and illicit commodities. The notable exception was one operated by Lin Tao Bao, a Fujianese, in Bolivia. The fees for their services in 1970s dollars averaged $1,800.

In the Fujianese seed community, established by ship-jumpers and stowaways, knowledge of the routes and operators was widespread. Ways were found for older sons, wives, daughters, and young children to enter Hong Kong, where they obtained CIDs and visas for entry to Bolivia, Panama, Guatemala, and Mexico. The smuggling gateway cities and the Mexican border lay only a plane ride away. By December of 1970, the *feixing hou-men*, the flying back door, was opened.

The momentous events in China between 1978 and 1980 had no effect on the total number of Fujianese migrants who used the feixing houmen.[11] But more open Chinese borders after 1979 accelerated the annual rate at which the feixing houmen made immediate families whole. By 1982, the gaps in the immediate family circles of most Fujianese seed immigrants were closed and emigration from Fujian ebbed far more quickly than it had flowed.

The feixing houmen profoundly altered the dynamics of Fujianese migration. In 12 years, more Fujianese by a factor of at least four entered the United States illegally than had entered legally *or* illegally during the preceding 30 years. The airplane not only quadrupled the absolute size of the U.S. Fujianese population; it shrunk the time interval required for the population to double, producing a nonlinear, or exponential, growth rate. At the same time it produced the reverse effect on the source population, depleting it of willing migrants at the same rate.[12]

Airborne smuggling could dramatically accelerate the rate of migration, but only migrant demand for the service could sustain and expand it. Logically, the reunification of Fujianese families should have diminished demand, both in the United States and in the source villages. Factually, the reverse was true: migration begat more migration. Instead of decreasing, the numbers of Fujianese desiring to migrate from source villages, and the numbers of those in the United States obliged to assist them, increased. What appeared to be the end of a migrant cycle was in fact only the second of the three phases that distinguish Chinese migration from all others.[13] It is essential, therefore, that the characteristics of the Chinese migrant cycle be developed before proceeding further.

Chinese Relational Migration

The 500-year course of Chinese migration has been driven almost exclusively by the pursuit of a single objective, expanding the economic base of the family. An economic strategy governs its order and progression, while bonds derived from *qinshu* (kinship) and *guanxi* (non-kin dyadic relationships) determine its extent. These factors have made Chinese migration unique.

A Chinese family has been called "a corporate entity in which the members cooperate to meet economic goals."[14] Each member is obliged to contribute to the family capital pool and the family is obliged to provide for each member according to apparent or expressed need. These mutually reciprocal economic obligations and others derived from parental and filial obligations bind the family together and are collectively referred to as *qinqing*. Obligations rooted in qinqing must be honored, and they are the most compulsive of the many other mutual-obligate bonds that shape Chinese society into vast networks formed of individual dyadic relationships (*guanxi*).[15]

The Chinese family is also a patriarchy in which descent passes through the male line and kinship is agnatically determined. Absolute authority is vested in the father, and the adult male children form a kind of mid-level management. As the father ages, the mantle of authority falls upon the eldest male. Typically, he discharges his duties through an administration composed of his adult male siblings. Regardless of birth rank, each brother has a several obligation to support his aging parents and a mutual obligation to assist his brothers. These take precedence over individual obligations that each brother may have as the head of his own household. In this way the Chinese family maintains itself as a cohesive social unit and an integrated financial entity.

The interlocking obligations that bind the Chinese family radiate outward to embrace all persons who are agnatic (related through male descent or on the father's side) or affinal (related by marriage) kin. In many of the source villages of Fujian, like those in Guangdong from which the Cantonese migrants came, virtually every inhabitant has some degree of mutual obligate-relationship with a neighbor derived from kinship ties. In both provinces, lineage and single-surnamed villages are typical and are common migrant sources. Lineage villages are composed of persons who trace their ancestry through the male line to a single, apical ancestor. As agnatic kin, they identify themselves as "close" and feel a strong sense of mutual obligation to assist one another. Similarly, the inhabitants of single-surnamed villages, who uniformly, or almost so, bear the same family name, view themselves as kin and have a shared sense of mutual obligation to assist their neighbors derived from these affinal ties.

The initial Fujianese seed migrants from source villages in the counties of Changle, Minhou, and Lianjiang were mid-level family management, the most productive adult males. Typically, as the demographic data show, they were married and headed households of their own.[16] They represented the tangible product of a "corporate decision" to expand the extended family's economic base and served as the instrument for its execution. Qinqing imposed obligations upon them to save, support, and assist family members at the source and in their subsequent migration, while patriarchal concepts, modified by earning capacity, dictated the order of future migration.

The implementation of this strategy produces a migration cycle consisting of three distinct migration phases, which are the unique template of Chinese migration. I refer to these phases as *economic, immigrant,* and *relational.* In the first, or economic, phase, the most productive males—the working-age, typically married brothers—migrate. They are the seed migrants who must, through diligent effort, establish roots, create a capital base, support family members at the source, and materially assist in the migration of their productive male siblings. The seed migrant's productive capacity is multiplied as each of his siblings migrate; and by each maintaining expenses at subsistence levels, a constantly expanding capital pool is created. The economic phase is complete with the migration of the last productive male sibling and his integration into what has become a U.S. branch of the "family corporation."

Drawing on the accumulating capital pool, the brothers assist in the migration of their remaining siblings and their own immediate family in the second, or immigrant, phase. In this phase, the stimulus for migration shifts from the economic to family reunification. Economic conditions act only as rate modulators, not as stimulators; adverse ones in China or highly favorable ones in the United States may accelerate the rate of migration, while the reverse conditions may retard it. Of the three phases, this is the most protracted.

Family migration order is determined primarily by the following criteria: productive potential, the most potentially productive to the most dependent; gender, males precede females; age, eldest precedes youngest, with exception of aged parents who are last, if they migrate at all; and degree of recognized family relationship, brothers and elder children precede wives, immediate family (with exception of a married sister whose husband will precede her) precedes the extended family (male family line precedes female [wife's] family line).

Coincident with or at any time after completion of the immigrant phase, migration enters the third, or relational, phase. In this phase, seed migrants are requested or volunteer to assist in the migration and settlement of persons with whom they have an obligatory bond. These persons may be kin or clan members with whom they have agnatic or affinal ties, or unrelated, but with whom they are tied through a guanxi partnership.

The migration and resettlement assistance rendered in the relational phase and in the immigrant phase, when it extends to in-laws (husbands of married sisters and the family line of wives), "reseeds" the migrant community with primary immigrants who repeat the cycle anew. As the migration cycle proceeds within families, it produces a migrant community in which every phase of the cycle may be present simultaneously.

Migration demand within the cycle reaches two distinct peaks: one at the beginning of the immigrant phase and the other in the relational phase. Demand for family reunification originating from family members in both the natal and nuclear households is highest at the beginning of the immigrant phase and steadily declines as each member emigrates.[17] Family reunification demand is limited and, if the seed migrant family tree is known, calculable.

Relational phase demand exhibits the reverse characteristics. The source of demand comes from less resourceful or more conservative potential seed migrants (those mid-level managers or other productive persons within a Fujianese family) who, stimulated by the economic success of other migrants, seek to emulate it by demanding that persons obligatorily bound to them assist in their emigration and resettlement. Because demand is stimulated by an evaluative process that depends on the dissemination of information, it is low at the start, increases linearly as word spreads, then exponentially as more proof of economic success is available (through the increased emigration of economically successful migrants).[18] Its limit, at any point in time, becomes the sum of all the unsatisfied obligate relationships of each member of the U.S. Fujianese migrant community.

Through these dynamic relationships, migration demand and migration form a positive feedback loop. Each successful seed migrant stimulates demand for migration by his family members. As family members emigrate in the immigrant phase, total migration demand in the source community is reduced. But as evidence of their economic success reaches the source community, migration demand rises among potential seed migrants, who migrate through assistance rendered by obligates in the U.S. population. Their economic success, in turn, increases migration demand in another immigrant phase. As this loop turns, source migration demand and migration reach exponential rates and the foreign population grows at exponential rates.

Capital—the ability of migrants to produce it and the belief by those at the source that migration will enable them to produce more of it—modulates the migration flow. The production of capital by migrants is essential to attract more migrants and to develop, expand, and sustain the smuggling industry. An expanding smuggling industry maintains an increasing rate of migration, causing the migration cycle to revolve at a faster rate, which increases the rate of capital production. Migration, capital production, and smuggling thus form another positive feedback loop in Chinese migration.

By 1982, Fujianese migrants had completed the economic and immigrant phases of their initial cycle of migration to the United States. Because the seed population was small in relation to the number of immediate family migrants and the feixing houmen shortened the intervals between arrivals, concentrating them in the period between 1979 and 1982, the rate of production of disposable capital could not keep pace with the rate of migration. Fujianese migration stalled, and it would require approximately four years for Fujianese migrants, whose numbers had quadrupled, to sufficiently replenish pools of disposable capital to permit Fujianese migration to enter its initial relational phase beginning in 1986.[19]

The smuggling industry did not wait. Beginning in 1982, it took the first steps in its evolution from mom-and-pop operations to integrated global enterprises. The timing and significance of the changes could almost convince an observer that industry participants anticipated the demand for their services that would emerge four years later.

Shetou—The Snakehead

To law enforcement, the alien smuggler—the *shetou*, or the snakehead—is a criminal, a human trafficker. To those who use the shetou's vital services, the shetou is a businessperson.[20] He or she is the point of contact between a migrant and an array of enterprises that, today, form a global marketplace of human smuggling services. In 1982, there were few shetou, no integrated smuggling enterprises, and no marketplace. To form a seamless transportation web capable of transporting high volumes of migrants across the vast distance between China and the United States, networks of Chinese smugglers, which existed in most intermediate countries, had to be woven into flexible strands and their smuggling operations expanded to include not only commodities, but human beings. Of all the overseas Chinese, only the Taiwanese had the global distribution, the developed smuggling infrastructure, the transportation routes, and the dialectal and ancestral connections to Fujianese migrants to create a global smuggling industry.

Development of the Taiwanese Human Smuggling Industry

The foundations for Taiwan's human smuggling industry were laid in December 1949, when Chiang Kai-shek's defeated Kuomintang (KMT) armies fled from eastern China to Taiwan and from western China to Myanmar and Thailand.[21] With the main body on Taiwan were the leadership and members of Shanghai's powerful Green Gang, who along with the Red Gang had installed Chiang Kai-shek as the KMT's leader, financed its operations, and, in the closing moments of the civil war, formed a rear guard enabling the army's escape. As an integral part of the KMT on the mainland, the Red and Green gangs formed the core of Taiwan's intelligence agency, the Intelligence Bureau of the Military National Defense (IBMND). They exploited their underworld guanxi to develop intelligence connections through other criminal groups that had fled the mainland, such as the 14K and Sun Yee On triads in Hong Kong. Composed of politically powerful and economically motivated criminals, the IBMND emerged as the most powerful institution in the KMT government and served the needs of politician and criminal with equal alacrity.

As the most visible antipole to a Communist China and with grandiose ambitions of its own to regain control of the mainland, Taiwan became a focal point for containing the spread of Communism. Beginning in the early 1950s with covert funding and training from the CIA, the IBMND turned the remnants of the KMT third army in Myanmar and Thailand into "Chinese Irregular Forces." They were a supposed intelligence arm and part of a potential mainland invasion force. In reality, they were the antecedents of the narco-insurgent armies in Myanmar and the heroin exporters of Thailand. The IBMND used cash generated from their heroin production as its principal source of finance and for personal enrichment of its leaders. It established import-export companies and agricultural stations to obscure its operations and secured Thai citizenship to cover its operatives. With recruitment of the Ma brothers, Ma Sik-Yu and Ma Sik-Chun, the architects of the modern heroin trade, the IBMND cemented Taiwanese control over smuggling routes from Thailand, Myanmar, Hong Kong, and China to the West.

Orchestrated by the IBMND, Taiwan spread its anti-Communist (anti-mainland) doctrine beyond Southeast Asia. Its motive was patent self-interest. Beginning in 1959, again with covert funding from the CIA, ambitious programs of economic and technical assistance were established in nations in Africa, Central and South America, and the Caribbean that were thought vulnerable to Communist influence. Coincident programs providing training in anti-Communist tactics and military hardware accelerated after Taiwan and South Korea cofounded the World Anti-Communism League (WACL) in 1966, which became a recruitment organ for the IBMND-operated Political Warfare College. Through these "foreign aid programs" Taiwan built networks of intelligence and influence in seemingly obscure and unimportant countries. Thousands of Taiwanese were transferred to work in aid programs, and thousands of "anti-Communist leaders" were brought to Taiwan for tactical and military training at the Political Warfare College. Many thousands more Taiwanese emigrated to these obscure countries, all of which coincidentally hosted pockets of overseas Chinese, to found and operate businesses related to import-export.

When China won the political "zero sum game," first in the United Nations and later in the United States, Taiwan dramatically expanded its aid and deepened its influence in these economic dependencies, many of which were newly emergent sovereign states. Its objective was to fuse them into a lobbying bloc for its readmission into the UN. With most of these nations controlled by right-wing politicians or military dictatorships, resident Taiwanese criminal entrepreneurs with connections to the IBMND, or the Taiwanese government, were cloaked with de facto diplomatic immunity that allowed them to serve Taiwan's interests and simultaneously advance their own. As the decade of the 1980s dawned, those interests that had been focused on the transportation of Golden Triangle heroin to North America turned to the transportation of people.

As successful heroin smugglers, the Taiwanese had solved the logistical problems common to the covert transportation of any controlled commodity over the vast distance from Southeast Asia to North America. Though the risk is many orders of magnitude less, the transportation of people is more demanding

logistically. Unlike heroin, people are highly visible and not easily hidden, and they require supportive services in transit. To
solve these problems, Taiwanese transporters first studied the
methods of the Cantonese who operated the feixing houmen
and then took over, adding their own innovations.

In the late 1980s, as it has been and will continue to be, the
Mexican border was the Achilles heel of the United States. Its
porosity permitted a stable illicit commerce in commodities and
people controlled by Mexican smugglers. Cantonese human
smugglers had a base of control in the much smaller Central
American countries where all smuggling routes converged. Guatemala and Belize, which form the strategic "neck" of the Central
American funnel and have substantial, easily crossed borders
with Mexico, served as locations to assemble migrants into
groups before transiting Mexico and entering the United States
by land. The Cantonese recognized that they had to contract
with the Mexicans to penetrate the U.S. border, but as astute
businesspersons, they knew that if they allowed the Mexicans
direct control of this stage, they might eventually lose substantial control over the entire enterprise.[22]

Throughout the feixing houmen period, control of the Central American neck had been in the hands of Cantonese families
headed by Vincente Leon Lau, but in 1981 that began to change.
Cut off from U.S. assistance since 1978, the right-wing military
government of Guatemala was firmly in the Taiwanese web of
foreign aid, military training, and matériel assistance. In exchange, Guatemala supported Taiwan's readmission to the UN
and permitted Taiwanese smugglers to operate freely. A Taiwanese group headed by a Mr. Li and a Mr. Dong (not their true
names) began to take control of these operations and to join
them to others in El Salvador, Costa Rica, Honduras, Nicaragua,
and Panama that were falling under Taiwanese control. By 1991,
this process would be complete and Taiwanese would have
functional control over transportation and transit routes beginning in Thailand and ending in New York, save those operated
by the Fujianese, Lin Tao Bao.[23]

Shetou Caozuo Fangfa: *Snakehead Methods of Operation*

From the peak that ended the first immigrant phase in 1982,
Fujianese migration began a slow but steady increase as it
entered the first relational phase in 1986. Spurred by the Taiwanese development of the transportation networks, the smuggling
industry developed the basic structure that exists today.

Networks created by guanxi partnerships between Taiwanese and Fujianese shetou made access to illicit transportation easier, and guanxi wove globally distributed specialist entrepreneurs into highly flexible networks to form the smuggling industry.

Mostly by letter, frequently through a returning relative, and sometimes by phone, pleas and demands for migration assistance from Fujianese in the source villages poured into the U.S. Fujianese community. The members of that community were established, had the funds and the obligations, and, most important of all, had guanxi with the smugglers. Thus, as in the feixing houmen period, the market for smuggling services was in the United States, not Fujian Province. Manhattan's Chinatown, the social and economic center of the fledgling Fujianese community, was the point of contact for those seeking illicit transportation services and those brokering them.

"Brokers" were Fujianese, veterans of the feixing houmen, who were known to have "strong" contacts with illicit transportation providers. If one in need of such services did not know a broker, someone in his guanxi network could be found to make the introduction. The deals they concluded, like the market itself, were more formal, but distinctly Chinese, and the services far more expensive. The terms, almost always oral, included a total payment, usually $18,000; a down payment, usually $1,000; undertakings of performance by the broker; and a final balance due on delivery. Each party, broker and client, were, in effect, primary guarantors of performance by others, the broker for the service providers and the client for the migrant. Because broker and client had a guanxi relationship, either pre-existing or newly established, neither could breach their obligations without incurring a loss of face (*mianzi*), and resultant social and economic ostracism, or risking rectification of a breach by a progression of informal means, culminating in terror-induced performance at the hands of a criminal gang retained by the aggrieved party.[24]

As the market grew more structured, so did the smuggling industry. Through his own guanxi network, the broker would contact a partner in Fuzhou City, who would, for a fee, use his or her guanxi network to obtain a valid Chinese passport and exit permission and arrange for the migrant's departure by air or land through Shenzhen to Hong Kong and reception by another Fujianese guanxi partner. The precise route from Hong Kong to the United States depended on the guanxi networks of the Fujian partners, but the universal means of transportation was commercial air.

One innovation that emerged and would persist in varying forms was the use of the U.S. transit without visa (TWOV) privilege, which permitted direct arrival in the United States. In general terms, TWOV aliens are permitted to enter the United States without a visa for the purpose of connecting to a flight for final destination outside the United States. Pioneered by a Taiwanese service provider based in Antigua who arranged an air routing from Hong Kong to Antigua through Europe that necessitated a final connection in Miami, the TWOV privilege was exploited by simply having the migrant slip away from the minimal security provided by the airline into the waiting arms of a U.S. contact who would transport him to Manhattan.

Air routes from Hong Kong ran in two general directions. The first was linked to Lin Tao Bao's operations based in La Paz, Bolivia. Lin is a Peruvian-born Fujianese, descended from coolies transported as labor by the Spanish in the nineteenth century. He was a successful businessman operating an import-export company with ties to Southeast Asia, Hong Kong, China, and Taiwan. He had also been a provider of illicit transportation to the United States since the ship-jumping period and in this role can be seen as one of the architects of organized Chinese smuggling.

As a businessman and a smuggler Lin had a wide guanxi net. It radiated outward from La Paz linking him to networks of resources in South and Central America, Mexico, and New York and to networks in Southeast Asia, Hong Kong, Taiwan, and China. His wife, a native-born Fujianese from Lianjiang County, declined to live in Bolivia and anchored the web in Fuzhou City. As his partner, she was the first true shetou.

During the feixing houmen period, Lin was the first to make systematic use of the photo-substituted passport. Using these passports, which were always Taiwanese and contained valid U.S. visas, his clients flew from Peru to Miami or New York and successfully entered as Taiwanese visitors. Being cautious, Lin obscured the Bolivian origin of his operation by transporting his clients to Lima, Peru, to board flights for the United States. The passports were collected at arrival by a U.S. network and, together with his portion of the proceeds, were delivered to Lin for another cycle.

Lin's methods, while efficient and successful, involved delay. Migrants had to wait for a limited stock of passports to be recycled and altered or wait for a replacement passport when one had completed too many cycles. To accommodate his clients while waiting, Lin established safe houses in La Paz, in the remote town of Santa Cruz in Bolivian Amazonia, and in Lima, adding capacity as needed. To protect the houses from sweeps by "corrupt" Bolivian police, Lin paid Bolivian immigration to secure residence permits and *cedulas* (identification cards), which also facilitated movement in Peru as well as satisfying an inquisitive U.S. immigration inspector as to the residence of a "Taiwanese" visitor arriving on a flight originating in Lima.[25]

In this period, as well as later, Lin's route benefited from the presence of Bolivian consuls in China who "accommodated" Lin's clients by issuing Bolivian visas in Chinese passports, allowing them easy exit from China, admission to Hong Kong, or to fly from China transiting Hong Kong.

When the delay and the volume of traffic on Lin's route created a Bolivian bottleneck, exceeding his capacity to move it forward or house it, he created a way station in Bangkok, Thailand. Migrants were diverted to await space in Bolivia. To create this, he tapped his guanxi network for persons to secure Thai visas in Hong Kong and for Thai-Fujianese to coordinate transportation and safe-house operations.

Lin's innovation was quickly emulated by other service providers. Bangkok's Chinatown, a sprawling warren of shops, hotels, and boarding houses located in the old section between the Hualamphong railway station and the Chao Phraya River and its Hotel Thaibei, became a safe holding center for migrant traffic on all routes. Later it would emerge as the center from which all smuggling routes radiated.

As do all Fujianese, Lin had a shared provincial ancestry with the Taiwanese, an affinity that makes them natural guanxi partners in all forms of business. And although the dialects of Min are different and essentially mutually unintelligible, Taiwanese speaking the southern and the migrants speaking the northern, Lin had a number of Taiwanese in his operations in Bolivia, Peru, and Ecuador. After he trained them, most moved to Guatemala to join the emerging Taiwanese smuggling network. Lin worked cooperatively with these Taiwanese and others in Nicaragua, Panama, and Costa Rica, because their overland routes through Mexico provided an outlet for pressure exerted by restive migrants and their relatives in Fujian and New York, angered by delays of five months or more in Bolivia or Thailand.

The second air route was far less organized than Lin's. From Hong Kong it proceeded westward through Bangkok to Europe and onward to Costa Rica, Panama, and Nicaragua or Belize.

Belize was a favored terminal point because holders of Chinese passports did not need a visa to enter and Nicaragua had consulates in China. The air terminal point was a function of network connections between the Hong Kong operator and those in Central America. Once on the ground, no matter in what country, all networks converged on Guatemala and from Guatemala overland through Mexico across the California or Texas border.

Each migrant carried to the United States increased the size of an essentially underground U.S. Fujianese population, isolated from the economic mainstream by its undocumented status. Although some who entered in the feixing houmen period had managed to obtain status, most had not. Access to a wider spectrum of jobs and expansion of job opportunities by Fujianese entrepreneurs depended on obtaining lawful status. Capital constrained migration and that constraint was removed in 1986.

The Modern Era: "Immigration Can Do Nothing," Immigration Does Nothing

The modern era of smuggling began on November 6, 1986, the effective date of the Immigration Reform and Control Act of 1986 (IRCA). Its amnesty provisions permitted undocumented Fujianese to obtain employment authorization (May 5, 1987), temporary residence and the right to travel (July 1987), and permanent residence (December 1988). Although IRCA's cutoff dates were intended to limit benefits to defined classes—entry by January 1, 1982 (undocumented aliens), agricultural employment by May 1, 1986 (special agricultural workers, or SAW) to qualify for benefits; and May 4, 1988 (undocumented aliens), November 30, 1988 (SAW) to apply for benefits—they were effectively rendered meaningless. Fujianese document vendors and agents opened offices in Manhattan's Chinatown; for a price they could document any dates and any employment and as "friends" or translators for a Fujianese applicant construct a plausible story for an INS interviewer. Litigation challenging early and improper INS regulations that "discouraged qualified applicants from applying for IRCA benefits" made the application cutoff date open-ended.

IRCA benefited Fujianese migrants and the smuggling industry in three essential ways:

1. It established the premise that "crime pays"; unlawful migration will be rewarded.

2. It created an expanding capital base by allowing established Fujianese to become entrepreneurs and the newly arrived to lawfully work.

3. It allowed travel by migrants and smuggling brokers. For the first time, those remaining behind could see the tangible economic benefits of life in America and newly arrived migrants would not have to endure a long period of family separation. Smuggling brokers based in the United States now had direct access to the migrant population.

As direct result of IRCA, by the fall of 1988 expanded air smuggling routes were carrying more than 20,000 Fujianese annually, the price for smuggling services had risen to $22,000, and the structure of the industry had evolved into its modern form. The smuggling "brokers" of Manhattan's Chinatown became smugglers, the shetou who traveled to Fuzhou City on advance paroles afforded them by IRCA or with newly gained green cards. As entrepreneurs they visited the villages from which they themselves had been smuggled or waited in Fuzhou City to be contacted through migrant guanxi networks. They sold a package of services from which they could expect to receive a gross profit of 36 percent, with the balance going to the service providers. Service providers like Lin had shetou in Fuzhou, making them a vertically integrated operation.

Service providers formed a flexible chain of entrepreneurs, each providing a critical service, that began in Fujian, passed through each transit country, and ended in New York, or a flexible web that radiated from a central point, like Lin in Bolivia or the Taiwanese in Guatemala.

At the U.S. terminus, Fujianese entrepreneurs formed "meeting and greeting organizations." Their function is to meet migrants at the point of entry, collect all travel documents, transport them to safe houses, hold them as collateral for the payment of balances due, and remit the proceeds and documents less their service fees of 10 percent. Gangs, first Vietnamese (Born to Kill, BTK), then Fujianese, collected unpaid debts. Attorneys retained by shetou secured the release of those caught and processed applications, and Fujianese agents and document vendors provided whatever services were required to secure approval of applications.

On June 5, 1989, in the aftermath of Tiananmen Square, President George Bush signed an executive order permitting all

Chinese nationals who had entered the United States on or before June 4, 1989, regardless of the means, to remain and to be employed upon merely proving nationality and date of entry. Several executive orders and presidential memorandums followed, culminating in Executive Order 12711 on April 13, 1990. It extended the benefits of the first order to those arriving on or before the effective date, permitted travel on advance parole, even to China, and directed that "enhanced consideration under the immigration laws be given to persons expressing fear of persecution related to forced abortion or coerced sterilization." All of IRCA's benefits and more were extended to a whole new class of irregular Fujianese migrants, who were now "refugees," fleeing past or threatened persecution or sterilization.[26]

Now, Fujianese migrants could be virtually certain of achieving some form of status that permitted them to work and travel. If they arrived before April 13, 1990, they received the benefits of the executive order. If they arrived after its terminal date without being caught, they could "document" an earlier arrival date. If they were apprehended and paroled, as many were, under the name used in their forged passport, they could use their actual name to document an earlier arrival date, and if their true name was known, they could document a new one. If they were detained they could be paroled and receive employment authorization upon merely filing an asylum application. And even those few with no plausible claim to benefits received permission to remain in the United States (extended voluntary departure) and employment authorization.

These endless permutations and combinations altered the cost-benefit equation for shetou and migrant alike. By December 1989 the balance was tipped so heavily toward the benefit side that the shetou fixed the value of their services at $32,000 per person and 50,000 Fujianese migrants were satisfied that the benefits received were worth the cost. In each of the next four years, 1990 through 1993, more than 100,000 Fujianese reached the same conclusion, generating an underground river of cash that flowed from the Fujianese migrant community to the smuggling industry at the rate of $9 million a day.

Smuggling became seasonal, shaping the annual migrant flow into a bell curve. The season begins just after the Chinese New Year with the departure of shetou from New York. Their assemblage in Fuzhou City and appearance in the source villages marks the start, and their gradual return to New York, beginning in August and complete by November, signals the end. The season's first migrants appear in New York by mid-March. Their numbers increase steadily, peaking in July and August, then fall steadily to November. Migrants "in the pipe-line," diverted to transit country holding centers because of heavy route traffic, lack of transportation, documents, or other difficulties, arrive throughout the year, forming a constant base-line of arrivals.

Feixing Qianmen—The Flying Front Door

Throughout most of 1989, the shetou assaulted the U.S. borders on the ground. Fujianese migrants were flown to Central America, assembled in truck-sized loads in Guatemala and Belize, then shipped through Mexico and across the California and Texas borders. Early in 1990, the ground assault turned into an air war; the *feixing houmen* became the *feixing qianmen*, the flying front door. Every international airport fell under attack and almost every international flight contained a Fujianese migrant.

Initially, stolen or "rented" Taiwanese, Japanese, Singaporean, and Thai passports containing valid U.S. visas were supplied to Fujianese, who were formed into tour groups or dressed as businessmen.[27] INS inspectors from Los Angeles to Miami and New York to San Francisco suddenly had to distinguish a Fujianese from a Taiwanese or Singaporean, tell a Chinese from a Japanese or Thai, and spot the aloof, English-speaking smuggling assistant accompanying the group among all the Asian faces in his queue. Inspectors on the West Coast were more adept than others in distinguishing Japanese from Chinese, but the linguistic and cultural challenge proved overwhelming and thousands were "inspected and admitted."

Passports could not be recycled quickly enough to accommodate those waiting to fly, and the useful life of photo-substituted passports plunged dramatically. Taiwanese consuls were paid for blank passports, their misdeeds covered by reporting huge quantities as stolen; other consulates were simply broken into and looted of blank passports. Forgers from Southeast Asia to Paraguay worked overtime to produce enough passports and U.S. visas. The results varied; those produced by former IBMND agents in Paraguay were almost undetectable, while some others could only fool an inspector processing a full 747 flight single-handedly.

By June 1991, overused passports, poor-quality forgeries, and more thorough INS inspections increased the detection rate, but the combined effects of Executive Order 12711 and a lack of detention cells required that apprehended migrants be released on parole without bond.[28] This removed the roadblock to increasing the flow by air. Now, passports were needed only to board flights, not to enter the United States. Migrants were placed on flights and the passports were collected from them in flight or after they had cleared exit controls and before boarding the plane. They were told by service providers from Brazil to the Philippines that no documents were needed, "America will receive you." Arriving flights contained as many as 68 migrants at a time with no documents; and despite record fines levied against them for landing inadmissible aliens, airlines kept carrying them. When the INS increased its West Coast detention space with new facilities on Terminal Island (San Pedro) and began detaining Fujianese migrants, service providers targeted airports like New York City's JFK with human tsunamis, inundating its 125-bed contract detention facility and delivering their cargoes directly to their destination.

The Seaborne Adjunct

Leaving post-Tiananmen China was more difficult. Chinese authorities made sweeps to root out wanted counterrevolutionaries, stepping up scrutiny at borders and at passport-issuing offices. In the freewheeling world of state capitalism, Chinese passports became more valuable. By early 1990, passport authorities required strong guanxi and a cash payment of $3,000 to issue a passport and exit permission. The shetou simply passed this additional cost on to their clients, increasing the down payment by a corresponding amount. Migrants could save this amount by illegally crossing a land border or departing by sea. Many without extra funds or who were unsponsored traveled by rail or bus to Kunming in Yunnan Province and south across the Myanmar border with the aid of Burmese smugglers to the Thai border near Chang Rai, then southeast to Bangkok with the aid of Thai smugglers. Beginning in late 1991, others chose to depart by sea.

Prior to that time, seaborne smuggling was an unpredictable and dangerous means of travel to the United States. Taiwanese fishing vessels able to carry a cargo of 12–18 migrants were contracted on an ad hoc basis. Their limited capacity, slow speed, and erratic departures and arrivals made them very unattractive to migrants and unprofitable for Taiwanese service providers. In May of 1990, with air routes operating above capacity, long delays in transit countries becoming common-place, and the added cost of air smuggling, a Taiwanese consortium proposed a novel solution. Mr. Li and Mr. Dong, who now controlled all of the routes leading to and from Central America, were the smuggling half of the consortium, and Taiwanese ship owners formed the other half. Together they proposed a seaborne smuggling service employing refitted cargo or mother-ship fishing vessels capable of carrying 100–500 migrants.

In January 1991, the consortium's representatives met with the shetou in Manhattan's Chinatown and offered to sell blocks of space in minimum units of 50 spaces for $300,000 payable in advance.[29] The shetou purchasers could use all the space for their migrants or broker the space to smaller operators. These arrangements permitted shetou to offer seaborne smuggling at $28,000 per migrant, with delivery guaranteed 40 days from departure.[30] Loading could be accomplished at the mouth of the Min River, a short distance from Fuzhou City, almost within sight of the source villages, and women and children could make the trip. The first vessels were under way in July 1991, and by the end of 1993, 54 had made the trip and 18 had been inter-dicted by the U.S. Coast Guard, including the disabled *East-wood*, carrying a record 527 migrants in February 1993, and the *Golden Venture*, grounded while trying to land off New York in June.

In a low-enforcement environment, seaborne smuggling of-fers many advantages to migrant and smuggler. But in the high-enforcement environment that developed in mid-1992 in the United States and later in China, the disadvantages came to out-weigh the advantages. The *Eastwood's* human cargo was worth almost $15 million, if delivered; when it was seized, the shetou had to make good on their guarantees and smuggle their repatri-ated clients by air to collect on their contracts. When fights between the captain and shetou representatives erupted aboard the *Nadje II*, leading to its detention in Mombassa, Kenya, the *Golden Venture* had to be sent to pick up migrants stranded for more than one year.

Simple economics, apart from the high-risk nature of the enterprise, made seaborne smuggling an adjunct to air. It reached its peak in 1992–1993, when approximately 7 percent of smuggled migrants entered the United States by seaborne means. In the same period, one 747 airliner departing Bangkok could carry more passengers than all but the largest refitted cargo vessels, and airlines offered 9,566 seats aboard 38 daily flights to JFK and Newark and 3,177 seats aboard 9 daily flights to Los Angeles.

The Transit Countries

Some shetou had the guanxi to obtain Chinese passports and visas, which permitted migrants to fly directly from China to the United States. These were costly for both smuggler and migrant. The average fee of $46,000 to $50,000 limited their use to the wealthy and criminals, political or common. Virtually all migrants leaving China passed through one or, in many cases, several transit countries before reaching the United States. Thailand emerged as an eastern terminus. Here, Taiwanese service providers were in full control from years in the smuggling industry and could operate openly without fear of interference from Thai national police. Thailand could be entered from China by the land route through Myanmar, and easily obtained visas and many flights connected it to Hong Kong. Its many Taiwanese- and Fujianese-controlled hotels and boarding houses in Bangkok and along the peninsula to the Malaysian border provided cheap housing where migrant groups could be assembled to wait for documents or for route congestion to clear. The many daily flights from Bangkok provided direct air routes to the United States and linked Bangkok to South and Central American land routes and Caribbean sea and air routes. In peak periods migrants could be and were moved by land to Malaysia or transferred by air to other holding facilities in Ho Chi Minh City, Vietnam.

In Central America, Guatemala and Belize became the western terminus. Taiwanese influence and Mr. Li and Mr. Dong's money allowed them to serve as the migrant assembly point for land routes through Mexico. Belize permitted visa-free entry for holders of Chinese passports and became the air gateway. In 1992, Mr. Li and Mr. Dong bought Said Mousa, Belize's immigration minister, ensuring that Fujianese migrants could legally remain for as long as necessary to make the trip north.

To streamline his operation, open a new air route to the United States, and connect to the Central American ground route, Lin Tao Bao relocated his operations from Bolivia to Sao Paolo, Brazil, in early 1992, making it another, smaller but active western terminus that connected with Thailand.

Between these eastern and western processing and holding centers, more than 43 countries played a transit role in airborne and seaborne smuggling. Some, like the Philippines, with large

Fujianese and influential Taiwanese populations, played major roles. Others, like Palau, whose economy is dominated by Taiwanese, played minor roles.

Everywhere, from Fujian across all the transit country links and in the United States, a clear division of labor and profits emerged. Taiwanese controlled all the transportation services and earned the largest percentage of the profits, and Fujianese were the shetou and the debt collectors and received a smaller percentage.

Xianzai He Weilai—The Present and Future

Beginning with the 1994 smuggling season, Fujianese migrant arrivals declined significantly to roughly 15,000 and continued declining in 1995, with arrivals dropping to the pre-IRCA baseline of about 5,000.[31] Within the same period, the United States dramatically increased enforcement activity against accessible elements of the smuggling industry and used coercive diplomacy to gain the cooperation of China and some transit countries. The coincidence led empirics to conclude that there was a direct causal link between the two trends. The results, they argued, proved that the shetou were both the inducement and instrument for Fujianese migration: Exposing the falsity of their promises, prosecuting their U.S. operatives, and inducing China and transit countries to prosecute foreign operatives produced the decline and continuing those policies will contain the problem.

Demographics and closed source intelligence compel a very different conclusion and imply a distinctly different future. Simply put, the shetou were victims of their own, not law enforcement's, success. The *absence* of effective enforcement, not enforcement, is responsible for the decline.

Three generations of Fujianese have emigrated from the source villages in Lianjiang, Changle, and Minhou counties over the last 50 years. From the inception, interaction between migrant and smuggler has been through the medium of guanxi. Migrants have found smugglers through their dyadic networks, and smugglers have been assured of the trustworthiness and creditworthiness of migrants through theirs. While guanxi has been highly effective as a social exchange mechanism for migrant and smuggler, it has also defined and limited the smuggler's client population to those in the source villages.

In the absence of law enforcement, migrant demand for smuggling services has driven their supply and migrant capital production has been the principal restraint. It required approximately 46 years for the U.S. Fujianese to acquire a sufficient capital production base to remove it as a restraint. During that period births in the source villages added to the client population and replaced those who emigrated.

When IRCA effectively freed U.S. Fujianese capital production, migrant demand and capital fueled the expansion of smuggling services. Source villages were emptied of migrants faster than reproduction could replace them. Between 1986 and 1994, migrant demand and the efficiency of the shetou's services doubled the U.S. Fujianese population twice, depleting the source village populations at the same rate. In some villages, like Hoyu in Changle County, 85 percent of the inhabitants, including virtually all those of reproductive age, are in the United States. In others the average is 50 percent, and none is without many families who have "relatives" in the United States. Across all these counties "women's villages", whose populations consist primarily of single and married women and paternal grandparents who have not emigrated, have become commonplace.

By 1993, without law enforcement to slow the rate of migration, the shetou had effectively depleted their client base. The Fujianese migrant cycle revolved so rapidly that by June, migration from virtually all source villages simultaneously entered a terminal stage characterized by the migration of women and children below the age of 15.

Experience with the Cantonese migration from Taishan shows that this stage will be protracted, but it may not be a significant source of migrants for the shetou. Lawful immigration is increasingly supplanting them as a means. Additional visas available for reunification of the families of legalization applicants under IRCA's amnesty program, now over, began the diversion of Fujianese migrants to lawful immigration. This trend continued with the Chinese Student Protection Act (CSPA), which provided some students with an additional quota to use for family reunification purposes. The trend appears sustainable, if the waiting period in family reunification quotas does not exceed its present five-year average.

Irregular migration from the source villages has not halted, but it has declined sufficiently to prompt action by Taiwanese service providers and Fujianese shetou. Faced with sharply reduced demand for their services and excess capacity, they responded like other enterprises. They consolidated, downsized, cut costs, and sought new markets. In 1994, Lin Tao Bao became a Taiwanese "profit center," effectively creating a unitary western terminus operation. Migrants using his Sao Paolo route are sent through Guatemala, and a small number using expertly altered passports are flown directly to the United States

Costs have been cut and losses to law enforcement contained by curtailing West Coast landings and channeling arriving migrant traffic to points closer to East Coast destinations. Seaborne smuggling from Fujian to the United States has almost been eliminated; not more than three boats arrived in 1995, and no more than one was expected in 1996.

Thailand still serves as the principal eastern terminus for assembling migrants after exiting China and as a commercial air feeder to old Central American and new Caribbean routes.

Cambodia is emerging as a new assembly point for migrants moving east toward Japan and west toward the United States and Europe. Migrants are moved to Phnom Penh from Bangkok or from China directly. The shetou now employ the excellent document-forging facilities in Bangkok to supply high-quality forged travel documents to waiting Chinese migrants, while avoiding the increased scrutiny of documents by airline personnel who have been trained by U.S. and Australian government document teams. Phnom Penh also reduces costs; bribes to officials are significantly lower, as are operating and maintenance costs.[32]

Guatemala and Belize have been retained as migrant assembly and processing centers, but land entry routes through Mexico now only run north to crossing points on the Texas and New Mexico borders. They feed safe houses that have been relocated to Chicago and western Pennsylvania away from the intense enforcement activity centered in New York's Chinatowns.

Caribbean operations controlled from Guatemala were expanded in 1994. The Dominican Republic, which had served as a low-traffic smuggling route to the United States for at least 10 years, was upgraded by resident Taiwanese to accommodate an increased flow. Migrants arriving by air from Thailand on Chinese passports are landed in Kingston, Jamaica, and after receiving a photo-substituted passport are transported by regional airlines to Santo Domingo. Others with photo-subbed passports supplied in Thailand enter the Dominican Republic directly. There, they are assembled in groups of between 5 and 30 and transported by small vessel to clandestine landing points in Puerto Rico. Once on U.S. soil, they are flown by domestic carriers to various airports on the East Coast.

Migrant traffic from Thailand is also sent to the Bahamas, where facilities have been upgraded to hold at least 1,000 people on main and at outer island locations. The Bahamas, like the Dominican Republic, had served as a low-traffic route since 1989, but its development into a medium-sized processing center was hampered by the apparent inability of resident Taiwanese to penetrate Bahamian immigration to ensure that arriving migrants would not be excluded on arrival. At the start of the 1994 season, this hurdle was cleared and migrants now arrive without difficulty.

Virtually all migrants are moved to the United States by sea using a variety of methods. The primary one employs small, high-speed vessels, similar to those used in off-loading narcotics, to transport up to 15 migrants to the Florida Keys where they are off-loaded. To transport larger loads of roughly 50 migrants, commercial vessels have been used to bring migrants to landing points in the Delaware and Chesapeake Bays and, in at least three instances, to the St. Lawrence Seaway, where they are off-loaded by raft in Canada and transported across unguarded border crossing points to safe houses in Albany, New York.

Service through the Bahamian route has proved to be quite rapid. Many migrants complete the trip from Fujian to Manhattan in five days. The Dominican Republic route has inherent delays attributable to assembling migrants for the Mona Channel crossing to Puerto Rico and greater risks. The high seas and poor condition of the often overloaded vessels make foundering and interdiction a not infrequent occurrence, and once landed in Puerto Rico, a large Chinese-speaking group attracts unwanted attention. The restructured Guatemala-Mexico land route requires the most transit time, but, with the exception of the Bahamian route, has the least risk.

Honduras, which at various times has served as a transit country for migrant traffic moving north from Panama and Nicaragua, as well as a vessel landing point for seaborne arrivals directly from coastal China, has emerged as a transit nation for another group of Chinese migrants, those involved in criminal networks. This darker facet of Chinese irregular migration was exposed with the arrest on July 15, 1996, of Jerry Wolf Stuchiner, the INS officer-in-charge (OIC) at the U.S. Embassy at Tegucigalpa, upon his arrival at Hong Kong's Kai Tak airport.

Stuchiner, who entered Hong Kong using his diplomatic passport, was in possession of five "officially issued" Honduran passports complete in all respects save one, the name of a bearer.[33] The passports were to be delivered to the Honduran consul in Hong Kong, Herby Dennis Weizenblut Oliva.[34]

Honduras, like Belize, enacted a special naturalization law on December 20, 1990, which permitted investors who agreed to invest in Honduras and paid the sum of $25,000 to acquire Honduran citizenship and a Honduran passport.[35] Documents produced before a special anti-corruption prosecutor in Tegucigalpa indicate that the law was promoted and passed by Hondurans who had formed an alliance with known Chinese enterprise crime figures for the sole purpose of facilitating the smuggling of Chinese.[36] Three Honduran consuls, the foreign minister, an ex-foreign minister, a secretary to the National Party, and many other highly placed Hondurans were implicated in the scheme.[37] It is alleged that following passage of the law, a U.S. company was established in Miami and a subsidiary created in Honduras. These were linked to a company formed in Hong Kong, which in turn controlled two additional Hong Kong companies. The Hong Kong companies were linked through Dickson Yao to guanxi networks of the Sun Yee On Triad.[38]

The function of the Hong Kong companies was to "recruit Chinese investors" in Honduras, transmit their funds for deposit in the central bank, and receive their naturalization documents on completion of the process. Their true function, however, was to receive total payments of as much as $100,000 per person and to launder the $75,000 through the Hong Kong corporations, then remit the funds to the Florida corporation, which, in turn, would remit some to Honduras and other amounts to Swiss bank accounts held in the names of the principals involved. It has been alleged that since December 1990, more than 20,000 passports were sold and more than $15 billion was collected.[39]

Stuchiner's involvement in the scheme is a source of serious concern to many agencies of the U.S. government, as well as other governments. Stuchiner pleaded guilty to possession of the five false travel documents and was sentenced in August 1996 to 40 months in a Hong Kong prison. In April 1997 his conviction was reversed on grounds that he had been charged improperly. Fifteen minutes later, however, he was rearrested by the Independent Commission Against Corruption for possessing equipment for making a false instrument, and in May 1997 he was sentenced to three months in jail; he was to be released and deported to the United States in July.[40]

The investigation of Stuchiner and its aftermath can be likened to a pebble tossed on the surface of a tranquil pond, with ripples crossing the globe from Hong Kong to Central America, the United States, and elsewhere. Stuchiner was no ordinary bureaucrat, but rather a main, if not the main, source of intelligence on Chinese alien smuggling when he served as the OIC of the U.S. INS office in Hong Kong from 1989 to 1994, a role that continued after his transfer to Honduras.[41] One thing is known with certainty: transferring Stuchiner to Tegucigalpa sent the fox to guard the chickens.

Replacing the declining Fujianese client base is more difficult than U.S. enforcement authorities imagine. The Taiwanese entered an existing market; they did not have to create one. Demand for service was well established and increased with each smuggled migrant. Making the market profitable merely required developing the infrastructure to permit a high-volume operation. Natural guanxi partnerships between Taiwanese operators around the globe made the creation of a flexible, high-volume transportation network relatively simple. And natural guanxi partnerships, derived from commonality of natal place, shared ancestry, and dialect, between Fujianese migrant and Fujianese shetou and between Fujianese shetou and Taiwanese operators created the essential market relationships and provided a mechanism to order them. To expand their client base, Taiwanese service providers must extend their network of guanxi relationships to shetou born in other provinces, who speak different dialects, and through them to potential migrants. These are unnatural guanxi relationships, and to create them the Taiwanese must bridge a formidable barrier of hostility and suspicion that separates Chinese who lack dialectal and cultural commonality.

They have clearly succeeded with the Wu-speaking shetou and migrants from the coastal city of Wenzhou, 240 kilometers to the northeast of Fuzhou, in adjacent Zhejiang Province. Generations of contact in coastal trade between Fujianese and Wenzhounese have made them sufficiently less alien to permit the formation of guanxi partnerships.

Wenzhounese have been irregularly migrating since at least 1970, when they began establishing seed colonies in Madrid and Barcelona. The social structure of their source towns and villages is strikingly similar to those in Fujian, and as a result

Wenzhounese migration has progressed relationally, displaying a nearly identical dynamic pattern and differing only in its smaller scale. Both the source migration rate and the rate at which migrants radiated from Spain to colonize other European countries tracked the removal of barriers to movement, employment and investment within the European Union (EU), increasing as those barriers decreased. About 1990, Wenzhounese EU colonies reached "critical mass" and their EU migration rate became superexponential.[42] Simultaneously, Wenzhounese began a U.S. migration through Taiwanese networks.

In 1990, their numbers were small in comparison to Fujianese, less than 1 percent of all arrivals. By 1993 they approached 7 percent, in 1994 jumped to 15 percent, and in 1995 were very close to 30 percent, establishing clearly that the Taiwanese have begun exploiting a replacement client base for their U.S. services, coincident with their dramatic expansion in EU services.[43]

Beginning with the 1994 smuggling season, closed sources of intelligence from within the shetou community revealed a shift in their marketing strategy in response to a changing market. Seemingly overnight, their booming sellers' market, in which they worked overtime to fill client orders, had become a buyers' market in which they had to work overtime to find clients. Collectively, they realized that for the first time they would have to develop a new client base and actively sell their services.

As prime beneficiaries of Deng Xiaoping's market economy fueled by Taiwanese investment, the more educated Fujianese residents of Fuzhou City, who consider themselves superior in every way to their crude, Min-speaking, country-bumpkin village cousins, have never been a significant source of clients for the shetou. Fuzhou City is a comfortable base of operations, but their client base was in the villages. Fuzhou City now contains almost one million new residents, members of the "floating population" from the interior provinces of Sichuan, Anhui, and Hunan. They are the laborers, filling jobs unwanted by the Fujianese of Fuzhou City at pay rates too low to attract villagers, many of whom now have remittances from the United States to sustain a higher standard of living. These new residents of Fuzhou City are a potential source of clients for the shetou, but only if they offered their services on markedly different terms.

These potential clients are seed migrants and they lack capital. Unlike the Fujianese, they do not have established foreign seed colonies to produce it. By borrowing at high rates of interest, many can obtain a down payment, but virtually none have the funds or borrowing capacity to pay the smuggling fees on arrival. For the first time, the shetou had to offer their services on credit with long repayment periods, secured only by the migrant's future earning capacity. Although these arrangements dramatically alter the relationship between shetou and migrant with potentially significant consequences for both, the shetou have offered them and migrants have accepted them.[44]

The years 1996 and 1997 should be watershed years for the shetou and the Taiwanese. They should mark the first time that the decline in the number of migrant arrivals in the United States is reversed and the provincial origins of the migrants shift from predominantly Fujianese to include Zhejiang, Sichuan, Anhui, and Hunan. If this is achieved, the U.S. borders will once again fall under assault as the Chinese migrant cycle advances—"Immigration has done nothing and Immigration can do nothing" to stop it.

Notes

1. *Mercury Newscenter,* Text, Presidential News Conference (June 6, 1993) (Internet).

2. The arrival of the Fujianese has created three Chinatowns, the original one in Manhattan and two new ones in Brooklyn and Queens.

3. See *Sale v Haitian Centers, et al.* This policy was implemented pursuant to a bilateral agreement between the Haitian and U.S. governments giving the United States permission to halt vessels transporting Haitian migrants on the high seas and implemented by a Presidential proclamation—Presidential Proclamation No. 4865, 3 C.F.R. 50–51 (1981–1983 Comp.), signed by President Reagan on September 29, 1981, which suspended the entry of undocumented aliens from the high seas. An NSC directive extended the proclamation to Chinese smuggling vessels even though no underlying agreement provided authority to halt such vessels on the high seas. A subsequent memorandum written by a State Department representative on the NSC suggested the United States had no asylum obligations to aliens "who had not entered" the United States and urged regularly restricting asylum applications to those who had made a formal entry. This has never been implemented, but the arguments with respect to the process that is due illegal entrants have been implemented by the Anti-Terrorism and Effective Death Penalty Act of 1996, which now limits such aliens to exclusion instead of deportation proceedings.

4. As a result of President Bush's executive orders and the strong influence exerted by "right to life" members of the president's staff, China's population control policy was the principal ground of asylum asserted by

Fujianese migrants apprehended by the INS. In 1992 alone there were 3,464 such applications filed.

5. The five-year period of extraordinary immigration benefits available only to nationals and citizens of China, which commenced on June 5, 1989, with President Bush's first post-Tiananmen executive order, was effectively ended by the closure of applications for permanent residence on June 30, 1994, under the Chinese Student Protection Act, Public Law 102–404, October 9, 1992, U.S. Statutes at Large 106 (1969).

6. Criminal justice professionals from these countries, speaking at the 18th International Asian Organized Crime Conference, April 29-May 3, 1996, Anaheim, California, cited illegal Wenzhounese migration and crime associated with it as the number one crime problem in their countries. Speakers at the Transnational Organized Crime Conference of Charles University, Florida State University, and the National Police Authority of the Czech Republic, held in Prague October 11–20, 1995, also cited illegal Wenzhounese migration and associated crime as a major criminal problem.

7. See Sterling Seagrave, *Lords of the Rim; The Invisible Empire of the Overseas Chinese* (New York: G. P. Putnam's Sons, 1995), 284–285.

8. As the established Chinese population in the United States, Cantonese had the oldest priority dates and dominated the available immigration quotas until 1994, when sufficient numbers of Fujianese had gained permanent residence and citizenship to permit them to act as relative sponsors.

9. The term *seed population* refers to a migrant group who entered a country with the intent of establishing a social and economic foundation to permit future migration from the source and have done so.

10. The earliest record in my database records the arrival of a Fujianese family patriarch aboard the *Black Star* in late 1941 at Hampton Roads, Virginia where he jumped ship. He had paid £100 to be a cook on its sinuous voyage across the war torn Pacific.

11. These events include the establishment of formal relations between China and the United States; U.S. recognition of the People's Republic of China as the only government of China; the opening of China to foreign investment; the transformation of China's economy from command to state-capitalism; and creation of special economic zones (SEZs) along China's southeast coast.

12. There are no accurate census data from which to estimate the absolute size of the seed population. What is known is that between 1940 and 1970 the source of its growth was almost exclusively ship-jumpers, and, based on that mechanism, its rate of increase (additions to the migrant population per year) is assumed to be constant and linear. A crude estimate of the time required for the population to double (doubling time) is approximately 15 years. More reliable data available from migrant interviews support the dynamic shift in migration rates between 1970 and 1982 and the magnitude of this increase in the Fujianese seed population.

13. Other Asian populations may exhibit the same migration characteristics, but there have been no studies to support this conclusion. There is no

question that the characteristics of Chinese migration are unique when compared with those of Western populations.

14. See Graham E. Johnson, "Family Strategies and Economic Transformation in Rural China: Some Evidence from the Pearl River Delta," in *Chinese Families in the Post-Mao Era*, ed. Deborah Davis and Stevan Harrell (Berkeley: University of California Press, 1993) pp. 103–136.

15. Like *qinqing* creates mutual-obligate relationships within the family, *guanxi* creates similar, but less compulsive, mutual-obligate dyadic relationships outside the family. A guanxi bond has two interlocking components, which between individuals form a social mechanism for accessing social resources and collectively creating social networks for the exchange of resources. The first of these is the right of each party to request performance by the other of the undertakings implicit in the bond (*renqing*). The degree to which a party feels compelled to perform is a measure of the strength of the bond. The second component is the obligation to repay (*bao*), which is incurred when the request is performed. The repayment must be a *renqing* of at least equal, but preferably greater, value to the performer. Each party's ledger of *renqing* and *bao* must remain balanced.

Guanxi partnerships are the source of migration assistance between non-kin. Guanxi networks are used by both migrant and shetou; migrants use them to locate and verify the performance of a shetou, and the shetou use them to locate migrant clients and check their creditworthiness. The networks form the structure joining globally distributed Chinese entrepreneurs into efficient, flexible transportation webs, linking migrants in China to any destination across the globe. Guanxi's "rules" are the foundation of commercial relationships: between migrant and shetou and among participants in the global transportation network. Guanxi's social order insures performance, but it creates a range of informal remedies to redress a breach of obligation that progress from mediation to physical terror, which guarantees ultimate performance. For a complete discussion, see: Willard H. Myers III, "Orb Weavers—The Global Webs: The Structure and Activities of Transnational Ethnic Chinese Criminal Groups," *Transnational Organized Crime,* Vol. 1, No. 4 (Newbury Park, Illford, Essex, UK: Frank Cass, 1996) pp. 1–36; Willard H. Myers, III, "Illuminating the Black Economy, Ethnic Chinese Transnational Enterprise Crime and U.S. National Security Interests, Reconciliation or Redefinition?," *Strategic Studies Series* (Washington, D.C.: National Defense University Press, 1997, in press).

16. See Willard H. Myers III, "The United States Under Siege, Assault on the Borders, Chinese Smuggling 1983–1992" (Center for the Study of Asian Organized Crime, Philadelphia, Pa., June 1992) cited in U.S. Congress Senate Report of the Permanent Subcommittee on Investigations, Committee on Governmental Affairs, *The New International Criminal and Asian Organized Crime* 102nd Cong. 2d. Sess., 1992 S. Prt. 102–129, p. 37; Myers, "The United States Under Siege, A Conspiracy of Silence, Chinese Smuggling 1983–1993" (Center for the Study of Asian Organized Crime, Philadelphia, Pa., December 1993); and Myers, *Fujianese Radiations in America: The Socio-*

Economic Consequences of Illegal Immigration (Center for the Study of Asian Organized Crime, Philadelphia, Pa., in press).

17. The natal household consists of grandparents, parents, and siblings. The nuclear household consists of the male siblings and their wives and children. These two households frequently reside under one roof or in very close proximity to one another.

18. Information about the economic success of migrants reaches the source community in many ways: letters; return visits by migrants wearing "expensive" clothes and jewelry and bearing "expensive" gifts for family and kin; and remissions to family, which permit those remaining to enjoy a significantly higher standard of living, which frequently includes the construction of a large home, equipped with modern appliances and a telephone. As the flow of such information increases, a "band wagon effect" is generated, which propels the linear growth rate of migrant demand to superexponential levels.

19. Although annual numbers of Fujianese illegal migrants dropped significantly between 1982 and 1986, illegal migration did not stop. It dropped to a base level and steadily increased throughout the four year period until it "exploded" again in 1986.

20. The term *shetou* is a Mandarin word translated as "snakehead" and is a slang term for an alien smuggler. In Chinese usage, any person connected with alien smuggling is a shetou, and human smuggling enterprises are referred to as shetou, snakeheads in a collective use of the term. Many news accounts from China refer to the arrest of "snakeheads" or "snakehead gangs" when reporting the "smashing" of alien smuggling operations. Operationally, a shetou is either an entrepreneur or an employee. As an entrepreneur, the shetou contracts with Chinese migrants desiring to enter the United States by illegal means, subcontracts with one or more "service providers" for the transportation and facilities needed for an illegal entry, collects the proceeds, and retains the net profits. As an employee, the shetou is compensated, based on the number of migrants he or she obtains, either by a service provider or by an integrated human smuggling enterprise, which provides all the capital, performs the services, and retains the profits.

Many of the most successful shetou are women. Chen Choi Ping, "Big Sister Ping" of Manhattan's Chinatown, has earned more than $10 million as a shetou. She has large real estate holdings in Chinatown and in Fujian, three restaurants, and three farms, two in New York and one in New Jersey. She and her partners dominate the supply of fresh produce to Chinese markets, and she operates the largest Chinese "underground bank" in the United States. Her farms provide ready employment for newly arrived migrants.

21. The documentation for this account of Taiwan's involvement in smuggling is drawn from the exhaustive research of investigative journalist David E. Kaplan. See generally, David E. Kaplan, *Fires of the Dragon* (New York: Atheneum, 1992). See also, Sterling Seagrave, *The Soong Dynasty* (New York: Harper & Row, 1985). For more recent information on the extent and development of the Taiwanese smuggling industry, see Myers, "Illuminat-

ing the Black Economy, Ethnic Chinese Transnational Enterprise Crime and
U.S. National Security Interests, Reconciliation or Redefinition?"

22. Colombian cocaine enterprise criminals were not so astute, and
Mexican polydrug enterprises are well on their way to controlling the North
American drug market.

23. The emergence of Taiwanese control of the Chinese human smuggling operations in Guatemala and Central America as well as a history of
Cantonese and Taiwanese operations and operatives is detailed in three
classified cables prepared by the U.S. embassy in Guatemala City and sent
to the Department of State beginning in July 1993.

24. "Gang terror" is the most frequent method of collecting unpaid
smuggling debts. Although characterized by law enforcement as near universal, it is in fact relatively rare, because the vast majority of debts are honored and paid when due. Its use is preceded by many other informal
remedies, which law enforcement seems to be unaware of or whose significance it fails to understand.

25. The "corrupt" Bolivian police were those who rounded up Lin's
Fujianese migrants to extort payments from him for their release. Non-cor-
rupt police enforced the law and rounded up migrants; they too received
payments for the release of migrants, and many joined the ranks of the corrupt police.

26. Between June 1989 and October 1, 1991, few Fujianese migrants
were caught and fewer detained. All those who were apprehended and detained in this period initially based their claims on involvement with the democracy movement and later on past or threatened persecution from
enforcement of population control laws. At the close of the 1991 fiscal year,
there were 1,387 Chinese asylum applications pending with the INS based
on both grounds. In fiscal 1992, 3,464 applications were filed asserting almost exclusively persecution based on population control as the ground. In
fiscal 1993, reflecting increasing apprehension rates, 12,992 asylum applications were filed with coerced population control now the exclusive ground.
As the start of fiscal 1994, 16,336 applications were pending. Like the rate of
Fujianese migration, the rate with which Fujianese filed asylum applications became superexponential in three fiscal years. Data source U.S. INS.

27. Passports are "rented" by paying their true owners for their use and
after a predefined period are returned to them. To many immigration officers, "all Chinese look alike" and in many cases rented passports were used
by Fujianese migrants without alteration of the photo. This was particularly
the case when there was a family resemblance between the passport holder
and the migrant.

28. Consider, if all asylum applicants in fiscal years 1992 and 1993 were
detained their numbers would exceed the available detention beds by a factor of at least 16.

29. Closed source intelligence, Center for the Study of Asian Enterprise
Crime [formerly Center for the Study of Asian Organized Crime], Philadelphia, Pa.

30. The delivery guarantee is a provision of all smuggling contracts. It provides, in essential terms, that the person smuggled will be delivered to the point of destination (New York City or its environs) free of law enforcement restraint and, if apprehended and repatriated, will be redelivered for no additional fee regardless of the number of additional smuggling attempts needed to achieve the objective, though some additional fees have been demanded and paid when a repatriated seaborne migrant is smuggled again by air. The guarantee of delivery has effectively blunted the enforcement strategy of rapid repatriation and enhanced the business reputation of the shetou who honor their guarantees.

31. It should be noted, paradoxically, that representatives of the U.S. Coast Guard dispute the findings of the Center for the Study of Asian Enterprise Crime based upon their interdiction and intelligence data. Those data reflect the following: for FY 1992, 9 vessels interdicted 793 Chinese aliens on board; FY 1993 12 vessels interdicted 2,464 aliens on board; FY 1994, 7 vessels interdicted 350 aliens on board, suspected off-loads of Chinese aliens directly into the United States, 6 vessels and 850+ Chinese aliens, suspected off loads of Chinese aliens in Mexico, Honduras and El Salvador, 3 vessels and 610 Chinese aliens; FY 1995, 4 vessels interdicted at sea 442 Chinese aliens on board, 3 vessels not at sea 47 Chinese aliens, suspected off loads of Chinese aliens directly in US 400, suspected off loads in Mexico, Guatemala, Honduras 616+, 52 suspected events calculated to involve 7,466 Chinese aliens; FY 1996 0 interdictions (nine months of fiscal year) suspected events in Mexico and Virgin Islands 317 Chinese aliens. Data Source: USCG, July 1996. Personal communication by USCG personnel to author July 1996. INS apprehension data reflect a vastly different picture. For FY 1994, 1,168 Chinese aliens were apprehended entering by all means, and for FY 1995, 759 Chinese aliens were apprehended entering by all means. Data Source: INS, July 1996. The difference between the USCG and INS data lies in the "suspected events." If one assumes that the USCG data are accurate, the INS apprehended only 9.5 percent of the Chinese aliens suspected of entering the United States in FY 1995, but 62 percent in FY 1994.

32. "Phnom Penh is new port of call for human smugglers," *Straits Times* (Singapore), May 21, 1997 (Internet).

33. William Branigin, "INS Agent Arrested in Hong Kong Alien-Smuggling Scheme Alleged," *Washington Post*, July 17, 1996, p. A28 (Internet); Associated Press, "Fed Accused of Alien Smuggling," July 16, 1996 (Internet). The names were to be added by the man Stuchiner was to deliver them to, Herby Dennis Weizenblut Oliva, the Honduran consul in Hong Kong and Stuchiner's friend and confederate in a high-stakes passport scheme. The names would be drawn from the top of a list of those who paid in excess of $100,000 each to acquire a passport.

34. Weizenblut served as the Honduran consul since December 1995. He was questioned by agents of Hong Kong's Independent Commission Against Corruption (ICAC) who made the arrests and released him because of his diplomatic immunity. The Honduran government sent the revocation of his diplomatic status through a circuitous diplomatic route, from

Tegucigalpa to London and from London to Hong Kong, which consumed five days. Constrained by Weizenblut's diplomatic status, ICAC officials watched helplessly as he boarded a hydrofoil to Macao and then flew to Bangkok, from whence he disappeared. Now an international fugitive wanted on an Interpol warrant filed by Honduras, Weizenblut has been reported seen in various "extradition-proof" countries.

35. The law is designated as Decree 26–90 and popularly known as the Special Naturalizational Law.

36. *El Tiempo* (San Pedro Sula, Honduras), "The Origins of the Chinazo," (22 July 1996) (in Spanish) (Internet). The scheme involving the sale of citizenship and the smuggling of Chinese is referred to in press accounts as "el Chinazo."

37. *La Prensa* (San Pedro Sula, Honduras) (5 August 1996) (in Spanish) (Internet). The central figure named in the plot is Rene Contreras, an ex-foreign minister. Also implicated are his current wife, Julie Ng, a former Honduran consul in Miami, Florida, and Hong Kong and an independently wealthy Chinese businesswoman with major interests in the shipping industry; Herby Weizenblut Oliva, then the Honduran consul in Hong Kong; Dennis Matamoros Batson, secretary of the National Party; Enrique Ortez Sequiera, liberal delegate before the National Election Tribunal; Roberto Antonio Callejas, ex-consul of Honduras in Miami; Carlos Kattan Salem, deputy minister, and Francisco Cardona Arguelles, ex-minister of administration; and Richard Cahan, a Hong Kong businessman.

38. The Miami company was Devonshire and Omega and the Honduran company was the Lempira Group. Upper Essex was formed in Hong Kong and directed by Richard Cahan, who represented Julie Ng and Rene Contreras. Cahan managed the Hong Kong operation through Reliance Agency Holdings Limited, and Sindy.

Dickson Yao is a central and "unifying" figure in much of this and other matters related to Chinese alien smuggling and Chinese enterprise crime in general. Since at least 1989, Yao served as a highly paid intelligence source for American enforcement and intelligence agencies, including the INS. Until Stuchiner was transferred to Honduras, he served as Yao's "handler." Yao has very strong links to the Sun Yee On and 14K triads. In 1993, he lured Ah Kay out of Fujian on behalf of the FBI so he could be arrested in Hong Kong and removed to the United States. He may have, at various times, worked for the CIA. He connects Stuchiner to the Hondurans and the Hondurans to large Chinese criminal enterprises in Hong Kong, China, and Taiwan. Since approximately 1990, he paid the salary of the Honduran consul in Hong Kong and $10,000 of the annual office expenses for the consulate. In addition, he paid the hotel bill of $14,500 for the February 1996 three-day stay of the current Honduran foreign minister, Delmer Urbizo Panting, and set up a meeting for him with Stanley Ho, the major casino figure in Macao, who is an honorary Honduran consul. Despite his powerful triad and law enforcement contacts or perhaps because of them, Yao was sentenced to only 18 months in prison after pleading guilty to possession of 500 Honduran passports of the type carried by Stuchiner. He is to be released in the late summer of 1997. Both his conviction and involvement deepen the sense of mystery that surrounds this entire matter. See Associated Press, "Honduras Probes Passport Scam," July 27, 1996 (Internet); *La Prensa* (San Pedro Sula, Honduras), "Arrested Chinese had paid the bill of Urbizo Panting in Hong Kong,", July 24, 1996 (in Spanish) (Internet); *Hong Kong Standard*, "Honduran Probe Continues," May 20, 1997 (Internet); Associated Press, May 21, 1997 (Internet) (reporting that Delmer Urbizo Panting is now under active investigation in connection with his involvement with Yao).

39. Associated Press, "Honduras Probes Passport Scam," July 27, 1996 (Internet).

40. After his initial arrest, Stuchiner remained silent and refused to cooperate in any investigations of his role and his connection to the "el Chinazo" affair, as it came to be known in Honduras. Initially, he planned to demand a trial in which he threatened to reveal intimate secrets of U.S. intelligence operations, but having a change of heart and strategy, he pleaded guilty to possession of the five false travel documents and was sentenced on August 17, 1996, to 40 months in a Hong Kong prison. The severity of the sentence compared with that meted out to his confederate, Dickson Yao, stunned him, as did the fact that he would be an inmate in Hong Kong after its handover to China.

Professing lack of funds, Stuchiner, himself a lawyer, took a pro se appeal to the Hong Kong Court of Appeal seeking a reduction of his sentence. On April 16, 1997, he appeared before the court and, to the shock of all present, the senior prosecutor for the Crown, Ian McWalters, confessed that Stuchiner had been convicted and jailed improperly—a travel document without a photograph did not meet the legal definition and none of the five bore any photographs. Stuchiner enjoyed 15 minutes of freedom as the conviction was reversed before he was rearrested by the ICAC on a charge of possessing equipment for making a false instrument. Between the time of his arrest on the new charge and his appearance in court for a plea sentence on the new charge, Stuchiner felt it was in his interest to begin talking. What he revealed is not known with precision, but it was said by the crown prosecutor that "the information given to ICAC investigators had been very useful" and it was alleged that he had received a death threat in his cell for his cooperation. On May 20, 1997, Stuchiner was sentenced to three months on the new charge. On June 27, 1997, he was released after receiving credit for time already served. For those five weeks, he was held in a "Resident Informer Cell" on the tenth floor of ICAC headquarters, a reward for his cooperation regarding James DeBates, his former subordinate, and for his cooperation in a major narcotics case initiated by ICAC and the Narcotics Bureau. Instead of being deported to the United States after his release, Stuchiner will be permitted to remain in Hong Kong to testify as a prosecution witness in the upcoming trial. Meanwhile, the Honduran attorney general has stated his intention to seek Stuchiner's extradition to Honduras to prosecute him in connection with his role and that of others in the el Chinazo affair. See Patrica Young, *South China Morning Post* (Hong Kong),

April 16, 1997 (Internet); Magdalen Chow, "Former Officer on Fresh Charge," *South China Morning Post,* April 30, 1997 (Internet); Magdalen Chow, "Jail Term Slashed for Ex-US Official," *South China Morning Post,* May 20, 1997 (Internet); Glenn Schloss, "Investigator from Honduras to Probe Scam," *South China Morning Post,* May 22, 1997 (Internet); *La Prensa* (Honduras), "Honduras Will Prosecute Diplomat, Jerry Stuchiner, If He Is Deported to the US," May 23, 1997 (Internet) (in Spanish); Associated Press, June 25, 1997 (Internet); Niall Fraser, "Passport Racketeer Walks Free from Relative Lap of Luxury," *South China Morning Post,* June 25, 1997, (Internet).

41. Stuchiner's involvement with Dickson Yao led him into many ventures unrelated to his duties, such as the export of Chinese laborers to Israel, and to supplementing his income and that of his assistant, James Debates, and Yang Chung-wei, a local consulate employee, through an elaborate bribery scheme that ensured approval of visa applications to those who paid. Stuchiner's involvement in the shadow world of Chinese alien smuggling goes back, it seems, as far as 1991. As these networks and links become more visible, the other denizens of the shadow world, intelligence officers and operatives, are worried, very worried, because they realize that Stuchiner may have been the shetou's Aldrich Ames. Chang Ting-ting, "U.S. Consulate Official Involved in Abuse of Power Case Is Suspected of Being Connected With 1995 Bribe-Extortion Scandal," *Hong Kong Ping Kuo Jih Pao* (in Chinese), April 14, 1997, 6.

42. "Critical mass" means the point at which seed migrant numbers are large enough to produce capital and generate source demand sufficient to create and sustain a market for organized smuggling services.

43. The increasing ratio of Wenzhounese to Fujianese migrants is what is significant. The annual number of Wenzhounese migrants arriving in the United States has increased far more slowly than the increasing ratios indicate, since the number of Fujianese arrivals in the same period has declined steadily.

44. The shetou have avoided the extension of credit because it increases their exposure to law enforcement and requires a permanent U.S. organization to supervise the collection of periodic payments. Most, if not all, payments for smuggling debts are now made in China or Hong Kong to minimize the U.S. enforcement risk. That risk is most acute when the migrant-debtor defaults or is unable to maintain a satisfactory payment schedule. When this occurs and non-violent collection methods fail, the progressive violence that ensues frequently leads to law enforcement involvement. As a debtor, the migrant has a relationship with the shetou that is potentially exploitive. In the extreme, it can amount to bondage or peonage where the debtor is physically restrained and required to work at a job selected by the shetou for wages that artificially prolong payment of the debt. This extreme form of migrant exploitation is characteristic of Thai migrant recruiters for the sex and garment industries, but has not been documented by the Chinese outside of China.

6

Immigrant Smuggling through Central America and the Caribbean

Anthony M. DeStefano

Illegal immigration into the United States, particularly from the Far East, has utilized a number of smuggling routes through Central America and the Caribbean. These regions, because of their proximity to the United States and the lack of meaningful law enforcement activity, have developed into significant points of transit for immigrants whose ultimate destinations are some of America's major metropolitan areas.

Many nationalities have used the area of Central America and the Caribbean as a transit point, including Cubans, Haitians, Ecuadorians, Colombians, Dominicans, Indians, Pakistanis, Chinese, and Eastern Europeans. This paper will focus on migration from the Far East, particularly that involving the Chinese. The paper will discuss the importance of the Central American nations (Honduras, Panama, Guatemala, Belize, El Salvador, Costa Rica, and Nicaragua), as well as islands in the Caribbean (Cuba, the Dominican Republic, the U.S. Virgin Islands, and the Lesser Antilles) to the human cargo situation, with a view toward forecasting trends and possible policy developments.

Central America: America's Immigration Underbelly

It was June 1994. The Sikh travelers from India boarded an old fishing boat in the Gulf of Fonseca, a body of water that serves as Honduras's outlet to the Pacific Ocean and shares its water with El Salvador and Nicaragua. There were 14 immigrants who, according to law enforcement officials, had paid as much as $8,000 per person to make the trip from Nicaragua to Honduras for later transit and illegal entry into the United States.

The Gulf of Fonseca has a reputation as one of the best natural harbors in the world. But on the day the Indian immigrants were traveling something went wrong. A patrol boat piloted by El Salvadoran immigration officials began to pursue the poorly maintained vessel. The captain, reportedly in contract with smugglers on shore, ordered the immigrants to jump into the water. Eight of them drowned. Their bodies were fished from the water by the smugglers and buried in a common grave.[1]

Death along the worldwide human cargo pipeline is nothing new. Untold numbers of immigrants have perished in their quest for new lives in the West, through either disease, murder, or misadventure. Indeed, traffickers seem to view their human chattel as an expendable commodity that will sustain some losses. In the normal course of the smuggling trade, the eight dead Indian nationals would hardly have made a ripple or caused any grief other than to their families. But those losses in the Gulf of Fonseca would later become an element of an unusual undercover operation, one that law enforcement officials said revealed the emerging significance of the region to the workings of immigrant smuggling cartels and combinations that service the global trafficking industry.

For Gloria Canales, a Costa Rican citizen, the importance of Central America as a human smuggling corridor was all too clear. In 1995, authorities in Central America would arrest the 45-year-old woman and contend that she was a focal point of smuggling operations through Central America into the United States. Officials alleged that an estimated 10,000 immigrants, many of them "exotics" from India, Pakistan, and China, were moved by Canales and her confederates through the smuggling routes northward to the United States. According to investigators, she was able to rely on a vast network of travel agents, guides, and other workers to move immigrants from Central America through Mexico and ultimately to major U.S. cities. Canales is also believed to have been involved in the corruption of a number of government officials in the countries that were important for people trafficking.[2]

If the worse allegations about Canales are true, her case illuminates how Central America and the Caribbean Sea have become the soft underbelly of the United States in the battle over the nation's borders and illegal immigration. Although Mexico remains a significant source of illegal immigration, it is Central America and the surrounding waters of the Caribbean that have become major transit points and source countries for the flow of migrants from around the world into the United States.

"Central America is a major conduit and source of illegal migrants entering the United States", acknowledged an interagency U.S. government working group on alien smuggling in late 1995. "In addition to being the source of 200,000 to 300,000 illegal aliens who attempt to enter the United States, it has emerged as a transit route for some 100,000 aliens from outside the region (primarily Chinese, South Americans, and South Asians.)"[3] The report also alleged that "several smuggling rings and hundreds of independent smugglers operate in Central America, including travel agents, guides, and support personnel."[4]

The Caribbean also is both the source of substantial illegal immigration and an increasingly important transit route for illegal migrants, with estimates showing that possibly hundreds of thousands of illegal migrants are utilizing that area, the working group reported.[5]

For most politicians and government officials who have been involved in immigration affairs, the U.S. border with Mexico has always loomed as the most important symbol of the nation's problem with illegal migration. Tens of millions of dollars and thousands of Border Patrol agents have been thrown at the southwestern border in various initiatives to stem the flow of illegal immigrants. But in a very real sense it is Central America and the waters of the Caribbean, not Mexico, that have become the southern border of the United States. Notwithstanding the highly publicized and politicized fence-building along the Mexican border with the United States, these areas deserve more attention than they have received from Washington in anti-smuggling initiatives.

Geography per se shows why Central America and the islands of the Caribbean have become of such strategic importance to the United States in the fight against illegal immigration. The isthmus of Central America covers a length of about 1,000 miles and connects South America, the homeland of a number of nationalities seeking entry to the United States, and Mexico, with its extensive border along the lower 48 United States. Mexico is the country of origin for hundreds of thousands of illegal immigrants who try to enter the United States each year. The latest figures from the U.S. Immigration and Naturalization Service (INS) show that 1.2 million people from Mexico were apprehended in 1995 attempting to cross the border, although a portion of that figure—perhaps as much as 50 percent, according to a recent fingerprint-matching study—represents repeated crossing attempts by the same individuals.[6] But significant numbers of immigrants, numbering more than 10,000 who were apprehended at the southwestern U.S. border with Mexico, come from Central American countries.[7]

Although it is geographically smaller than Mexico, Central America poses a number of problems for immigration policymakers in the United States bent on controlling the flow of illegal aliens over the southern land route. The borders of the region's countries are intricate and cross varied terrain. While smugglers may have sophisticated all-terrain vehicles, border police in such places as Honduras are basically assigned to fixed crossing points. When Honduran immigration officials have to give chase, they are often outfoxed by their more mobile adversaries, who may also have heavier and more sophisticated firepower.

The Central American isthmus is also, by definition, surrounded by water on two sides. On the western side is the Pacific Ocean, often an avenue for smuggling ships crossing from China's Fujian Province or Taiwan. On the east is the Caribbean Sea, whose islands are serving as major landing points for immigrants attempting to enter the United States from Europe or the Far East. Coastlines of Central American nations are dotted with small, obscure landing zones. The close proximity of the countries also permits easy passage between them by boat; a small boat can handle the journey from Belize to Honduras. Coastal patrols are rare or nonexistent. In short, the geography of Central America and the Caribbean, as well as the relative lack of sophistication of law enforcement, make it a good place through which to smuggle people overland or by sea.

But it is not geography alone that accounts for the popularity of Central America and the Caribbean as major transit points for illegal immigration. Politically, the area has been unstable for years. El Salvador and Guatemala have experienced civil wars and coups that have made it difficult for governments to work effectively and survive, let alone attend to such matters as immigration. There is also a long-standing, pervasive problem of government corruption. Reports have circulated for years—some have emerged this year—of immigration officials engaging in corruption to assist smuggling enterprises. In 1995, Belize witnessed the removal of a number of immigration officials after it was alleged that they had taken payoffs to help immigration traffickers.[8] Government officials in Honduras have also charged that some government employees there assisted the Canales enterprise.[9] As one U.S. official said, Central America in particular has been wide open to the people smugglers because of the culture of bribery that has developed in the area.

Allegations of corruption are not limited to Central American immigration officials. In July 1996, the INS was shaken by news that a 19-year veteran of the agency, Gerald Stuchiner, was arrested on charges that he was involved with the smuggling of Chinese aliens through Central America. Stuchiner, long considered one of the key INS investigators into Chinese organized crime, was allegedly in possession of five forged Honduran passports. News reports, citing unidentified U.S. officials, said that Stuchiner, who was instrumental in orchestrating the arrest of Canales, was apparently in league with corrupt Honduran officials in a ring separate from hers.[10]

A number of socioeconomic factors help to explain why Central America in particular has developed into a haven for migrant smuggling. The Central Americans are greatly attracted to the notion of a better life elsewhere, as prevailing wages in their homelands are so low. Not only are residents of Central American countries well aware of how much better life is to the north, but they are also aware that there is a constant demand in the United States for their relatively cheap labor. Washington, as one commentator recently pointed out, is allowing the labor market to exist as a magnet for aliens through lack of significant workplace enforcement of the immigration laws.[11] The kinds of economic conditions that exist in Central America, coupled with the migratory pull of life in the United States, make illegal migration an acceptable aspiration and response.

There is also the belief that some governments, such as those of Nicaragua and El Salvador, view emigration (legal or illegal) by their citizens as a source of valuable foreign capital through remittances sent back to the homeland.[12] Why then, it is argued, should Central America seriously fight illegal immigration if it is a source of such capital? One Honduran official said that the smugglers are often viewed as heroes in her country. Given the benefits some immigrant cultures see arising from illegal migration, it is not hard to see why smugglers have such a steady clientele and are so successful in the cultural milieu within which they operate.

The Initial Phase of Trafficking

Immigrant smuggling through the Caribbean and Central America into the United States developed in a significant way at least as far back as the 1980s. According to Zheng Xin Wei, a Chinese immigrant from Fujian Province, smugglers in China helped him transit from the Far East to Guatemala in 1989. With the help of forged passports and visas, Zheng, who revealed details of his life through his attorney, said he was able to land without a problem in Guatemala where a ring of "Spanish" smugglers took him under its wing and, along with a group of other Chinese, drove a truck to Mexico. It was in Mexico, Zheng recalled, that he traveled over mountains for about 10 days with his compatriots to wait for the right moment to walk across the border to the United States. Once on American soil, Zheng traveled to Flushing, Queens, where he later started his own career as an immigrant smuggler.[13]

Zheng's story is important if only to serve as a reference point in time. If his story is true, the smuggling route taken by Zheng was well traveled before the 1990s, the period when U.S. officials finally became acutely aware that immigrant smuggling was a major problem. The smuggling organizations that the Chinese immigrant said helped him must have been in place and operational well before he began his trip in 1989. It took a series of smuggling ship incidents, most notably the running aground of the *Golden Venture* off Jacob Riis Park in New York City in June 1993, to awaken Washington and the American news media to the business of illegal immigration from the Far East in a dramatic and deadly fashion.

But although the major smuggling ship cases created a sensation for a time, immigrant smuggling through Central America and the Caribbean had already been big business for many years. One U.S. official said that Central America has served as a transit point for illegal migration since the mid-1970s. The story of Zheng aside, news media reports show that in 1992, small groups of immigrants from China were being discovered transiting through the areas, usually in small boatloads that were crossing the Caribbean from South America. In fact, it was in South America where sizable populations of overseas Chinese took up residence, if only for a short time. Reports from U.S. law enforcement officials asserted that Asian agribusinesses developed in the area and sometimes used Chinese nationals as workers.[14]

In keeping with the overall trend of Chinese immigrants aspiring to travel to the United States, many South American nations soon began serving as jumping-off points for further travel to the north. Though reliable information about smuggling in the early 1990s is not extensive, one Bolivian official has stated that her country served as a major stepping stone for smugglers prior to 1993. In an interview with *New York Newsday* in 1994, Victoria Shepard, head of immigration services in Bolivia, said that Asian immigrants used her country as a transit point because of rampant immigration corruption there before she took over in 1993. One INS official said Bolivia had in fact been a smuggling haven for years, with the same also having been reported about Peru.[15]

The *Golden Venture* Incident and Its Aftermath

Over the years, Chinese living in South America could attempt to get to the United States in a number of ways. Air travel was the fastest but the most vulnerable to INS interception. Overland travel, while longer and more arduous, would take migrants into Central America, which developed sizable transiting populations of Chinese. Short boat trips were also possible to Central American coastal waters.

On June 6, 1993, the *Golden Venture* ran aground near New York City with some 285 illegal Chinese immigrants on board. The vessel was one of a number of smuggling ships that had attempted the voyage from the Far East to the United States that year. Some vessels appear to have gone undetected and dumped their human cargo on U.S. shores. But others, like the *Golden Venture*, were either intercepted or ran into trouble within U.S. territorial waters, leading to the apprehension of the crew and passengers.[16]

Later research would indicate that boat smuggling from the Far East represented only a small portion of illegal immigration from China.[17] Such trips were arduous and filled with hardships such as sickness, bad weather, and meager food supplies. Sexual attacks on passengers by the smugglers were not uncommon. But although the boat traffic may not have been a major means of smuggling aliens into the United States, the *Golden Venture* incident and others like it jolted the American public and Washington. The scenes of shivering, blanket-swaddled immigrants on beaches in Queens, New York, served as a dramatic metaphor for the problem of illegal immigration.

The U.S. government's response to the numerous smuggling incidents in 1993 was to announce a policy of interdiction and diversion of smuggling ships at sea; ships would be intercepted by the U.S. Coast Guard and diverted to the shores of Mexico and Central America.[18] Once the immigrant ships were diverted, the people on board were sent back to China. In one well-known episode, 119 Chinese passengers aboard the *Jin Yinn*, a Taiwanese fishing vessel, were taken into custody in Guatemala in May 1994. From there, the International Organization for Migration (IOM), an international group, arranged for the repatriation of all the immigrants to China. The government of Taiwan agreed to cover the cost. The crew of the *Jin Yinn* were turned over to Taiwanese officials in Guatemala after assurances were given to the U.S. Department of State that criminal charges would be filed. (It was later discovered, however, that Taiwan would not prosecute the crew, a situation that led to anger from Washington when it was publicized.[19])

In addition to the vessel interdictions, federal law enforcement officials announced a series of investigations and indictments aimed at breaking up Chinese smuggling rings. One such probe was the Federal Bureau of Investigation case in New York that led to the indictment of Ah Kay, Chinatown's Fuk Ching gang leader, and his associates on alien smuggling and racketeering charges. In Boston, federal officials brought charges against a group of Chinese and Vietnamese for bringing in a boatload of Chinese to the port of Bedford and later transporting the passengers to a warehouse in Brooklyn. Federal prosecutors in San Francisco also brought charges against those believed to be responsible for smuggling ships. There were additional INS actions, including overseas programs in which federal officials schooled foreign airline personnel in Europe and the Far East on how to spot fraudulent passports and travel documents. Clearly, the heat had been turned up by law enforcement in the wake of the *Golden Venture* incident.

But, while the arrests and indictments earned the federal government much-needed publicity and broke up some smuggling gangs, such increased pressure, coupled with the policy of diversion of smuggling ships at sea, made other venues more hospitable to the smugglers. Law enforcement sources and news accounts indicated that smuggling vessels, instead of approaching the U.S. shores, angled farther south to such places as Ensenada on the west coast of Mexico, Guatemala, and Honduras, where it was safer to unload immigrants. The Caribbean also became a venue where smugglers played hide-and-seek with the U.S. Coast Guard.

Air traffic routes into the Caribbean and Central America also became key migrant shipping lanes. Asian travelers who were willing to put up with circuitous routes—and many were—could be sent by smugglers to the stops that were the most advantageous. One INS official described how Chinese migrants, after reaching Hong Kong from Bangkok, could fly to Moscow and then to Cuba. After landing in Havana, the Chinese could then fly directly to Nicaragua, said the official. This route was also being taken by Indo-Pakistani travelers. They would leave Bombay and fly to Europe, usually Amsterdam, and then land in Surinam, where no visa was required of them, said the INS official. From Surinam, the travelers could go to Colombia and then either fly to Nicaragua or take a boat to small islands off the Nicaraguan coast.[20]

Caribbean island routes also became useful to smugglers. One method had Chinese immigrants traveling to the Dominican Republic where traffickers would load travelers into 40-foot boats known as *yolas* and sail across the Mona Passage to Puerto Rico. Once the boats reached Puerto Rico, the migrants were essentially "home free" inside the United States, as the commonwealth, for immigration purposes, allows relatively easy flights to the U.S. mainland, without rigorous INS checks. But the Mona Passage route was sometimes perilous and shark-infested. Moreover, by late 1994, the Coast Guard had gotten wise to the route and was making numerous interceptions.[21]

If pressure developed on one route, the smugglers and the immigrants could find alternatives. By 1995, other water-borne routes that developed to handle the flow involved the U.S. Virgin Islands. In one case, 18 Chinese were caught in October 1995 when they landed on the north shore of St. Thomas.[22] They described how they had sailed to the U.S. territory from Cuba. The experience they described was similar to that of a group of 27 Chinese from Fujian Province who had landed on the eastern shore of St. Thomas in August 1995 and had been caught by the INS.[23] By 1996, law enforcement sources said attention was also being paid to the presence of Chinese immigrants in the island republics of Dominica and St. Vincent and the Grenadines in the West Indies, and they reported smugglers were using those areas as staging posts for boat trips to U.S. territorial waters.[24]

Clearly, although U.S. officials had put pressure on some smuggling organizations through prosecutions and Coast Guard interceptions, the net effect of those moves was to make Central America and the Caribbean more attractive to smugglers. So, by mid-1995, one State Department official admitted that tens of thousands of Chinese immigrants were being warehoused (i.e., waiting for travel) in Central America as part of smuggling operations destined for the United States. The official, Robert Perito, head of the State Department's office of International Criminal Justice, said that reports from American officials traveling in Honduras, Belize, and Costa Rica cited brisk traffic in immigrants, who came to the region by air through Europe. Perito explained that the relaxation of travel restrictions by Beijing had made it easier for Chinese citizens to get passports. Corrupt provincial officials then put exit permits and visas into the passports, allowing the immigrants to travel to Europe and elsewhere.[25]

The Role of Official Corruption

Apart from geography, a substantial reason why Central America and the Caribbean have become smuggling highways is the official corruption that has plagued those areas, including their immigration services and governments. Except for Honduras, no Central American nation has until recently had any laws prohibiting immigrant smuggling. But all nations in that area have relevant statutes and procedures dealing with normal immigration. Smugglers have been able to compromise immigration and other government officials throughout those areas through corruption, in effect making government their partner in the crime of immigrant smuggling.

"Alien smuggling is abetted by high levels of official corruption and the bribing of officials who often provide active assistance to move illegal migrants", said the U.S. working group report in 1995 about Central America.[26] Through bribery and other corrupt acts, government officials subvert laws controlling the movement of people across national borders and contribute to the thriving business of providing false documents (i.e., passports, visas, and travel permits) so necessary for the trafficking of immigrants. The allegations of such corruption have involved governments large and small.

Mexico: According to news media reports in July 1994, the directors of Mexico's National Immigration Institute office in Tijuana were allegedly receiving large payoffs to help smuggling gangs move immigrants into the United States. Investigators said that the payments were coming from trafficking networks involved in the smuggling of Chinese, Indians, Iranians, and Central Americans into the United States.[27] Prior to the surfacing of the payoff allegations, U.S. officials had complained to the Mexican government that there was suspected corruption in Tijuana. The charges against the immigration service were made in a report prepared by the director of the Center for Human Rights in Tijuana, based on a year-long investigation. Soon after the report was publicized, a top immigration official as well as two of his deputies were removed from office by Mexico's interior minister, Jorge Virgilio.[28]

In May 1996, U.S. officials, in announcing the arrest of Gladys Garza Cantu on charges of alien smuggling through Central America, alleged that she had worked closely with several Mexican police officials. One of those officials was charged in the federal indictment with having been paid $9,200 by Garza for moving several Indian immigrants through the border town of Reynosa.[29]

Belize: In the spring of 1995, the government of this small Central American nation was rocked by a scandal involving the improper sale of entry and residence permits to Chinese and Taiwanese nationals. Those types of documents are often used to facilitate the movement of illegal immigrants to the United States. Two officials of the government's immigration department were arrested on conspiracy and forgery charges.[30]

Honduras: Government officials in Honduras have reported that Gloria Canales, the Costa Rican woman suspected of being a key smuggler throughout Central America and parts of South America, may have made payments to a wide variety of government officials to facilitate movements of people over the borders. As of this writing, Canales is only facing charges of helping to smuggle 14 Indian immigrants into Honduras in 1995. But Honduran authorities have said that they have evidence she was prepared to bribe an Honduran immigration official—who was actually an undercover operative—with a $16,000 down payment to get the immigrants into the country and then out to Guatemala.[31]

Angelina Ulloa, the director of immigration for Honduras, has stated that she believes corruption was rampant within her office before she took over in 1994. She also stated that corrupt employees were able to help Canales elude arrest by tipping her off to the undercover investigation that targeted her.[32]

While not an example of official corruption, Honduras was also rocked by a scandal involving the sale of visas to Chinese citizens. The scam exploited a provision in Honduran law that provided for a small number of special visas—about 1,800—to be given to investors who were going to pump money into the local economy. According to Ulloa, some local Chinese businessmen fraudulently produced 18,000 such documents and sold them at about $25,000 each. The fraud netted an estimated tens of millions of dollars, said Ulloa, adding that there have been arrests of the Chinese nationals believed to have been involved.[33]

Panama: A former immigration director of that country, which has a Chinese population of 100,000 and is believed to be a major transit point for Asian immigrants seeking entry into the United States, was fired for allegedly taking bribes from alien smugglers.[34]

Guatemala: As in Panama, a former immigration director was fired for accepting bribes from smugglers.[35]

Case Study: Gloria Canales

Because alien smuggling was until recently not considered a crime anywhere in Central America but Honduras, there do not appear to have been any major criminal investigations of suspected traffickers in that area until 1994. It was then that officials came across the name of Gloria Canales. A 42-year old Costa Rican citizen and mother of five, Canales had been unknown to law enforcement officials until they heard about a mysterious woman in Central America who may have had a connection to Chinese boat smugglers. Further investigation determined that the woman suspected of such ties was Canales.[36]

According to a number of law enforcement sources interviewed, U.S. authorities considered launching an investigation of Canales, to be based in Washington. For reasons that remain unclear, however, the U.S.-based investigation was not approved by the INS, according to Department of Justice officials.[37]

Nevertheless, any U.S. decision that may have been made not to actively pursue Canales did not prevent her from remaining a subject of interest to American and Honduran immigration officials, who launched their own probe in 1995. The inquiry was, for all practical purposes, run out of Tegucigalpa, the Honduran capital, with active involvement by the INS agent attached to the American embassy there. The unprecedented joint U.S.-Honduran investigation provides a case study of how regional cooperation among Central American nations can be useful in developing intelligence and mounting undercover operations leading to arrests related to the human trafficking business. The arrest of Canales in December 1995 was viewed by American immigration policymakers as a significant success, although the later arrest of the INS case agent on corruption

charges cast a pall over the results. The Canales case also underscored a key point for American policymakers: active and continuing U.S. cooperation is also necessary in the area—if only to
serve as a catalyst for local police agencies newly emboldened in
efforts to attack the immigrant trafficking syndicates.[38]

Until 1994, little was known about Canales's personal life. A
heavyset woman, Canales lived with a common-law husband in
a large home behind metal fences and gates on an estate that was
sumptuous by Costa Rican standards. Law enforcement officials
suspected she was part of an alien smuggling enterprise that
stretched back eight years and had moved everything from
Ecuadorians and Colombians to so-called exotics—meaning
immigrants from China, India, and Pakistan. Canales, officials
have said, allegedly used bribery and other acts of corruption to
facilitate her smuggling business. Believed by immigration officials to have moved tens of thousands of illegal immigrants
through Central America, Canales was also viewed as being a
subcontractor or partner to other South Asian smugglers working in South America.[39]

The targeting of Canales and her subsequent arrest followed
a sea change within the hierarchy of the Honduran government's immigration authority. In 1994, Angelina Ulloa took over
command of the unit, which, by her own admission, had been
suspected of corruption and malfeasance for years. Ulloa had
previously been part of the intelligence establishment of Honduras and no doubt had the right political connections and friends
to permit President Oscar Reina to pick her for the immigration
job. While some of her claims about the work of previous admin-
istrations should be looked at with the skepticism due any
appointee's statement about job performance, Ulloa said in a
1996 interview that under her tutelage, the immigration department of Honduras had seen a hundredfold increase in fees
remitted to government coffers.[40]

U.S. law enforcement officials appeared comfortable enough
with Ulloa, whatever her political connections, to help out in the
investigation aimed at implicating Canales in alien smuggling.
Key help in the operation, said Ulloa, came from an INS special
agent in Tegucigalpa. With INS assistance, Ulloa and her staff
devised an undercover operation that attempted to exploit the
brazen attitude believed to have surrounded Canales because of
her years of running businesses in Central America.[41]

Sonny Reina, the man who headed Ulloa's computer operations in Tegucigalpa, was picked as the undercover operative

who would approach Canales with an offer to help in smuggling, said Ulloa. Reina told Canales that Ulloa was an "ignorant woman" who could be fooled and suggested that for a fee he could assist in the movement of some Indian immigrants through Honduras, said Ulloa. The price discussed, she said, was around $100,000 for about 80 immigrants, with a down payment of $17,000 actually paid to Reina. Law enforcement officials said that the plan called for Canales to enter Honduras with the illegal immigrants, at which point she would be arrested.[42]

But the plan was thrown into disarray, said Ulloa, by corrupt employees in her agency who alerted Canales to the undercover plan. The target of the investigation never appeared after 14 Indians landed at Tegucigalpa from Nicaragua for a bus trip to Guatemala and further travel north. Agents later intercepted the bus and the Indian immigrants were then deported by Honduras.[43]

Having never stepped inside Honduras, as the undercover plan had called for, Canales was not arrested. For months, she apparently stayed inside Costa Rica, eluding capture. Honduran authorities decided it would be futile to seek her extradition from her home country. Finally, in late 1995, U.S. officials learned from confidential sources that Canales had traveled to Ecuador. With the assistance of Interpol, the Honduran government served an arrest warrant on the government of Ecuador, where authorities finally arrested Canales. An extradition battle erupted in Ecuador. In the end, however, Canales was ordered out of Ecuador and to Honduras. Because officials wanted to avoid having to send her anywhere near Costa Rica and risk her being freed on some legal technicality, she was flown to Miami and then to Tegucigalpa on December 13, 1995.[44]

Costa Rican officials continued to cooperate with U.S. and Honduran officials in the Canales case by executing a search warrant on her home. According to law enforcement officials, the search provided evidence that Canales had extensive worldwide contacts in an alien smuggling business. Among the documents seized were letters addressed to "Gloria" and "Dario" that appear to discuss smuggling fees, document and passport transfers, and problems with some of Canales's associates in the United States, according to officials. The search also uncovered immigration and visa stamps for El Salvador, Ecuador, and Panama. Telephone records from the Canales house, also part of the search inventory, showed calls to India, Guatemala, Nicaragua,

Mexico, Colombia, and Panama, as well as Arizona and New York.[45]

According to Dr. Wilfred Alvarado, head of the Direccion Investigacion Criminal in Honduras, one of the most revealing finds in the search of the house was evidence that Canales had asked some of her immigrant clients to steal jewelry in Costa Rica as a means of paying for their smuggling fees, which reportedly ranged around $8,000 per person. Costa Rica had been plagued by reports of gangs of "Hindus" who stole jewels and Canales may have been the cause, said Alvarado.[46]

Jorge Burgos, the Honduran lawyer for Canales, said she has not been charged in the deaths from the 1994 incident and is only being held on charges that she was involved in the smuggling of the 14 immigrants to Honduras in 1995. As to those charges, said Burgos in an interview with an American reporter, he will be able to prove that the Indian immigrants had entered Honduras legally and that no crimes were committed in their traveling. Burgos also denied that Canales was involved in the deaths of the immigrants in the Gulf of Fonseca incident.[47]

But Honduran and U.S. officials thought they had a big catch in Canales and touted the arrest as a major achievement in an initiative against smuggling. If Canales was as bad as U.S. and Central American officials said she was—that she brought in 10,000 illegal immigrants to the United States and had a massive operation involving hotels, travel agents, and other operatives to help the smuggling operation—her arrest helped document how extensive smuggling operations have been in Central America. It also showed that nations in that area could work together in a meaningful way to attack alien smuggling, if only on a case-by-case basis.

As of this writing, however, the Canales case may have been tainted by the arrest of the INS agent involved, Gerald Stuchiner. News reports at the time of Stuchiner's arrest in July 1996 in Hong Kong indicated that he was under investigation for possible corruption at the same time that he was involved in the Canales case.[48] Some reports suggest that the probe of the INS agent was centering on his suspected involvement with corrupt Honduran officials in the procuring of fake travel documents for Chinese immigrants who wanted to travel through Central America.[49] While one Honduran consul general in Hong Kong was briefly detained and questioned in the Stuchiner affair in Hong Kong, it is unclear at this writing which level of Honduran officials in Honduras may have been under suspicion along with

Stuchiner. As a recognized expert in alien smuggling, Stuchiner had access to Honduran officials at all levels within that nation's immigration and investigative branches of service. In any case, the allegations against Stuchiner could provide Canales with ammunition to challenge the case against her in Honduras and cast doubts on the credibility of any evidence the U.S. or Honduran officials may present in court. In short, what seemed to be the finest efforts of the INS and Honduran officials to date in the fight against alien smuggling may turn out to be a major embarrassment.

In August 1996, after resigning from the INS, Stuchiner pleaded guilty to having fake passports in his possession and was sentenced to 39 months in prison. In April 1997, however, the charges against him were quashed because it was discovered he had been charged under the wrong part of the law in Hong Kong. He was rearrested in Hong Kong on a different immigration-related charge, and in May 1997 he was sentenced to a shorter, three-month prison sentence, according to news agency reports.

In fairness, it should be noted that the INS has not rested its efforts on the Canales case. The arrest of Gladys Garza Cantu, mentioned earlier, disrupted at least one route moving some hundreds of aliens (compared to the thousands believed to have been moved by Canales) through Central America and Mexico.

The Foreseeable Future

Both the Canales and the Cantu cases, and the allegations surrounding them, underscore how important Central America and the Caribbean have become as alien smuggling routes into the United States. That being the case, the federal government should develop and implement a coherent overseas strategy to address the problem. The reason is simple: despite the highly publicized attention paid by the federal government to disrupting smuggling operations along the southwest U.S. border, the key major traffickers will continue to stay in business because the demand for smuggling remains high. Wide disparities between rich and poor, developed and developing nations, persist, as does the economic motivation for migration. Taking out one key trafficker is not enough; other networks appear ready and willing to take her place. Ironically, any enforcement action also increases the difficulties faced by future investigations.[50]

The Canales case showed that bilateral efforts can work if the legal framework is in place. At the very least, that means that nations in Central America, and elsewhere for that matter, must have laws on the books making alien smuggling a crime. Until recently, Honduras was the only Central American nation to have enacted such a law. As of this writing, Nicaragua and Panama have statutes on the books, and El Salvador is expected to have a law take effect in July 1997.[51] Unless a nation criminalizes alien smuggling, it will continue to be considered a safe haven for smugglers.

Drafting alien smuggling laws is only one piece of the puzzle, however. There must be effective legal and enforcement mechanisms in place within a country to enforce such laws. For much of Central America and the Caribbean, immigration police and prosecutors are outgunned—both figuratively and literally. For instance, in Honduras immigration agents are stationed at nine border crossing points and the main airports, leaving 6,000 kilometers of border area within three countries fair game for smugglers.

"There is no money for border control," said Angelina Ulloa in an interview. By contrast, she said, alien smugglers have more advanced weapons, safe houses, sophisticated radios, four-wheel-drive vehicles, and officials on their payroll. Her colleague, Dr. Alvarado, said that his investigative office has a budget of $10 million but has to use it to fight not only alien smugglers but narcotics traffickers and a $50-million stolen car business that brings in vehicles from the United States. He also said he needs three times the number of agents he currently has working for him, which is about 540. Clearly, the task of fighting alien smugglers is more daunting when officials face such disparities in resources, particularly when the smugglers have access to a market estimated to generate $5 billion in gross revenues and access to Far East criminal organizations of ancient lineage.[52]

Illegal migrant trafficking appears to be a well-developed phenomenon, with numerous syndicates and organized crime groups at many levels taking part in the activity. Nonetheless, there seem to be clear signs that the global community is finally taking some tangible steps to combat the smugglers. This is not to say that immigrant smuggling will disappear overnight—the demand is simply too great and the economics too lucrative for the traffickers to halt their business in the face of more law enforcement activity. But with organizations such as the International Organization for Migration acting as a catalyst, nations are slowly taking more concerted action. The IOM sponsored an international trafficking conference in October 1994 and a number of Western governments, including the U.S. government, have been involved in working group discussions to share intelligence on the trafficking problem. Although not bold initiatives, these early steps are important because they place the subject of trafficking on the table for more significant diplomatic efforts.

Central American governments also appear to recognize that regional cooperation is an important step in dealing with the trafficking issue. In 1995, a regional seminar on migrant trafficking was held and a comparative study was initiated to review Central American legislation related to trafficking. There have also been calls for more discussions and consultations among the regional states.[53]

Have any of these embryonic efforts at controlling smuggling had any effect on the real world of the people traffickers? There is anecdotal evidence to suggest that efforts to step up enforcement, even on a piecemeal basis, have had an impact in Central America. One U.S. agent has said that before the arrest of Canales, the average price for an illegal immigrant to be smuggled through Central America was about $45. But after the Canales arrest and a few other interceptions of Chinese immigrants in small boats near Honduras, the average price has jumped to more than $1,000. Clearly, the smugglers were perceiving an increased risk to their activity and were passing along a higher price to reflect the added difficulty of smuggling through the area. The higher fees may deter some Central Americans from transiting through the area. But they are unlikely to deter the Chinese and the Indo-Pakistani immigrants, who have already paid tens of thousands of dollars to reach the West, from making the trip, said one INS official.

The INS is mindful of the fact that combating international alien smuggling rings requires a concerted, international approach. "This administration will build a web of enforcement across the sea, and across our borders to stop these activities and punish the perpetrators of these crimes," the INS said in a public statement issued in March 1996.[54] But some critics would quarrel with the INS claim that it is able to move fast enough to build that web. Having asked Congress in fiscal year 1995 for 45 new overseas investigative posts, the INS was able in FY 1996 to get authorization for only 15.[55] The process of filling those spots has proved to be time-consuming and may only be accomplished after FY 1997 is well under way. Some INS officials are also concerned about whether those new hires will be saddled with bureaucratic work on such mundane topics as green card and visa applications, in addition to trying to run investigations.

No matter how long it may take the INS to hire new overseas investigators, the smugglers in Central America and Mexico are still at work. The latest available data show a continuing stream of illegal immigrants. In 1995, more than 1.2 million Mexicans were apprehended along the southwest U.S. border. The same INS statistics show that Central America is also serving as a source region, as well as a transit region, for illegal immigration, although the actual number of apprehensions of people from that area is still quite small.[56] Yet, while INS officials are not catching large numbers of migrants from Central America, other statistics indicate that people from that area are actively transiting further north. For instance, Honduran officials reported that in 1995 Mexico deported 26,000 Honduran citizens out of a total of 120,000 deportees.[57]

As underscored by the Canales case, Central America and the Caribbean are crucial transit areas for alien smuggling to the United States and deserve greater attention. If the United States is serious about combating traffickers, it should strengthen the INS presence in those areas and develop significant working relationships with law enforcement officials there. As of this writing, the agency has only one resident agent for all of Central America. Four more agents were scheduled to be assigned to the region by July 1997, however. The INS presence in the Caribbean was also scheduled to be increased in the summer of 1997, officials said. Clearly, to infiltrate and potentially eliminate the well-organized cartels of people smugglers, a substantially greater commitment of financial and human resources will be necessary for the foreseeable future.

The views and opinions expressed in this essay are those of the author and do not necessarily reflect the opinions of *Newsday* or its management.

Notes

1. Interview with Dr. Wilfredo Alvarado, director of Direccion Investigacion Criminal, Republic of Honduras, on May 14, 1996. A confidential

news source with the U.S. Immigration and Naturalization Service also confirmed the details of the drownings.

2. Anthony M. DeStefano, "People Pipeline," *Newsday*, June 2, 1996, pp. A5, A43.

3. *Presidential Initiative to Deter Alien Smuggling: Report of the Interagency Working Group*, Washington, D.C., December 1995, 4.

4. Ibid, 4.

5. Ibid, 5.

6. Doris Meissner, Foreign Press Center Briefing with INS Commissioner Doris Meissner, Washington Foreign Press Center, October 23, 1995.

7. Apprehension figures provided to the author by the U.S. Immigration and Naturalization Service in May 1996.

8. Economist Intelligence Unit (EIU), "Belize: Country Update," EIU ViewsWire, October 3, 1995.

9. DeStefano, "People Pipeline," p. A43.

10. William Branigan, "Immigration Agent Arrested in Smuggling Scheme," *Washington Post*, July 16, 1996 (Domestic wire service version ed.).

11. Wade Graham, "Masters of the Game: How the U.S. Protects the Traffic in Cheap Mexican Labor," *Harper's*, July 1996.

12. Myron Weiner, "Nations Without Borders: The Gift of Folks Gone Abroad," *Foreign Affairs* 75, no. 2 (March/April 1996): 128–134.

13. Anthony M. DeStefano, "From India to Costa Rica, And Then on to New York," *Newsday*, June 3, 1996, p. A7.

14. Information about this early period of Chinese migration is derived from newspaper accounts, notably those appearing in the *Los Angeles Times*, as well as the author's own interviews over the years with law enforcement officials.

15. Anthony M. DeStefano, "Havens No More," *New York Newsday*, November 2, 1994, p. A25.

16. Marlowe Hood, "Riding the Snake," *Los Angeles Times*, June 13, 1993, sec. Magazine, 12.

17. Anthony M. DeStefano, "Study: Emigrés Flee to U.S. for Money," *New York Newsday*, May 11, 1994, p. A26.

18. Josh Friedman and A. DeStefano, "Their Cargo is Human," *New York Newsday*, June 12, 1996, 4.

19. Details from a report of the Central News Agency, Taipei, broadcast June 20, 1994. The author and a colleague also interviewed U.S. officials, some confidentially, about their reaction to Taiwan's lack of prosecution in this case.

20. DeStefano, "People Pipeline," p. A5.

21. Ashley Dunn, "After Crackdown, Smugglers of Chinese Find New Routes," *New York Times*, November 1, 1994, p. A1.

22. *Associated Press*, October 30, 1995, AP Worldstream, ed.: Pages.

23. Lynda Lohr, "St. John Drop Point for Illegal Chinese Immigrants," *Associated Press*, August 12, 1995, AP Worldstream ed.: Pages.

24. Interviews by the author with confidential news sources.

25. Anthony M. DeStefano, "Human Cargo: Ready, Waiting," *New York Newsday*, March 29, 1995, p. A2.

26. *Presidential Initiative*, 4.

27. Gregory Katz, "Mexican Officials Linked to Ring that Smuggled Aliens into U.S.," *Dallas Morning News*, July 23, 1994, p. A1.

28. Ibid.

29. Numerous newspaper reports in May and June 1996, including those in the *New York Times* and *Newsday*.

30. EIU, "Belize."

31. DeStefano, "People Pipeline," p. A5.

32. Ibid, p. A43.

33. Anthony M. DeStefano, "Directing Government Changes," *Newsday*, June 2, 1996, p. A5.

34. William Branigin, "Costa Rican's Arrest Lifts Veil on Growing Smuggling of Illegal Aliens," *International Herald Tribune*, December 27, 1995.

35. Ibid.

36. DeStefano, "People Pipeline," p. A5.

37. Earlier interest in Canales was stated to the author by confidential law enforcement news sources and appeared in *Newsday* on June 2, 1996.

38. DeStefano, "People Pipeline," 3.

39. Background on Canales appeared in *Newsday* on June 2, 1996, based on interviews with Honduran government officials.

40. Angelina Ulloa was interviewed by the author in May 1996 at her office in Tegucigalpa, Honduras. Much of the substance of the interview appeared in *Newsday* on June 2, 1996.

41. Ulloa interview.

42. Ulloa interview and interview with Dr. Wilfredo Alvarado, head of the Direccion Investigacion Criminal, in May 1996.

43. Ulloa interview.

44. Ulloa and Alvarado interviews.

45. Alvarado interview. Copies of some of the materials taken from the Canales home were made available to the author by a confidential news source.

46. Alvarado interview.

47. Jorge Burgos was interviewed by the author, over the telephone and with the help of an interpreter, on May 23, 1996.

48. Branigin, "Immigration Agent Arrested."

49. Ibid.

50. This statement is based on interviews with law enforcement officials in a variety of disciplines about the difficulties of penetrating criminal syndicates.

51. Interview on May 30, 1997, with a spokesperson for the U.S. Department of State.

52. Alvarado interview and DeStefano, "Directing Government Changes," p. A42.

53. "Trafficking in Migrants: Some Global and Regional Perspectives" (paper submitted by the International Organization for Migration to Puebla, Mexico, conference, March 1996, p. 11).

54. Office of Public Affairs, U.S. Immigration and Naturalization Service, "Backgrounder: Cracking Down on Alien Smugglers," March 1996, p. 10.

55. Anthony M. DeStefano, "War on Smugglers: INS Maps Strategy . . ." *Newsday*, June 3, 1996, p. A7.

56. Apprehension data provided to the author by the INS in May 1996.

57. Ulloa interview.

7

Canada's Growing Role as a Human Smuggling Destination and Corridor to the United States

Kenneth Yates

During the past decade, Canada has witnessed an increasing stream of illegal migration from East Asia. A growing body of evidence suggests that organized transnational crime syndicates are facilitating much of this migration and are viewing Canada as both a smuggling destination and a transit country to the United States. For the Canadian law enforcement community, migrant trafficking from East Asia represents one of this decade's most serious security and law enforcement challenges.

Currently, it is difficult to determine how "snakeheads" (a literal translation of the Chinese word *shetou*, which refers to human smugglers) recruit their clients in the source countries. Why this is so is not certain; however, one can strongly infer that there is an orchestrated effort by the smuggling organizations to maintain secrecy about their identities and operations. Almost all aliens currently entering Canada as political asylum refugees are highly evasive when answering any questions put to them by law enforcement officials regarding the smuggling organizations that may have brought them into Canada.

Based on my experience with alien smuggling investigations stemming from East Asia for the past six years, the method most commonly used by smugglers to solicit their clients in China's Fujian Province (where most aliens currently originate) is word of mouth. Words and reputations spread like wildfire throughout Chinese communities wherever they exist, and it is this "gossip network" and *guanxi* (connections or contacts) that the smugglers rely on to generate business.

Once the client and snakehead find each other and all fees are determined and agreed on—fees can range between U.S.$35,000 and $45,000 depending on the final destination (either Canada or the United States)—the snakehead receives a deposit of between U.S.$5,000 and $10,000. The smugglers then require that their client provide names, telephone numbers, and addresses of relatives in both Fujian Province and North

America. This information, once verified, allows the smuggling organizations to obtain down payments from those relatives as payment for one or more segments of the journey. For example, after a migrant travels from Fujian Province to Bangkok, Thailand, for example, the smuggling organization might demand another payment from the migrant's relatives once their arrival in Thailand is verified by telephone. Once that fee is paid, the next segment of the trip would commence. An alternative financial arrangement would be for the organization to simply accept a deposit prior to the journey. Once they successfully deliver the migrant to the final destination, they then attempt to collect payment in full *prior* to releasing the alien.

After migrants pay the initial deposit, the smuggling organization initiates the procedures necessary to facilitate the migrant's exit from China to either Hong Kong or Bangkok. This includes an air flight from Fujian to Guangdong and a forged exit visa for tourism or to visit bogus relatives in Hong Kong or Thailand. Genuine exit visas obtained from corrupt government officials in Fujian or Guangdong are also used in this segment of the smuggling process.

Having exited China, the migrants are taken to Hong Kong and placed in safe houses to await their forged travel documents, such as passports and entry visas to Canada, which are generally counterfeited. In order to avoid having the migrants detected during their journey to North America (a trip that often involves passing through several countries), the smugglers will doctor the passports in such a way that they reflect the migrant's race, gender, and general age group. Because this is a time-consuming process—obtaining suitable documents may take several weeks or longer—the smugglers often will fly their clients to Bangkok, Thailand, where they are placed in hotels and are told to wait for their instructions, airline tickets, travel documents, and dispersal.

High-quality document forgers in both Hong Kong and Thailand are a critical component of the organization. Passports are obtained by several methods, and most migrants travel on genuine passports that have been subjected to photograph substitution. These passports either have been stolen or have been bought from dishonest holders around the world, who sell them for prices ranging from U.S.$2,000 to $5,000 and then report them stolen to authorities. Corrupt government officials in source countries or diplomatic missions overseas are an additional source of passports.

Why North America?

No doubt part of the reason individuals wish to leave China is because of the political oppression exerted by the Chinese government. Nevertheless, even after taking that fact into account, one has to recognize that most of the aliens smuggled to North America have little or no economic future in their homeland. Most earn meager wages and have virtually no prospects for improving their socioeconomic status.

Those migrants who are cooperative upon their arrival in Canada often state that living anywhere else in the world could not be worse than their life at home. We must bear this in mind when considering the motivational factors of the aliens, and what they are prepared to endure upon their arrival, including the possible consequences if their smuggling fees are not paid in full, such as; kidnapping, extortion, torture, forced prostitution, and even murder. Thus, most of the migrants are economic migrants who are utilizing criminal enterprises to deliver them to a much more prosperous country. Although many nations in Western Europe and East Asia have emerged as Chinese human smuggling destinations, the continent of choice remains North America, particularly the United States. Tradition extending back to the gold-rush era of the 1800s plays a great role in this choice to go to the "Golden Mountain."

The presence of ethnic networks also greatly influences the decisions of would-be immigrants. Many smuggled migrants have relatives or fellow villagers already living in such cities as New York and, more recently, Los Angeles. With respect to Canada, and particularly Toronto, those Fujianese who are criminally inclined regard this locale with its large Southeast Asian population, as almost virgin territory. It is well-known that a number of them find the thought of easily-obtained social assistance to supplement their income—whether criminal or legitimate—to be very attractive. Of course, Canada's system of free medical care also serves as an inducement for would-be refugee claimants to ponder.

Another serious consideration that must be taken into account is the fact that once the aliens have arrived on North American soil, little action, if any, will be taken by government to repatriate them. This represents absolutely no deterrence to anyone considering a future here, either as a refugee claimant or illegal alien. From the alien's perspective, therefore, smuggling is a type of financial venture that is virtually guaranteed to succeed.

Dispersal from Thailand and Travel Routes to North America

After the smuggling organizations deliver the migrants to Bangkok from Hong Kong or China, they place them in inexpensive, lower-class hotels to await their documents and travel itinerary. The migrants are also given instructions on what to expect upon arrival at their destination. This "coaching" takes place so that the migrant will know exactly what to say to immigration authorities to gain political asylum.

Bangkok's role as a preferred human smuggling dispersal point (compared with Hong Kong or other Asian cities) reflects the fact that Thai authorities do not consider alien smuggling a high priority. In recent years, there has been evidence of collusion by some Thai officials on duty at the airport facility who have allegedly allowed migrants to arrive and stay in Bangkok. Such conditions provide an excellent environment for the smuggling organizations to flourish and operate in.

Recent intelligence indicates that Cambodia is also being used as a dispersal point for aliens. Although the reasons behind this trend are not clear, they are probably quite the same as Thailand. Routing of migrants from the Far East varies depending on the various travel documents available for use at the time. Visas play a major role in determining whether aliens can be routed through particular nations. Because air carriers are now subjected to hefty fines and/or seizure of airliners when they allow travelers with bogus documents to board their aircraft for Canada, airline employees are taking much more care when they inspect passengers and their travel documents during the preboarding stage. (Financial penalties are seldom paid, however, and one West European airline company is alleged to owe hundreds of thousands of dollars in unpaid fines.)

To facilitate smuggling along multiple routes, the trafficking organizations prefer to use Singaporean, Malaysian, and British overseas passports because Canada does not require entry visas for those passports. We have also found that the organizations frequently use passports from China, Japan, and South Korea.

Europe currently appears to be one of the routes most favored by the smuggling organizations, although they continue to use any and every route available that will get them into Canada. Recent intelligence reports indicate that the organizations are not relying on escorts as much as they did in the past; however, there appears to be a network of individuals in various European nations who are working for the organizations and are simply a telephone call away and ready to render assistance when necessary. This may involve negotiating the release of aliens if they are detained or obtaining fresh counterfeit documents for the next portion of the trip.

A similar pattern is seen in South and Central America, where a network is in place to provide a second set of documents to enter North America after completion of the first leg of the journey from the Far East to, for example, Argentina.

Airline travel is the most rapid, efficient method of smuggling aliens. Rented or owned ocean-going vessels such as the infamous *Golden Venture*, although more profitable because of the number of people who can be moved at one time, are simply no longer a safe, viable proposition if the smugglers want to evade detection. These smuggling vessels have attracted vast attention from both U.S. government agencies and the media and can be easily tracked by any number of resources, including satellites, naval patrols, coast guard vessels, and aircraft, which can successfully interdict the smugglers in international waters. One also has to consider the inhumane treatment of the aliens aboard ship, which has been reported in great detail by the media and simply further strengthens public ridicule toward the smugglers.

In contrast, once smugglers load their clients into a commercial aircraft bound for North America—migrants typically travel alone or in pairs to avoid attention and therefore detection—they have essentially accomplished their goals. Migrants cannot be interdicted mid-flight, and thus the smuggling organization's mission is already a success. There is a general consensus among many Canadian law enforcement officials that the migrant trafficking organizations will continue to rely on commercial aircraft in combination with high-quality forged documents. Thus, if governments are to attain any success in stemming the flow of illegal aliens, they must interdict the aliens prior to their boarding aircraft that are destined for North America.

Arrival of Aliens in Canada

As signatories to the 1951 Geneva Convention on the status of refugees, both the United States and Canada, if abiding by the spirit of that treaty, are *bound* to accept anyone claiming political asylum unless there are very strong grounds for refusal. For many law enforcement officials, however, the treaty has created a veritable monster for the 1990s. In its desire to exhibit true compassion, the Canadian federal government abides by the treaty faithfully, but in the process Canada unfortunately has emerged as a global haven for bogus and nondeserving political asylum claimants.

Canada, I am told, has a reputation of welcoming almost everyone arriving at its ports of entry, even though many government officials know that the majority of refugee claims are bogus. Front-line immigration officers are obligated to allow would-be refugees free and unhindered entry into Canada, and this fact is well known throughout the world. This "open door policy" must change, however, if we are going to deter the growing number of nondeserving individuals claiming political asylum at our doorstep.

Entering Canada is a relatively simple procedure for several reasons, one being the large number of overseas flights arriving daily at the nation's airports. In Toronto, for example, an average of 33 overseas international flights arrive daily. In 1994, more than 19,477 overseas flights arrived at Canada's four main international airports: Vancouver, Toronto, Montreal, and Halifax.[1]

Before leaving Bangkok, the alien has been instructed by the smuggling organization to do one of four things:

1. Prior to landing in Canada, destroy his or her travel documents and flush them down the lavatory into the aircraft holding tanks and then, upon arriving at customs/immigration, claim political asylum.

2. During the flight to Canada, hand off the counterfeit travel documents used on the journey to the escort (if one is being used) and claim political asylum upon arrival. Bilingual escorts are used by some organizations to facilitate their clients' unhindered entry into Canada. Usually, the escort will accompany four to six aliens on flights from Bangkok via Europe to Canada and will repossess all counterfeit passports, which will then be recycled by the organization.

3. Proceed through customs/immigration inspection at the airport terminal as a bona fide visitor. This method is usually reserved for aliens who use genuine and unaltered passports actually issued to them and obtained through corrupt means from secondary countries. The chances for being detected and refused entry with this

method are slim to none; however, if the migrant is caught, he or she will then claim political asylum (remember, they cannot be refused entry as a refugee claimant).

4. Last, simply claim political asylum, with or without counterfeit documents.

After international flights arrive in Canada, passengers disembark and walk to the customs inspection areas. Most aliens arriving from Fujian Province arrive at the Vancouver, Toronto, and Montreal airports.

Current evidence indicates that a number of refugee claimants are delaying their entry into the customs inspection areas by hiding in bathroom facilities for several hours so investigators cannot ascertain which flight they arrived on. This is obviously an orchestrated ploy by the smuggling organizations to have the migrant evade detection.

Once the aliens have been discovered in bathroom facilities, or after they enter the customs inspection area, they will immediately claim political asylum. The aliens are then referred to the immigration authority where the refugee process commences. (It is important to remember that once any person has stepped onto Canadian soil, that individual enjoys *all* the legal rights a Canadian citizen has under the constitution—Charter of Rights and Freedoms). Immigration officials will then question the alien as to why he or she is claiming political asylum. They will also inquire into whether the alien was assisted by an organization to arrive in Canada, what routes/airlines they used to arrive in Canada, and whether they have relatives or friends in the country. (Note: there is no offense for a person claiming refugee status to have utilized counterfeit travel documents or to have been assisted by an organization to reach their destination.)

The interview process takes several hours, and unless there is some substantial reason for detaining aliens in custody, they are set free on their own recognizance promising they will appear for an immigration hearing. Photographs and fingerprints of the claimant are obtained prior to the release. (Note: if a late night flight arrives and refugees claim political asylum when there is no interpreter available, they are simply given a form, printed in Chinese characters, to fill in. This form, or questionnaire, is in lieu of an interview and will result in the release that night of the refugee claimant unless there are extraordinary circumstances as to why they should not be released.)

This procedure is normal across the country. Because of funding limitations, there are simply not enough detention facilities to hold someone for Immigration Act violations, and with governments attempting to balance budgets, this scenario is unlikely to change.

The majority of refugee claimants entering Canada do not appear for their immigration hearings. This indicates that they have probably been smuggled into the United States. During the interview process, most refugee claimants, having been coached by the smuggling organization, will claim that they have been persecuted by the Chinese government because of that nation's birth control laws or some other set of circumstances that they consider to be human rights violations. To reinforce this currently favorite reason of birth control, a male alien will often state that his wife, who is still in China, was forced by the state to have an abortion because she became pregnant again after her first child.

Prior to the birth control reason, Tiananmen Square (the 1989 government crackdown) was the all-time favorite and resulted in thousands of successful refugee claims in Canada alone. No doubt, there will be scores of other reasons dreamed up by the smuggling organizations that will be successfully used by future refugee claimants. If there are sufficient grounds to hold a person in custody after claiming political asylum, they are usually released several months later after someone—usually a smuggling organization worker or someone chosen by them—posts a cash bond in the range of Can$8,000 to ensure that the refugee appears at an immigration hearing about one month after release.

Post Release of Aliens

Once the migrants have successfully entered Canada, the North American members of the smuggling organizations commence their activities. Upon release by immigration officers, the alien enters the airport concourse and finds a pay phone and then contacts the local snakehead with a telephone number that has been supplied by the smuggling organization in Bangkok. Another scenario is for the snakehead to be notified by other organization members overseas of the pending arrival of the alien or aliens at the airport on a specific flight. The snakehead will then wait in the airport terminal for the alien to be released by Immigration. This method allows the organization to ensure that the alien will not evade payment of the transportation fees.

Once the snakehead or one of his "employees"—typically just a lower-level runner who works for the organization—meets the alien, they take them to safe houses where they are confined until all final smuggling fees are paid. If the alien has already paid his fees, he may only stay in the safe house for a number of hours or days until the second or last segment of the smuggling operation can be commenced.

During this segment of the smuggling journey, if the aliens have not paid their fees, the smugglers begin calling relatives or friends of the migrants who are living in either Canada, the United States, or China. They demand that the relatives immediately pay the smuggling fees, or else the alien will be harmed. This process may take several days or perhaps even weeks or months, depending on whether the relatives can pay the money demanded. In the meantime, the aliens are virtual prisoners in the safe houses, and many of them are locked in rooms and then beaten. In some cases, the smugglers or their agents will put a gun to the alien's head while he talks to his relatives back home desperately trying to raise the funds that will secure his release.

Those aliens who have been fortunate enough to have had their fees paid then face the last cross-border journey into the United States. This journey can be accomplished by a number of methods:

1. Land crossing via car with counterfeit Canadian or U.S. identification. This vehicle is typically driven by a legitimate Canadian or U.S. resident.

2. Land crossing hidden in the trunk of a car driven by a legitimate Canadian or US. resident. Non-Asians are preferred by the organizations during this segment in order to minimize suspicions of illegal activity by U.S. customs and immigration inspectors.

3. Land crossing hidden in the rear of a legitimate commercial vehicle such as a tractor trailer or van containing products for delivery into the United States. This method involves the smuggling of multiple aliens at one time. Non-Asian truck drivers are also frequently used with this method.

4. Land crossing from Canada into the United States via an unmanned portion of the border. This method is becoming less favored, however, because of the number

of aliens intercepted through the use of technical equipment.

5. High-speed boats and/or snowmobiles across the St. Lawrence River from Canada into New York State. This involves the organization using Native Indians to smuggle aliens from a Canadian reservation to an American reservation. This method is probably the most successful and results in very few aliens being intercepted.

6. Inflatable rafts. This undoubtedly is the most dangerous method and has tragically resulted in a number of drowning deaths. Asians, usually Vietnamese "freelancers," are commonly used to smuggle the aliens across the Niagara River near Buffalo, New York, in cheap "play" rafts purchased at local stores. Aliens paddle their way in these small inflatable rafts across a treacherous stretch of water that is several hundreds of yards wide.

Once the aliens arrive on American soil, the smugglers or their agents drive them to a pre-arranged meeting place such as a restaurant in the Buffalo area. There they are met by drivers who invariably take them to New York City where they are either dropped off or taken to a safe house where they are to be confined until the final smuggling payment is received by the organization. This confinement may also last for months, and nonpayment has resulted in severe beatings and murder at this stage of the journey.

The Challenges Facing Law Enforcement

Despite the fact that human smuggling organizations operate an organized, geographically dispersed illegal immigrant enterprise, recent successes in Canada suggest that the phenomenon can be effectively combated. In 1990, I became involved in an Asian alien smuggling investigation that dealt a major blow to the alien smuggling industry operating in Canada. The probe, which lasted six months, was conducted jointly by Toronto's Combined Forces Asian Investigative Unit-CFAIU (my unit), the Royal Canadian Mounted Police, Canadian immigration, the U.S. Immigration and Naturalization Service, the Royal Hong Kong Police, and Hong Kong immigration.

Eventually the investigation, code-named Overflight, led to the arrest of the head of a human smuggling organization and most of his "employees" both in Toronto and halfway around the world in Hong Kong. This organization had smuggled more than 1,200 illegal Chinese immigrants into Canada within the past two years. All had claimed political asylum upon their arrival, and about 450 of the original group were ultimately smuggled into the United States.

A distinguishing characteristic of this smuggling operation was the dramatic increase in crimes committed by the smuggled migrants themselves. Within two years after their arrival in Canada, more than 450 of the original 750 or so refugees who decided to stay in Canada had registered at least one felony conviction. Toronto and Vancouver, in particular, experienced an epidemic of crime perpetrated by these new Asian criminals who were identified as the infamous *"Dai Huen Jai"* or Big Circle Boys.

The smuggling organization had earned more than Can$12 million for bringing these so-called refugees into Canada and the United States, some of whom were discovered to be residents of Hong Kong and not the Chinese province of Guangdong—formerly known as Canton. So what are the problems facing law enforcement? They are numerous, but not insurmountable. Let us first closely scrutinize what we are dealing with.

As with most criminal enterprises, human smugglers are dealing with a commodity—human beings. Why? Because smuggling humans across international borders delivers huge profits with virtually no chance of getting caught. Even if the smugglers are caught, the penalties are minimal in most countries and serve as no deterrent whatsoever.

Human smuggling organizations are transnational, whereas our police resources are limited by our own national borders. Although the existence of Interpol can aid in an international investigation, the institution is simply not capable of, or geared to, the long-term investigations that are necessary to effectively curtail the smuggling problem. Under these circumstances, it is clear who has the advantage. Any effective battle against transnational human smuggling will require that law enforcement agencies from multiple countries develop the capability to conduct investigations cooperatively and with integrity.

Finally, a major concern for our department, and indeed for many police agencies throughout North America, is limited funding. In Canada, of all the various organized crime groups, ethnic Asian groups impose the largest burden on police resources. By necessity, virtually all major Canadian cities have Asian Investigative Units. Many of these are task forces comprising municipal, provincial (state), and federal agencies that can both expedite investigations through various bureaucratic obstacles and share the heavy burden of operation costs.

Investigations lasting months on a national or multinational level can cost millions of dollars. Where does the funding come from? Simply put, the resources and funding must be made available by government on all levels. Any money spent on proactive investigations that neutralize alien smuggling organizations will save the taxpaying public millions of dollars in the future. Fortunately in Canada, Command Officers at virtually all levels of law enforcement recognize and understand the inherent consequences of alien smuggling and the impact it has on crime levels on both the domestic and international front. This understanding helps generate support for greater funding of law enforcement activities that can effectively combat alien smuggling.

Policy Recommendations

Alien smuggling is perceived by many as a federal problem— after all, it is the federal government that has jurisdiction over immigration matters (as is true in the United States). Yet, in practice, alien smuggling is actually a post-entry criminal activity and for this reason it is everyone's problem: federal agencies alone simply cannot suppress the smuggling activities. It is therefore incumbent on law enforcement at all levels of government to participate in solving the problem, bearing in mind that the federal government by fiscal necessity must be responsible for the majority of the funding.

To enhance future law enforcement efforts, it might be useful for both Canada and the United States to establish formal multi-agency anti-smuggling task forces in those urban areas that are identified as destination points, such as New York City or Toronto. The sole purpose of such task forces would be to identify and subsequently disrupt or neutralize smugglers within a particular jurisdiction. With that objective in mind, all agencies involved would benefit from the reduced numbers of aliens vis-à-vis the reduced amount of crime involved in that arena and also the reduced amount of crime perpetrated on the general public by the additional aliens who would have been brought in by the smugglers.

To go one step further, given that smugglers operate on a multinational basis, could considerations be given to the establishment of formal multinational anti-smuggling task forces? (I emphasize *formal* in both initiatives to ensure accountability and greater effectiveness). Recent evidence suggests that a growing number of nations, particularly in Eastern and Western Europe, are being selected by human smuggling organizations as final destinations or transit points. Given this reality, would it not be prudent for those nations, in addition to North America, to combine their intelligence gathering and resources as part of a unified effort to neutralize the problem? The smuggling organizations recognize no borders; we in law enforcement therefore should also dismantle borders and work in the "global village" the world has become.

In addition to the establishment of task forces, consideration should also be given to the convening of a conference specifically to deal with Asian migrant trafficking. The annual International Asian Organized Crime Conference (IAOCC) is an excellent example of a meeting in which agencies and law enforcement personnel share ideas, experiences, and initiatives for the benefit of all participants. An Asian Smuggling Conference could benefit anti-smuggling efforts in the same way, bearing in mind many of the crime problems faced by participants of the IAOCC are caused by aliens smuggled into our respective nations.

Simply put, if future Asian alien smuggling is not reduced or eliminated, the effects on society will be the equivalent of "pouring gasoline on a well-established fire" and will—if not dealt with in a swift, sure manner—become too entrenched to eradicate.

Note

1. *Statistics Canada: Aviation Statistics Center.* Most recent data available as of April 25, 1996.

8

Safe House or Hell House? Experiences of Newly Arrived Undocumented Chinese

Ko-lin Chin

In 1979, the United States established diplomatic relations with the People's Republic of China.[1] A year later, China immediately liberalized its emigration regulations to qualify for most-favored-nation status.[2] Since then, tens of thousands of Chinese have legally emigrated to North America.[3] Because of the immigration quota, only a limited number of Chinese whose family members are U.S. citizens or who are highly educated have the opportunity to come to America legally.[4] Consequently, some Chinese turn to the so-called snakeheads or professional smugglers for help.[5]

In New York City's Chinatown, the arrival of large numbers of legal and illegal Chinese migrants has forced the community to expand its territory into Little Italy and into the eastern part of the Lower East Side of Manhattan, an area once populated by Jewish immigrants.[6] One researcher suggests that as many as 8,000 Chinese are covertly entering the United States every month.[7] According to official estimates, in 1991 approximately half a million Chinese were living in the United States illegally.[8]

There are mainly three ways by which a Chinese migrant can enter the United States.[9] One technique is to travel to Mexico or Canada from China and then enter the United States by crossing national borders.[10] The second method primarily involves air routes to major American cities via any number of transit points, which can be in any city around the world.[11] Some unauthorized Chinese also arrive in Florida from South America by small airplanes. Between August 1991 and July 1993, a third means, entering the United States by sea, became a popular method. A large number of Chinese are smuggled into the United States in fishing trawlers. In June 1993, the ship *Golden Venture*, with more than 260 passengers aboard, became grounded in shallow waters off a New York City beach. Ten passengers drowned while attempting to swim ashore.[12] In all, between 1991 and 1993, 32 ships, with as many as 5,300 Chinese, were found in the waters near Japan, Taiwan, Indonesia, Australia, Singapore, Haiti, Guatemala, El Salvador, Honduras, and the United States.[13]

U.S. immigration officials estimate that at any given time as many as 4,000 Chinese are temporarily waiting in Bolivia ready to be shuttled to the United States by smugglers. Another 4,000 are believed to be awaiting entry into the United States in Panama. Thousands more are in Haiti and other parts of the Caribbean, or in Peru—all waiting anxiously to get into the United States. U.S. officials maintain that Chinese smuggling rings have connections in 51 countries that are either part of the transportation web or are involved in the manufacturing of fraudulent travel documents.[14] According to a senior official, "at any given time, 30,000 Chinese are stashed away in safe houses around the world, waiting for entry".[15]

Unlike undocumented Mexican migrants, who enter the United States at little or no cost,[16] each illegal Chinese migrant must pay the smugglers about $30,000 for their services.[17] Because thousands of Chinese are smuggled out of their country each year, people trafficking is a very lucrative business. A senior immigration official estimated in 1993 that Chinese organized crime groups are making more than $1 billion a year from human smuggling operations.[18] Other observers have suggested that Chinese smugglers are gaining about $3 billion annually from the human trade.[19]

Upon arrival in the United States, undocumented Chinese are reported to be locked up in safe houses operated by people hired by the human smugglers to collect the passage fees. The migrants are released only after their families or relatives pay off the smuggling charges. In the process, many Chinese migrants are believed to have been physically and sexually assaulted by the debt collectors.[20] Aside from anecdotal reports in the media, however, no research has ever been conducted to examine how and why illegal migrants are being abused in the safe houses by their captors. Specifically, we do not know how widespread this practice of confining illegal migrants is, how long the migrants are confined in the safe houses, or what measures the debt collectors use to ensure prompt payment of the smuggling fees. We also have little information about how families and relatives of the migrants deliver the payment, how the speed of payment affects a migrant's safe house experience, or how female migrants are being sexually abused by their captors. Based on data collected for a study of undocumented Chinese, this paper examines the patterns and processes of smuggling-related aggression in the safe houses located in the United States.

Methodology

This research, funded by the National Science Foundation, was conducted in New York City's Chinatown, a well-established social, cultural, and economic center for Chinese living in the New York metropolitan area. Interviews with 300 illegal immigrants were conducted by Fuzhounese-speaking interviewers in a field office located near Chinatown. A Chinese person would have been eligible to participate in the study (regardless of their immigration status at the time of the interview) if he or she had entered the United States after January 1, 1987, without authorization.[21] The year 1987 was selected as a watershed because I wanted to include only immigrants who came to America after the Immigration Reform and Control Act (IRCA) was implemented.[22] This allowed me to collect data on the subjects' experiences in America for up to six years.[23]

I used two techniques to recruit subjects for this study. First, I developed sources of potential subjects through ethnographic contacts with individuals who could provide the research team with access to undocumented Chinese. Many social workers, church workers, members of advocacy groups, business owners in the Chinese community, and my Fuzhounese interviewers are often in contact with unauthorized Chinese, and they were asked to refer subjects to me. After having exhausted the referrals from social workers, business owners, and interviewers, I adopted traditional "snowball" referral methods: I asked the subjects who were referred to me by friends and interviewers to refer colleagues, friends, or relatives who had illegally entered the United States.[24]

The interviews with illegal entrants were conducted face-to-face, utilizing a standardized questionnaire. I first wrote the questionnaire in English, then translated it into Chinese and pretested and revised it to assure validity and reliability. A bilingual research assistant coded some of the open-ended questions prior to data entry. I conducted a reliability check to assure accuracy and consistency in coding. Table 1 shows the personal characteristics of the respondents of this study.

Data collected from illegal migrants sometimes may not be valid because they are afraid of official repercussions due to their illegal status.[25] Both the quantitative and qualitative data

Table 1
Respondents' Characteristics (N=300)

	N	Percent		N	Percent
Sex			**Number of**		
Male	238	79	**children**[b]		
Female	62	21	None	7	3
			One	46	22
Region of origin			Two	88	43
Changle	146	49	Three	47	23
Fuzhou	62	21	Four or more	19	9
Tingjiang	56	19			
Lianjiang	23	7	**Employed in**		
Others[a]	13	4	**China?**		
			Yes	246	82
Education			No	54	18
Elementary	87	29			
Junior High	130	43	**Occupation**[c]		
Senior High	69	23	Professional	30	12
College	14	5	Store Owner	68	28
			Clerical	40	16
Marital status			Blue-collar worker	85	35
Married	205	68	Farming/fishing	23	9
Single	93	31			
Widowed	2	1			

Respondents' age in years: mean, 31.8; median, 32; mode, 30.
a. Seven from Minhou County, one from Fuqin City, and five from Zhejiang Province.
b. For subjects who were married or widowed.
c. For subjects who were employed in China. Monthly income in yuan: mean, 998; median, 350; mode, 200. The exchange rate is approximately 8.50 yuan = 1 U.S. dollar.

collected for this study, however, appeared to have high validity. Because the interviews were conducted by Fuzhounese-speaking female interviewers in a private, natural setting located near the Fuzhounese community, the respondents seemed to be relaxed throughout the interviews. Moreover, after the survey instrument was tested with 10 illegal migrants in a pilot study, I eliminated questions that appeared to have caused uneasiness among the respondents.[26] Finally, because they were themselves illegal migrants who were living among the Fuzhounese, the interviewers could easily relate to the respondents of this study. The interviewers were not only capable of understanding the experiences of the respondents, but were also able to ensure the reliability of the subjects' responses.

Findings

In 1993, the first media reports appeared about the existence of safe houses for undocumented Chinese in Los Angeles, New York City, and northern New Jersey. For example, in May 1993 a journalist described how immigration officials in Newark, New Jersey, were shocked by the discovery of 61 Chinese migrants in a garage in Jersey City.[27] A year later, authorities found 63 smuggled Chinese at a house in the small, rural community of Mitchelville in Prince George's County, Maryland.[28] In sum, between 1993 and 1994, law enforcement and immigration authorities in Los Angeles and New York City raided at least a dozen safe houses packed with Chinese migrants. The authorities were stunned to find so many people being crowded in tiny basements or rooms that were poorly maintained.

As the authorities began to learn that many undocumented Chinese were being confined in safe houses after they entered the United States, terrifying accounts about female migrants being gang-raped and forced to participate in sex games also came to light. For example, when the authorities raided a safe house in New York, they discovered a young woman who was being sexually exploited by her captors.[29] Similar nightmarish circumstances have been reported in the media.[30] There were also reports that the debt collectors not only sexually abused the female migrants but also forced them to work in houses of prostitution.[31] Debt collectors were delivering their female captives who were late in their payments to massage parlors in the evening and bringing them back to the safe houses in the morning. In 1995, when a female migrant was gang-raped, had a finger cut off, was hit over the head with a television set, and strangled to death in a safe house, the authorities and the public were shocked and outraged by the extremely brutal crime.[32]

There are no reliable data to suggest how many safe houses exist in the New York metropolitan area. Queens police authorities estimated in 1993 that, in Queens alone, there may have been 200 to 300 safe houses being used to hold newcomers.[33] Although the authorities might have overestimated the number of safe houses in order to make the point that this was a serious problem, it was the cruel and unusual treatment of migrants in these safe houses that concerned the police and the public the most.[34]

Rate of Detention in Safe Houses

It is highly unlikely for Chinese migrants to pay their traffickers the entire smuggling fee before they arrive in the United States.[35] To ensure that the smugglers will deliver the "service," Chinese "customers" normally pay the smugglers only a down payment (about $1,000 to $3,000), and the second portion of the trip's price is paid upon arrival in New York City.

According to my survey, not every migrant who owes money to the smuggler is detained after he or she enters the United States. Smugglers allowed some of my respondents (about 36 percent) to go free immediately after they arrived at their final destination. Still, of the 300 survey subjects, 191 (64 percent) were locked up in a safe house after their arrival in America. An analysis of the quantitative data suggests that the migrants' personal characteristics are not associated with the likelihood of being confined. In other words, a migrant's sex, marital status, region of origin, educational level, and so forth have little to do with whether he or she is going to be confined in a safe house. The data do suggest, however, that younger migrants are more likely to be detained than older migrants (see table 2).

The data also suggest that smuggling-related variables are more likely to affect a newcomer's chance of being detained (see table 3). Less than half (41 percent) of the subjects who left China by air were detained, whereas almost 9 out of 10 (89 percent) who left China on boats were confined by debt collectors after they entered the United States. Method of entry also appears to be associated with the risk of detention. Subjects who flew into the United States had a detention rate of only 53 percent, whereas those who arrived by sea had a detention rate of 83 percent. Border-crossers had a detention rate of 72 percent.

Year of arrival is one of the most important smuggling-related variables associated with the likelihood of detention. Only 4 out of 10 of the migrants who arrived in 1988 or before were confined, but the rate of detention increased dramatically thereafter. By 1993, more than 8 out of 10 migrants were being locked up upon their arrival. Even after controlling for smuggling method, the relationship between year of arrival and detention rate remains strong (data not shown).

**Table 2
Associations between Personal Characteristics and
Safe House Detention Rate**
(N = 300)

Safe house detention rate for the sample = 64%

	Sample N	Detained N	Percent
Sex			
Male	236	150	64
Female	62	41	66
Age*			
20 or less	40	31	78
21–30	98	68	69
31–40	108	66	61
41 or more	52	26	50
Marital status			
Single	93	66	71
Married	203	123	61
Widowed	2	2	100
Region of origin			
Changle	146	97	66
Fuzhou	61	38	62
Tinjiang	55	36	66
Lianjiang	23	12	52
Others	13	8	62
Education			
Elementary	57	39	68
Junior High	159	104	65
Senior High	68	40	59
College	14	8	57
Have relatives in America?			
Yes	208	130	63
No	88	59	67

Notes: Number of missing observations: Sex=2; Age=2; Marital status=2;
Region of origin=2; Education =2; Have relatives in America? =4.
* $p < .05$.

Table 3
Associations between Smuggling-Related Variables and
Safe House Detention Rate
(N=300)

Safe house detention rate for the sample = 64%

	Sample N	Detained N	Percent
Method of departing China*			
Air	83	34	41
Land	121	73	60
Sea	94	84	89
Method of entering America*			
Air	141	74	53
Land	122	88	72
Sea	35	29	83
Year of arrival*			
1988 or before	23	9	39
1989	42	19	45
1990	49	24	49
1991	61	39	64
1992	62	50	81
1993	61	50	82
Method of finding **one's snakehead****			
Friends/relatives abroad	36	18	50
Friends/relatives in China	222	141	64
Subject initiated the contact	29	22	76
Smugglers initiated the contact	11	10	91
Made a down payment?			
Yes	240	158	66
No	58	33	57

Notes: a. Number of missing observations: Methods of departing China = 2; Methods of entering America = 2; Year of arrival = 2; Methods of finding one's snakehead = 2; Made a down payment? = 2.
* $p < .001$.
** $p < .05$.

Another factor apparently associated with the risk of detention is the way a migrant found his or her snakehead. A migrant who contacted a foreign-based snakehead through friends and relatives abroad was least likely to be detained. The most vulnerable were those who were approached by China-based snakeheads; about 9 out of 10 migrants recruited by this method were later confined in safe houses.

Contrary to the assumptions of U.S. authorities, the data suggest that migrants who pay more for their trips are not necessarily less likely to be detained. In fact, the data indicate the opposite; those who agreed to pay extra were more likely to be confined. The data also suggest that, although migrants who were detained had tended to pay less of a down payment than those who were not detained, the difference was not statistically significant (data not shown).

Length of Confinement

For my respondents who were detained, the average length of stay in a safe house was about 11 days. Both the median and modal stay was 7 days. More than 62 percent of the detained subjects were released within a week. My data suggest that most Chinese migrants tried to come up with the balance due to their smugglers within the grace period of 7 days.[36]

According to the data collected for this study, migrants who arrived by air were both less likely to be detained and more likely to pay sooner than those who entered the country either overland or by ship. Although border-crossers were less likely to be detained than passengers arriving on sea vessels, they tended to spend more time in the safe houses than the latter group did. The data indicate that the average length of stay was 7 days for subjects who flew in, 10 days for those who arrived on sea vessels, and 15 days for those who crossed the border. Also, migrants who paid a down payment were significantly more likely to have had a shorter stay (9 days) than those who came without paying a down payment (22 days). Moreover, the data suggest that those who came recently were more likely to be detained longer than those who arrived in the past. For example, detained subjects who arrived in 1988 or before spent an average of 6 days in the safe houses, whereas those who arrived in 1993 spent an average of 12 days. Even though a migrant's relatives in America may not be a factor in determining whether he or she is going to be detained, they do appear to play a role in the early release of migrants. Subjects who had relatives living in the United States were detained an average of 10 days, whereas those without relatives were confined for 15 days.

How a migrant found his or her snakehead has important implications not only for the likelihood of being detained but also for the length of confinement. Subjects who found their snakeheads via friends and relatives abroad spent an average of only 3 days in the safe houses, whereas those who found their snakeheads through friends and relatives in China were confined for an average of 11 days. Those who found their snakeheads themselves and those who were approached by the snakeheads were not only more likely to be detained, but also more likely to spend a substantially longer period in the safe houses than the first two groups (23 days versus 13 days).

Methods of Payment

Little is known about how trafficked migrants pay the human traffickers for their "services." Law enforcement authorities have suggested that many smuggled Chinese are not required to pay their smugglers in advance nor immediately after their arrival. Instead, they suggest, the migrants go to work after arriving in America and pay the smugglers from their monthly income.[37] The authorities further propose that, because money lenders or human traffickers charge high interest rates, it may take the migrants many years, if not a lifetime, to repay the money they owe to their friends, relatives, or smugglers. Thus, the labels "indentured slaves" or "indentured servants" have often been applied to undocumented Chinese by American authorities.

My interviews with undocumented Chinese suggest that, contrary to the assumptions of the U.S. authorities, human traffickers are unwilling to collect the smuggling fees from their "customers" on a monthly basis. Their common practice is to demand that migrants pay the entire smuggling fee immediately upon arrival in America. Some of the respondents we interviewed were relatives of the snakeheads, and even they were asked to pay as soon as they arrived in New York, although they were sometimes allowed to go free while still owing the smugglers a small portion of the balance.[38]

According to the data collected for this study, of the 288 undocumented Chinese who owed the smugglers the second portion of their smuggling fee when they arrived at their final destination, 110 (38 percent) said their entire balances were paid in the United States by families and relatives in America. Another 107 (37 percent) stated that their families in China made final payments in China, and 47 respondents (16 percent) said that their balances were paid partly in China and partly in America. The rest, 24 subjects (8 percent), made payment outside of China and America, usually in a transit country or area such as Hong Kong, Thailand, Singapore, or Bolivia. These findings contradict law enforcement authorities' notions that most, if not all, smuggling-related payments are made in the United States.[39]

Nevertheless, methods of payment adopted by smuggled Chinese are changing over time. During earlier waves of illegal migration among the Chinese (1988 and earlier), more than three out of four respondents paid the entire balance to the smugglers in the United States. By 1993, the percentage of subjects using this method had dropped to 24 percent, about one out of four. Almost half of the subjects we surveyed who arrived in 1993 paid the smugglers the whole balance in China, and almost one out of five made payments both in the United States and China.

Methods of payment also seem to be related to the region of origin of the subjects. The majority of those from Tingjiang and Lianjiang still prefer to pay the smugglers in the United States, whereas people from Changle are more likely to pay the smugglers in China.[40] When a newcomer places a call to China, family members will make every effort to collect from friends and relatives who promised to borrow the money needed to pay the smuggling fees. Some migrants rely on their families and relatives in America to pay for their passage. A Fuzhounese take-out restaurant owner who has been living in the United States for 15 years told the author that so far he had paid for the delivery of three relatives. But because he could not afford to sponsor any more relatives from China, he had changed his phone number and made sure that his relatives in China could not have access to it.

As mentioned above, more often than not, smugglers demand that migrants pay their entire balance immediately after their arrival in the United States. Only 39 of the 300 subjects we interviewed (13 percent) were allowed to make another payment after one payment was made on arrival. Only 13 subjects (7 percent) were allowed by their snakeheads to owe them money. These subjects are probably close friends or relatives of the snakehead who arranged for their passage.

General Tactics of the Debt Collectors

In New York City, debt collectors, or enforcers, are hired by the snakeheads to operate the safe houses and collect money.[41] They perform the following tasks: (1) rent a house or an apartment to function as a safe house;[42] (2) go to the airports and other points of entry to meet the newcomers and transport them to the safe house; (3) help the newcomers to get in touch with and coerce their friends and relatives in America or China to pay for their passage as soon as possible; (4) if the payment is made in China, release the migrant once the China-based snakehead informs the U.S.-based snakehead that the money is duly paid; (5) if the payment is made in New York City, arrange a meeting with whoever agrees to pay, collect the balance, and turn the migrant over to his or her sponsor;[43] and (6) provide meals to the migrants while they are in custody.

In general, migrants whose families and relatives are projected to deliver the payment expeditiously are treated well by the debt collectors. More often than not, however, the debt collectors are not certain who among their captives is going to make payments promptly. As a result, the enforcers work under the assumption that most migrants will not pay quickly unless they are being coerced to do so, and they therefore adopt many tactics to make life inside the safe houses as unpleasant and expensive as possible for the migrants. First, the enforcers often charge the migrants an exorbitant price for phone calls. To pay the smuggler, a migrant needs to call family and relatives in China or the United States. To prevent the migrants from making unnecessary phone calls, and to ensure that they persuade their family or relatives to pay after the initial phone call, debt collectors normally charge $100 per call to China.

Second, debt collectors usually charge the migrants extra fees if they overstay their grace periods. According to the respondents we interviewed, debt collectors charged them $100 a day for each day they spent in the safe house after the grace period. Third, debt collectors regularly offer little food to the migrants. Some migrants are completely denied food or drinking water. Fourth, the enforcers frequently yell at the migrants in their custody. The purpose is to create a frightening atmosphere within the safe house. Fifth, the debt collectors often intimidate the migrants. They also frequently say things to scare their captives into thinking that the sooner they pay the better. Female migrants are often reminded about what might happen to them if they do not pay on time.

Sixth, the debt collectors often sexually harass the women. A subject told us how these activities were carried out by the enforcers: "The beautiful girls were invited by them [enforcers] to go out and have fun." Another female respondent said: "There were five of them [debt collectors], and they evaluated us in public as to who is attractive and who is not." Finally, migrants may be beaten. Physical punishment in the safe houses is not limited only to those migrants who have difficulty coming up with the balance. According to our subjects, assaults against fresh arrivals are also a possibility.

Most migrants we interviewed indicated that they had had a nightmarish experience while they were being detained by the debt collectors. Generally, only those who were close friends or relatives of their snakeheads were not harassed.

It is not clear whether these tactics are effective in persuading the migrants' families to pay the smuggling fees any sooner than they would otherwise. This is because the timely delivery of payment could be affected by many factors that are not controlled by families or the migrants. The balance of approximately $27,000 to $29,000 (about 240,000 yuan) is a large sum of money for most families in China; for an average wage earner, this could be equivalent to 20 years of his of her salary. Although the migrants may not have the money deposited in a bank prior to their departure, they still come because they have already figured out how the money can be secured once they have arrived in America. The majority rely on members of their extended families and close friends who promised to lend a certain amount of money to the migrants' families.

Once the family has received a phone call from the migrants in the United States, they will immediately approach those members of the extended family and close friends who have pledged to loan money. This may require a few days because most financial transactions in China are made both in cash and in person. This means a family must usually go door to door to collect the money in person. Often, it takes a considerable amount of time because so many relatives and friends have to be visited. Some of those who had agreed to loan money may default for various unforeseen reasons.[44]

Even if the family has no problem collecting the money from the supporters, disputes between the migrants' families and the snakeheads can also cause a delay in payment. For example, additional charges such as legal fees, bail money, and expenses for overseas phone calls may add to the balance without the knowledge of the family. And when the family is asked to pay an additional few thousand U.S. dollars, they may either become reluctant to pay or need more time to find the extra money.

Moreover, even if the payment is delivered promptly by the migrants' family in China to the China-based snakeheads, the latter still need to inform the snakeheads at the U.S. end that payment has been made. Because the snakeheads are handling a large number of migrants simultaneously, omissions and mistakes occur that can delay the release of migrants from the safe houses.

Life inside the Safe Houses

Chinese migrants can be categorized into five groups according to how quickly the balance of the smuggling fee is paid: (1) those who pay immediately (within a few hours or the day after their arrival); (2) those who pay within the grace period; (3) those who do not meet the deadline but render the payment not long after the due date; (4) those who have major difficulties in making the payment and who make the payment only after overstaying the grace period for a month or so; and (5) those who pay several months after the grace period. I shall discuss how these five groups of people are treated by their captors and how female migrants are subjected to sexual assaults.

Experiences of migrants who paid promptly. Some of my respondents paid the snakeheads the balance of the smuggling fees a few hours after they reached New York City. As a result, they were not abused by the debt collectors. They were sometimes even commended by the smugglers and debt collectors for their punctuality. For example, a subject told us what his snakehead said after he had paid promptly: "My snakehead said I am a *how jiao* [literally, good feet; meaning reliable]. I paid him right after I got here." Some of the financially well-to-do respondents were treated rather cordially by the debt collectors. Moreover, respondents who were smuggled into the United States by snakeheads who happened to be their close friends or relatives were not abused in the safe houses.

Some respondents, aware that they might be subject to harsh treatment in the custody of the debt collectors after arrival in

New York, called home just before they boarded the plane headed for the United States and instructed family members to make the payment immediately. By doing so, they did not have to spend time in the safe houses. Most migrants, however, are unwilling to pay the full amount until they have arrived at their final destination.

Ordeals of migrants who did pay on time. Paying within the grace period may not protect a smuggled migrant from being abused by the debt collectors. Many of my respondents' families and relatives remunerated the snakeheads within the grace period, but the migrants were still subjected to a variety of exploitations and abuses.

Some of them were beaten severely, as testified to by a 40-year-old male respondent from Fuzhou City:

> The place I was kept was hell. We ate, lived, and urinated in the same place. More than a dozen people were confined in a room. We were starved all the time. The air was awful. Often, people cried in their sleep. The debt collectors treated me poorly; others who were there longer than I were treated even worse. They yelled at or beat us whenever they wished. Often, people were beaten until they were bloody. I believe there was one person who didn't come out alive.

Another informant, a 32-year-old male from Changle, also likened safe houses to hell as depicted in the movies. He disclosed some of the cruel and unusual practices commonly adopted by the enforcers to make sure that the safe houses have a hellish atmosphere:

> They fed us awful food. You can say they did that intentionally to force us to pay as soon as possible. They locked us in a basement without any sunlight. I don't know how hell is like, but the basement was like the hell we saw in the movie. The debt collectors often used various methods to force us to pay promptly. Some were soaked with cold water when the weather was very cold. Some were shackled to prevent them from moving. Some were asked to move heavy objects, and so on.

Sufferings endured by migrants who failed to pay on time. Once a migrant overstays the grace period, his or her relationship with the debt collectors may change dramatically. That is, the debt collectors may begin to intensify their cruel and unusual punishment of the migrant. Some of their common tactics include the following. First, migrants are asked to do housework such as cooking meals, cleaning the house, and so on.

Second, the debt collectors may stop providing the migrant with food and drinking water. Or, to prevent the migrant from starving to death, only porridge might be served once a day.

Third, migrants are shackled. Some are handcuffed so that they cannot move around. During several police raids of safe houses, law enforcement authorities have discovered evidence of the practice of shackling captives to metal bed frames or other heavy objects.

Fourth, the migrant is showered with cold water. To punish the overdue migrants, debt collectors may pour cold water onto the migrants and leave them to shiver in the cold. The purpose of this practice, according to one respondent, was to "clear my mind so that I will be able to think of a way to pay [the smuggling fees]." Another subject who experienced the same type of punishment told the interviewer: "At the safe house in New York City, they showered us with cold water. I was ordered to kneel down for half an hour. They did not treat us like human beings. We were beaten often."

Fifth, some migrants are threatened by their captors. Male migrants may be warned that they could be slaughtered, and female migrants may be told that they could end up working in a house of prostitution. Most Fuzhounese female migrants come from rural areas populated by rather conservative Chinese families. The thought of being forced to work as a prostitute could be a major shock to young female migrants who may not have even dated before. According to a 20-year-old female migrant from Changle, the enforcers threatened not only her but also her parents over the phone:

> Whenever I talked to my mother over the phone, she asked me in tears how I was doing. Because I was scared, I cried. At that moment, the debt collectors yelled at me and threatened that if my family did not come up with the balance soon they would sell me to a prostitution house. When my family heard the threat over the phone, they got panicked. Later, my family went all out to borrow money from loansharkers. Those debt collectors spend all their time talking dirty to the women.

Sixth, migrants are kicked and beaten. Physical abuse is probably one of the most popular practices adopted by the enforcers to punish those migrants who are behind in payment. Almost every migrant we interviewed had personally witnessed at least one incident of beating in the safe houses. According to a respondent, "During the eight days I was there, I saw five people being either beaten or kicked because they had problems coming up with the money." Once the migrants arrive in the safe houses, the captors make it clear to them that they will be assaulted if their families and relatives do not pay after a certain period. To frighten not only the victim but also the victim's family and relatives, migrants are often attacked while they are talking to their families over the phone.

Some of my respondents were beaten so severely that they required hospitalization. Apparently, however, the smugglers do not seek medical attention for their captives. According to a 30-year-old Tingjiang male subject:

> Some who were there for a while and could not come up with the money were beaten badly. You can see their bones through their wounds but the snakehead would not allow them to see a doctor. He only gave them some Chinese medicine and asked them to take care of their wounds themselves. Some were beaten so badly that they could not even move.[45]

Sometimes, the enforcers will try to prevent their victims from bleeding by putting a book on top of the victim's head before striking their head with a hammer.

One respondent told us that he was not only punished by the enforcers in a safe house, but also forced to inflict pain on other migrants on behalf of his captors. Another respondent stated that he was not allowed to lie down to sleep and was often attacked by the enforcers with iron bars and gun handles.

Nightmarish experiences of migrants who were held captive for months. A small number of Chinese migrants may have to spend a few months in the safe houses because their families and relatives, for various reasons, are unable to come up with the hefty smuggling fees. This often happens because the migrants have been tricked by the "little snakeheads" in China into believing that they do not have to pay upon their arrival in the United States. They may be told, for example, that they can make payments from their wages in America. But, as mentioned above, the U.S.-based snakeheads are determined to collect the entire fee immediately once the migrants are smuggled in. For them, what had been said by the recruiters or little snakeheads in China is of little significance.

A 20-year-old female subject was allowed to work and pay the smuggling fee on a monthly basis, but the catch was that she had to work in the snakehead's massage parlor as a prostitute:

> Initially, I was told by my snakehead that I would pay him the balance periodically by working in his so-called company. I thought that I will pay him $1,000 a month while working in his garment factory. After my arrival, however, he said that this could be done only if I worked in his massage parlor. When I refused to work for him, he demanded the $20,000 balance immediately.

Debt collectors have many ways of punishing those migrants who have arrived in the United States and failed to pay for many months. One common tactic, as described above, is to force the female migrants to work in prostitution houses. Law enforcement authorities in New York City have often asserted that the snakeheads had forced many Chinese female migrants who could not afford the clandestine trip to work in massage parlors or prostitution houses. For example, a girl from China was forced to work as a prostitute for two years repaying the smuggling fee while getting paid only $1,000 a month.[46] According to a 40-year-old male from Fuzhou City, he believed that one of his female counterparts had been forced to work in a prostitution house after her family failed to pay the smuggling fee:

> In the safe house, there was a woman detained for almost six months. She was locked all day long in the basement. She was offered very little food. At night, she was driven by the *ma jia* [enforcers] to where I don't know, then the next morning she was brought back.

Some were threatened with guns. Some were not allowed to lie down and were ordered to sleep only in a sitting position. A 30-year-old female migrant from Changle disclosed that she had heard that some migrants might be having their fingers being chopped off by the debt collectors:

> After we arrived in New York City, we were kept in a house in Flushing. Fourteen females were locked in one room, and

the men were kept in an adjacent room. There were many people kept in the house. At the beginning, the food was not bad; however, later instead of three meals a day, it was changed to two meals. I didn't meet the snakehead. The debt collectors treated us all right. But the Vietnamese hired by the debt collectors to watch us were not nice. They often threatened the males with violence. A male had his small finger chopped off and it was sent to the victim's relatives in America to urge them to pay as soon as possible. I heard about this; I didn't see it myself. But I heard of people crying all the time who were kept inside the safe house.

Some who were punished regularly for a certain period of time said they became accustomed to it and that their sense of fear disappeared. A 19-year-old male from Tingjiang reported that

I was locked up for five months in a safe house located in a suburban area. Thirteen people were being confined. We did not have enough food or enough clothes. Even now, whenever I think about my experience in that safe house, I become frightened. I was beaten about once a week because my family was having a hard time coming up with the money. In fact, I was lucky; others were beaten every other day. They beat us with sticks. Those who were locked up together could not help one another. That's why we just let them do whatever they wanted to do. I can't really describe what kinds of people they are. After being there for a period of time, I had no sense of fear anymore because being punished became a daily routine.

Rape inside the Safe Houses

After being subjected to sexual harassment and assaults in transit points or ships throughout the arduous trip from China to the United States, female migrants are once again vulnerable to sexual exploitation in the hands of debt collectors and enforcers after their arrival in America. It is not clear what percentage of the Chinese female migrants are being sexually abused in the safe houses. According to a 17-year-old female respondent, the snakeheads condone this type of activity within the safe houses, presumably to ensure speedy payments of the smuggling fees:

They kept me in a basement with more than 20 women. The debt collectors attacked those who did not come up with the payment on time. When they punished us, they made sure that our families in China were listening to our screaming over the phone. Inside the safe house, it was really a tragic and horrifying scene. If a girl owed money for a long time, she would be raped by the debt collectors. Some women who were raped reported to the snakehead what had happened to them and the snakehead reacted by saying: "That's not forcible rape. That's convenience sex." You can tell they did not treat us like human beings at all.

Another 20-year-old female migrant also told us how indifferent a debt collector could be when it came to raping women in the safe houses:

During my stay at the safe house, one night a girl was dragged to the basement by the debt collectors. One of them turned around and told us sarcastically: "They are having 'war' downstairs." We heard the girl in the basement crying and yelling. Later, she came upstairs sobbing. She did not eat anything for two days. We all knew she was raped and I was very scared. That little girl was very pretty; she was only 17.

Some victims can be subjected to gang rape. According to one subject who was locked in a safe house, "there was a woman who came along with me. A debt collector asked her to go to his room and he raped her. She was often raped by five debt collectors in turn."

Some women were sexually attacked while they were talking to their families in China. The debt collectors are apparently willing to do anything to send a message to family members of the migrants that they want the passage fees promptly. A 45-year-old male from Changle told the interviewer that "after we arrived in New York, there was a change in the group of debt collectors":

Unfortunately, those women who were raped on the ship were again raped by this new group of debt collectors. These guys even raped a woman while she was talking to her family over the phone, so that the family was forced to come up with the money in a hurry.

Conclusion

After enduring so much suffering throughout their arduous journey, many Chinese migrants arrive in the United States only to discover that the worst is yet to come. It is inside the safe houses in the New York metropolitan area where they are being repeatedly punished and tortured by debt collectors who do not hesitate to use cruel and unusual measures to force their captives' families and relatives to deliver the smuggling fees as soon as possible.

In the basements that are often described by my subjects as hell or prison, the migrants are subjected to a variety of abuses. The debt collectors, whose humanity my subjects often questioned, have developed many ways to create a hellish atmosphere within the safe houses to assure that the migrants will be desperate to leave as soon as possible.

We do not know how Chinese migrants are affected by their traumatic experiences in the safe houses. Is it possible that some of those who have been confined in the safe houses for a prolonged time and repeatedly abused and tortured may have suffered permanent psychological damage? According to a 29-year-old male from Changle, a migrant did become mentally disordered after his release from a safe house:

> There was a male who came along with me on the same ship. After he arrived here, his family could not come up with the balance and he was beaten badly by the enforcers. Later, he became crazy and verbally disorganized. He is a Changle Chenkuang person.

Another subject told me about a female migrant she knew who had been detained in a safe house for several months. During that time, she was repeatedly raped and physically abused by her captors. The young woman was released only after her family paid the smuggler. Due to her months of abuse in the safe house, she is paralyzed and cannot go to work to fulfill her American dream, a dream that had prompted her to initiate the illegal voyage from China to America.

Clearly, Chinese migrants have heard that they will be treated badly in New York if they cannot come up with the money for the trip on time. It is highly unlikely, however, that they could have imagined that they would be treated worse than animals in a place they often call the "Golden Mountain" or the "Beautiful Country."

Notes

1. Chinese living in the United States may have come from the People's Republic of China (PRC), the Republic of China on Taiwan (ROC), Hong Kong, or other countries. In this paper, China refers to the People's Republic of China, and Chinese, unless otherwise indicated, denotes immigrants from, or citizens of, China. I will use the word "Taiwan" to indicate the Republic of China, and "Taiwanese" to refer to migrants from, or citizens of, Taiwan, although many people in Taiwan consider their country an independent China and themselves Chinese.

2. Alan Dowty, *Closed Borders: The Contemporary Assault on Freedom of Movement* (New Haven: Yale University Press, 1987).

3. Min Zhou, *Chinatown: The Socioeconomic Potential of an Urban Enclave* (Philadelphia: Temple University Press, 1992).

4. In 1994, 54,000 Chinese legally migrated to the United States. That year, China was the second highest source, after Mexico, of legal immigration to America.

5. In the Chinese communities of America, undocumented Chinese are often called *renshe* (human snakes) because of their ability to wiggle through tight border controls. Human smugglers are labeled *shetou* (snakeheads), so named because of their image of slithering from point to point along clandestine routes. The smuggling activity is known as "digging snakes." Some Chinese consider these terms derogatory, but the majority do not.

6. Richard Bernstein, "Immigrants Both Renew and Unsettle Chinatown," *New York Times*, June 9, 1993, p. B2.

7. Willard H. Myers III, "The United States Under Siege: Assault on the Borders: Chinese Smuggling 1983–1992" (Center for the Study of Asian Organized Crime, Philadelphia, Pa., 1992).

8. T. J. English, "Slaving Away," *Smithsonian* (February 1991): 10–14.

9. Throughout this paper I will often use the words "Chinese migrants," "undocumented Chinese," or "unauthorized Chinese" to refer to illegal Chinese immigrants.

10. William Glaberson, "6 Seized in Smuggling Asians into New York," *New York Times*, May 5, 1989, p. B3.

11. Donatella Lorch, "Immigrants from China Pay Dearly to be Slaves," *New York Times*, January 3, 1991, p. B1; Prasong Charasdamrong and Subin Kheunkaew, "Smuggling Human Beings: A Lucrative Racket that Poses a Threat to National Security," *Bangkok Post*, July 19, 1992, 10.

12. Jane Fritsch, "One Failed Voyage Illustrates Flow of Chinese Immigration," *New York Times*, June 7, 1993, p. A1.

13. Al Kamen, "U.S. Seizes Illegal Aliens from China," *Washington Post*, September 5, 1991, p. A5; Diana Jean Schemo, "Survivors Tell of Voyage of Little Daylight, Little Food and Only Hope," *New York Times*, June 7, 1993, p. B5; U.S. Immigration and Naturalization Service, *Vessels That Are Known to Have Attempted to Smuggle PRC Nationals into the United States* (Unpublished report, August 17, 1993).

14. Dan Freedman, "Asian Gangs Turn to Smuggling People," *San Francisco Examiner,* December 30, 1991, p. A7; Al Kamen, "A Dark Road from China to Chinatown: Smugglers Bring Increasing Flow of Illegal Immigrants to U.S.," *Washington Post,* June 17, 1991, p. A1; Seth Mydans, "Chinese Smugglers' Lucrative Cargo: Humans," *New York Times,* March 21, 1992, p. A1.

15. Gwen Kinkead, *Chinatown: A Portrait of a Closed Society* (New York: Harper Collins, 1992).

16. John Crewdson, *The Tarnished Door: The New Immigrants and the Transformation of America* (New York: Times Books, 1983); Robert C. Jones, ed., *Patterns of Unauthorized Migration: Mexico and California* (Totowa, N.J.: Rowman and Allanheld, 1984); Wayne Cornelius, "Impact of the 1986 U.S. Immigration Law on Emigration from Rural Mexican Sending Communities," *Population and Development Review* 15, no. 4 (1989): 689–705.

17. Undocumented Chinese interviewed for this study (N=300) reported having paid smugglers an average of $27,745 per person to be smuggled to America. The subjects arrived in the United States between 1988 and 1993. According to Chinese migrants who arrived in America in 1996, passage fees have been increased to approximately $36,000 per person.

18. "Asian Gangs are Making a Billion Dollars a Year from Alien Smuggling" (in Chinese), *World Journal* (New York), January 20, 1993, 3.

19. Pamela Burdman, "Huge Boom in Human Smuggling—Inside Story of Flight from China," *San Francisco Chronicle,* April 27, 1993, p. A1. Estimates of the scope of the Chinese human trade and the revenues/profits of the human traffickers are cursory at best because there is little reliable information on how many Chinese are being smuggled into America every year and how much money the smugglers make per migrant. Undoubtedly, these two variables (number of smuggled migrants and profits per migrant) may change dramatically from year to year and from one smuggling route to another. As a result, all pertinent estimates should be year and route specific.

20. Seth Faison, "Queens Arrests in Kidnapping Include Victim," *New York Times,* October 22, 1993, p. B3; Dennis Hevesi, "8 Captives are Freed in Brooklyn," *New York Times,* June 27, 1993, 27; Patricia Hurtado, "Chinese Kidnap Suspects Detail Scheme," *New York Newsday,* June 11, 1993, 33.

21. Students and professionals from China who remained in the United States beyond the terms of their admission were not included in this study because their socioeconomic status in China and experiences in the United States are significantly different from those of Chinese who entered the United States clandestinely. Likewise, undocumented Chinese from Taiwan and Hong Kong who stayed beyond their visas were also excluded.

22. The law allows unauthorized migrants who arrived in the United States before 1982 and migrants with recent agricultural employment experience in America to obtain legal status.

23. Interviews were conducted in November and December of 1993.

24. Patrick Biernacki and Dan Waldorf, "Snowball Sampling," *Sociological Methods and Research* 10 (1981): 141–163. I am aware that the use of

purposive sampling techniques will limit the generalizability of my research findings in a strict statistical sense. Due, however, to the lack of information about the population of undocumented Chinese in New York City,
random sampling was not feasible.

25. Julina Samora, *Los Mojados: The Wetback Story* (Notre Dame, Ind.:
University of Notre Dame Press, 1971).

26. Three questions about the subjects' attitudes toward the Chinese
government were included in the original questionnaire. During the pilot
study, however, I found that all 10 migrants interviewed were reluctant to
talk about the Chinese government because they were concerned that their
families in China might be persecuted by Chinese authorities for their
comments. The subjects in the pilot study were also unwilling to reveal
what village they were from, even though they were willing to tell us
which county or city they came from. Moreover, the subjects were not eager to disclose exactly how much money they were sending home monthly.
As a result, all three questions were eliminated from the revised questionnaire.

27. Evelyn Nieves, "Chinese Immigrants Kept Padlocked in Warehouse," *New York Times,* May 26, 1993, p. B5.

28. Jon Jeter and Pierre Thomas, "Chinese Hostages Found in P.G.
House; 63 Held," *Washington Post,* April 7, 1994, p. A1.

29. "Police Arrested Three Men One Woman After Chinese Illegals Es-
caped from a Safe House; A 16-year-old Girl was Sexually Assaulted and
Pregnant" (in Chinese), *Sing Tao Daily* (New York), November 18, 1993, 31.

30. Ying Chan, "America Still Their Goal," *New York Daily News,* July 5,
1993, 6.

31. "Voyage to Life of Shattered Dreams," *New York Times,* July 23, 1993,
p. B1.

32. Seth Faison, "Brutal End to an Immigrant's Voyage of Hope," *New
York Times,* October 2, 1995, p. A1.

33. "There may be 200 to 300 Safe Houses in Queens, Police Assumed"
(in Chinese), *World Journal* (New York), June 30, 1993, p. B1.

34. Vicki Torres, "2 Men Tell of Torture at Hands of Smugglers," *Los Angeles Times,* October 3, 1993, p. B1.

35. According to this study, almost all (296 out of 300, or 99 percent) of
the Chinese migrants interviewed owed money to their smugglers after
they entered the United States.

36. Some Chinese migrants sign a contract with their smugglers before
they are smuggled out of China (an example is appended at the end of this
note). It is not clear how prevalent the practice is. The contract outlines the
rights and responsibilities of both the migrants and the smugglers. One provision in the contract clearly indicates that the migrants may be subjected to
confinement in the United States and that they are responsible for paying
the balance of their smuggling fee within seven days after they reach New
York City.

Smuggling Contract

Party A (client) would like to go abroad and he/she hereby asks Party B (snakehead) to assist him/her. Based upon the foundation of a common goal, both parties agree to the following terms:

1. Both parties concur that the total fee for Party A to go to the United States is $30,000. Party A will provide Party B with a copy of his/her identification card and an application fee of $1,000, and with an additional $2,000 after travel documents are secured (The $3,000 will be deducted from the $30,000 total fee after Party A arrives in the United States). Party A will also present Party B with the address and phone number of a relative in the United States who will serve as the sponsor. Party B will give Party A the name of a relative of Party B in China as the guarantor.

2. Party B will be responsible for obtaining a passport and a visa for Party A. (All expenses are included in the $30,000 fee). If Party A fails to make the trip within three months after the agreement is signed, Party A has the right to terminate this agreement, and Party B will return the application fee to Party A.

3. After Party A leaves China, Party B shall be responsible for all expenses abroad. Party A shall not have to bear any expense until his/her arrival in the United States.

4. If there are accidents on the trip, Party B shall be responsible; however, if the mishaps are the direct result of Party A not following Party B's instructions and arrangements, Party A shall bear the consequences of these accidents.

5. If Party A is arrested, both parties will split the bail money. The bail money is not included in the $30,000 fee. Half of the bail money has to be paid by Party A or his/her family or sponsor.

6. If Party A is repatriated back to China and is fined by the Ministry of Public Safety, Party B will pay part of the fine out of the $1,000 application fee. The rest of the fine shall be paid by Party A. The $2,000 down payment will not be returned to Party A by Party B, since this money is needed to cover the expenses for securing travelling documents and buying air tickets.

7. If Party A is sentenced to prison, Party B shall not bear any responsibility. While Party A is on the road, neither party shall terminate this agreement; Party B shall not sell Party A to another smuggler, Party A shall not change snakeheads.

8. After Party A has arrived in the United States, his/her sponsor shall be bound by this agreement. If the sponsor fails to do so, Party B has the right to hold Party A as a hostage. If the balance of the total fee is not paid within 7 days after Party A's arrival, Party A will be charged $100 a day to cover meals and lodging.

9. After Party A arrives in the United States, he/she shall not attempt to escape from the control of Party B. If Party A does escape, his/

her sponsor and family in China will still need to pay the balance of the total fee.

10. This agreement becomes valid after both parties sign it. After Party A arrives in the United States and the balance of the smuggling fee is paid, this agreement is terminated.

Signature of Party A _____
Signature of Party B _____
Date: _____

37. Some U.S. officials even suggest that migrants may have been forced to work in chain restaurants and other business firms owned and operated by human smugglers for relatively low wages. According to these officials, human smugglers are not only charging the migrants an excessive fee for the journey, but also controlling and exploiting them for many years after they are smuggled into the United States. This assumption has yet to be substantiated, however.

38. It is not difficult to understand why smugglers are reluctant to keep the migrants on hold for a prolonged time to further exploit them. First, the smuggling rings may simply not have the manpower to keep track of a large number of migrants. Those who are set free to go to work may just vanish in a large and free country like the United States and never be seen again. Second, migrants are the best evidence a prosecutor has to successfully indict a smuggling network. Thus, it is only natural for the smugglers to terminate the relationship between themselves and the migrants as soon as possible. Third, the smugglers have to invest a large sum of money to move their "customers" from China to America and they cannot afford to tie up their financial resources for many years. They need to collect money from the newcomers in a relatively short period to cover their expenses, to expand their operations, and to enjoy their illegal gains.

39. U.S. Senate Committee on Governmental Affairs, *Asian Organized Crime: Hearing before the Permanent Subcommittee on Investigations of the Committee on Governmental Affairs,* October 3, November 5–6, 1991 (Washington, D.C.: Government Printing Office, 1992).

40. This may be due to the fact that the early wave of Fuzhounese migrants came mainly from either Tingjiang or Lianjiang. Therefore, many more families in these two areas may have a family member or close relative living in the United States. Changle, on the other hand, also has a large number of overseas Chinese, but they are more likely to be found in Southeast Asia.

41. In the media and law enforcement reports, the terms *debt collectors* and *enforcers* are often used interchangeably to denote people hired by the snakeheads to operate safe houses and collect money from the migrants' families and relatives. As a result, I too will not differentiate debt collectors from enforcers. Nevertheless, according to some of my subjects, two groups of people are running the safe houses. *Enforcers* are hired by debt collectors to oversee the daily operations of the safe houses and are mainly responsible for punishing those who are late in their payments. *Debt collectors* may

show up at the safe houses only occasionally; their main responsibility is to collect the money from the migrants' families or relatives.

42. Sometimes debt collectors may simply use their own houses or apartments as safe houses.

43. Normally, the meetings between the migrants' friends or relatives and the debt collectors take place in Chinatown. One of the popular meeting places is believed to be in front of the Confucius Plaza, a large public-housing project located on Bowery Street. When the two parties meet, the migrant's friend or family member will toss a bag of money into the car of the debt collectors. After the debt collectors take a quick look at what is inside the bag, the migrant will then be allowed to switch cars.

44. According to data collected for this study, it took an average of three months for my respondents to travel from China to the United States. About 10 percent of the subjects spend more than six months on the road. As a result, by the time a migrant's family approached relatives and friends for the money they had promised to lend, it might have been several months since the initial pledge was made. Unfortunately, many things can happen within several months in an ever-changing Fuzhou area that might cause lenders to change their minds or force them to default on their promises.

45. There is no reliable information on how many migrants may have been beaten to death in safe houses by captors who were desperate to collect the smuggling fee from their families. According to rumors in the Fuzhounese community, some Chinese herbalists working in the ethnic enclave are occasionally summoned by the snakeheads to the safe houses to attend to severely wounded migrants who could die if left untreated. A Fuzhounese herbalist told the author a story she heard about another Fuzhounese herbalist. The herbalist was awakened by the phone at three o'clock in the morning. The caller was a snakehead and asked the doctor to rush to a place to save a patient on the brink of death. Sensing that this was a serious incident, and knowing that he was conducting business in the community without a license, the herbalist refused to help. The next day, the snakehead called the herbalist again and asked for compensation for the death of the patient. The snakehead told the herbalist that he was responsible for the death of the migrant because he did not come. The snakehead threatened the herbalist. Out of fear, the herbalist paid the snakehead about $10,000 and abruptly closed down his small clinic and vanished from the community.

46. "A Bar Girl Smuggled into the U.S. is Working as a Prostitute to Repay the Smuggling Fees" (in Chinese), *Sing Tao Daily* (New York), June 11, 1993, 30.

About the Contributors

Ko-lin Chin is an associate professor at the School of Criminal Justice, Rutgers University-Newark, in New Jersey. He is the author of *Chinese Subculture and Criminality* (Greenwood Press, 1990), *Chinatown Gangs* (Oxford University Press, 1996), and coeditor of the *Handbook of Organized Crime in the United States* (Greenwood Press, 1994). He is currently conducting a study on illegal Chinese immigrants in the United States.

Anthony M. DeStefano is an assistant city editor for *Newsday* in New York City. From 1986 until 1995, he was a reporter for *New York Newsday*, where he covered criminal justice and immigration issues. He has written extensively about alien smuggling, particularly the case of the ship *Golden Venture*. Mr. DeStefano was part of the *Newsday* team that won the 1992 Pulitzer Prize for coverage of the August 1991 subway crash in Manhattan. He has been recognized by the New York State Bar Association for his outstanding work in the area of public information.

Jack A. Goldstone is professor of sociology and international relations at the University of California, Davis. He is the author of *Revolution and Rebellion in the Early Modern World*, which won the 1993 Distinguished Contribution to Scholarship award of the American Sociological Association, and has published many articles on population and social conflict, including "The Coming Chinese Collapse" in *Foreign Policy* (1995). Dr. Goldstone is currently a member of the Task Force on State Failures created by Vice President Al Gore.

Marlowe Hood is a Paris-based journalist who has written extensively on China and Asian migrant trafficking. From 1986 to 1989, he was Beijing bureau chief for the *South China Morning Post*. Currently an editor at *Agence France Presse* and a lecturer at the Institut Français de Presse, he is also writing a book on corruption in post-Mao China.

Ling Li is a migration specialist with the International Organization for Migration (IOM). Previously a research officer at IOM's Geneva headquarters, he edited its quarterly publication *Trafficking in Migrants* and coauthored a study on Chinese migrants in central and eastern Europe (Macmillan, forthcoming). After a brief assignment at the Beijing bureau of the *New York Times*, he returned to the IOM and is now working at its Washington, D.C., mission on global liaison activities, including assisted voluntary return programs for trafficked migrants.

Willard H. Myers III is the director of the Center for the Study of Asian Enterprise Crime in Philadelphia. A former practicing attorney specializing in U.S. immigration and nationality law, he has written widely on Chinese irregular migration and global Chinese smuggling networks. He has testified before the U.S. Congress on Asian organized crime and is a consultant to intelligence and enforcement agencies in the United States, Canada, and Australia. He was the technical adviser for the television documentary "The Dragon of Crimes," produced by the Canadian Broadcasting Corporation and the A&E Network.

Paul J. Smith is a research fellow with the Asia-Pacific Center for Security Studies in Hawaii. At the time of this writing, he was an adjunct fellow with the Pacific Forum/CSIS in Hawaii where he specialized in international migration and Chinese politics. He has prepared reports on these subjects for the Council on Foreign Relations' Asia Project and the United Nations International Migration Bulletin. His essays on international migration topics have appeared in such publications as the *Christian Science Monitor, Defense News, International Herald Tribune, Japan Times, Korea Times, Survival (IISS Quarterly)*, and *Washington Times*.

Kenneth Yates is a detective with the Metropolitan Toronto Police Service and is considered one of Canada's leading authorities on Asian organized crime and migrant trafficking. He was named Police Officer of the Year in 1993 for his efforts in "Project Dragon," a probe that netted more than $60 million worth of heroin. He also spearheaded the probe "Project Overflight," which undermined an alien smuggling ring that had delivered more than 1,200 illegal immigrants from China into Canada and the United States. He has testified at hearings of the U.S. Senate Subcommittee on Asian Organized Crime.

Index

Note: Italicized letters *t* and *n* following page references indicate tables and notes, respectively.